The Origins of Graphic Design in America, 1870–1920

Ellen Mazur Thomson

The Origins of Graphic Design in America

1870–1920

Yale University Press

New Haven & London

Designed by Nancy Ovedovitz and set in Century Expanded type by The Composing Room of Michigan, Inc. Printed in the United States of America by Edwards Brothers, Inc., Ann Arbor, Michigan.

Library of Congress Cataloging-in-Publication Data
Thomson, Ellen Mazur.
The origins of graphic design in America, 1870–1920 / Ellen Mazur Thomson.
p.   cm.
Includes bibliographical references and index.
ISBN 0-300-06835-2 (cl : alk. paper)
1. Graphic arts—United States—History.   2. Commercial art—
United States—History.   I. Title.
NC998.5.A1T56   1997
741.6'0973'09034—dc21   96-52342 CIP

A catalogue record for this book is available from the British Library.

The paper in this book meets the guidelines for permanence and durability of the Committee on Production Guidelines for Book Longevity of the Council on Library Resources.

1   3   5   7   9   10   8   6   4   2

Contents

Acknowledgments vii

Introduction: Making Ideas Visible 1

1. Contexts and Connections 8

2. The Trade Journals 36

3. Career Transformations 60

4. Professionalization 85

5. The Great Divide 105

6. Women in Graphic Design History 133

7. At the End of the "Mechanical Revolution" 159

v

Contents

Appendix A: Periodicals of Importance
in American Graphic Design, 1852–1920 165

Appendix B: "New Kind of Printing Calls
for New Design" 184

Notes 191

Index 215

Acknowledgments

An earlier version of chapter 2 appeared as "Early American Graphic Design Periodicals," in *Journal of Design History* 7,2 (1994): 113–26. It is reprinted in revised form by permission of Oxford University Press. An earlier version of chapter 6 appeared as "Alms for Oblivion: The History of Women in Early American Graphic Design," in *Design Issues* 10,2 (Summer 1994): 27–48, and in *Design History: An Anthology*, ed. Dennis P. Doordan (Cambridge: MIT Press, 1995), 63–85. It is reprinted in revised form by permission of MIT Press Journals.

Much of the research for this book was undertaken at the Library of Congress in Washington, D.C., and I am deeply indebted to the staff for their skilled and patient assistance. Librarians at the Museum of American History, Smithsonian Institution; the Gelman Library, George Washington University; the Women's Museum Library in Washington, D.C., the New York Public Li-

Acknowledgments

brary; the Rare Book Collection of the Butler Library, Columbia University; the Indiana University Libraries; and the Wisconsin State Historical Society also provided invaluable help.

For early encouragement of my research I thank Caroline Hightower, formerly at the American Institute of Graphic Arts, R. Roger Remington of the Graphic Design Department, Rochester Institute of Technology, and Jack Robertson at the Kimball Fine Arts Library, University of Virginia. Betty Jo Irvine at the Fine Arts Library, Indiana University, helped me in the final stages. Jeremy Aynsley of the Victoria and Albert Museum, and Victor Margolin at the University of Illinois, Chicago, were generous and careful editors for earlier versions of two chapters, and Dr. Margolin kindly steered me through some analytical difficulties later on. Joan Boudreau and Helena Wright of the Division of Graphic Arts, National Museum of American History, Smithsonian Institution, introduced me to the complex world of early reproduction technology; I gratefully acknowledge their assistance. I also thank Nathan Gluck of the American Institute of Graphic Arts for sharing both archival materials and his wealth of knowledge about the institute's history and Myrna Davis of the Art Directors Club for providing me with material on the association's origins. Judy Metro, Yale University Press, its readers, and Laura Jones Dooley, in her thoughtful editing, greatly improved my manuscript.

I thank my parents, Miriam Becker Mazur and Abraham Mazur, for their support and enthusiasm for my work despite its distance from their own fields of interest, and my sons, Josh and Jack, for their good-humored tolerance. My deepest appreciation goes to my husband, Jamie Thomson, who carefully read through many incarnations and drafts and was unstinting in his encouragement. His pointed and good-humored criticism has kept me focused and seen me through.

The Origins of Graphic Design in America, 1870–1920

Introduction: Making Ideas Visible

The concept of graphic design and the professional graphic designer evolved in the United States during the last three decades of the nineteenth century. Before the Industrial Revolution, compositors, printers, typographers, and artist-engravers designed as part of their craft. The transformation of press and paper technology combined with advances in photography and photomechanical reproduction and in transportation and business practices to encourage specialization and professionalism. By 1900 a new group of professionals had emerged, involved no longer in production but in the design of typography, illustration, publications, and advertisements. These designers worked in the art departments of advertising agencies and book and magazine publishers or they freelanced. By 1922, when the term *graphic design* first appeared in an article by William Addison Dwiggins, design professionals had created a discipline that combined visual art with mass communication.[1]

1

Introduction

1. "Steel and Copperplate Engraving." Horace Greeley et al.,
The Great Industries of the United States (1871).
General Collection, Library of Congress.

This book examines the evolution of professional graphic design practice in the United States. It begins in 1870, shortly after the Civil War, at a time when the technological changes we associate with the Industrial Revolution were beginning to transform American society, and it concludes fifty years later, in 1920, when World War I had ended but before the advent of Modernism. As an investigation of origins, this book is not a full-fledged history of late nineteenth- and early twentieth-century graphic design—it contends that graphic design practice evolved at the intersection of printing, typography, advertising, and illustration in the span of these fifty years. When people in these fields began to think self-consciously about designing for mass audiences and faced new design problems, they began to identify themselves with a new profession. What designers did—in printing, advertising, illustration, and publishing—how they learned to do it, what they called themselves, and how they organized themselves and their work forms the subject of this book. In particular, this study describes when and how these workers recognized a common interest and how they redefined themselves to create a new professional identity. In other words, why did illustrators, typographers, photographers, advertising artists, printers, cartoonists, art directors and advertising art managers, layout men, and lettering men come to believe that they shared more than the methods of reproduction technology?

The terms used to describe graphic design activities during this period and for many years thereafter were used loosely and interchangeably. Art historians early in the nineteenth century used the word *design* in two ways: in the broad sense of "planning" or "conceiving" and in the narrow sense of "drawing." The first American art history text, written by William Dunlap in 1834, was entitled *A History of the Rise and Progress of the Arts of Design in the United States*. In his introduction, Dunlap defined design "in its broadest signification" as "the plan of the whole." Design included visual art, "the art of representing form"— that is, sculpture, painting, engraving, and architecture. Dunlap further distinguished two meanings of the word *graphic:* the first referred to letter forms in printing, and the second, of more recent usage, referred to pictorial forms in reproducing images—that is, to engraving.[2]

To complicate matters, the phrase "graphic arts" was commonly used, but its meaning seems to have been elastic. It continues to plague graphic designers today: witness the recent debate over renaming the American Institute of Graphic Arts (AIGA).[3] "Graphic arts" in contemporary literature has retained its

2. "Wood Engraving." Horace Greeley et al., *The Great Industries of the United States* (1871). General Collection, Library of Congress.

3. "Lithography." Horace Greeley et al., *The Great Industries of the United States* (1871). General Collection, Library of Congress.

dual associations with graphics; it is used to describe the printing crafts, especially production processes, and to describe fine art printmaking, prints made in limited editions by artists. Graphic design as a profession existed before Dwiggins's article and the terminology used during the period under study is inexact, so I use "graphic design" here as the founders of the AIGA did when they defined their profession in 1913. Graphic design and graphic designers refer to the profession and the professionals involved in *"all arts and crafts intended to make ideas visible."*[4]

The history of graphic design, like the discipline itself, has its roots in more developed historical traditions: in printing history, advertising history, and art history. Histories of printing have tended either to concentrate on changes in technology, especially the development of printing presses and type-casting devices, or on the contributions of individual printers and typographers. Advertising historians have largely ignored the visual aspects of advertising and the careers of advertising designers, concentrating instead on the work of advertising agents, copy writers, and agency heads. Histories of art and art education are inclined to treat graphic design as a poor relative—undeniably present but slightly disreputable and inconvenient to include within their general scheme. This has begun to change with the publication of studies that straddle the domains of printing, art, and design history.[5] In *Trading Words*, Claire Badaracco focuses on book composition and display advertising to show that between 1900 and 1940 the mass-market literary economy transformed printed culture. Michele Bogart's *Artists, Advertising, and the Borders of Art* examines the history of American illustrators as they attempted to negotiate between the demands of the commercial (advertising) world and the prevalent ideals of fine art. In *The Tyranny of Taste*, Paul Lubbock studies the political economy of design and shows how over four centuries British design became an instrument of public policy. My book, though it is also deeply indebted to older disciplines, expands the framework of historical inquiry to include institutional structures and shifting social contexts. I have, therefore, referred to changes in mass production and distribution, a developing transportation system, the struggle for women's rights, theories of art education, and the growth of the labor movement as they shaped the development of graphic design.

Richard Hollis has argued that graphic design in the United States did not really begin until European Modernism came to America in the 1930s and did not reach its authentic form until 1950.[6] Although designers from Europe who emigrated to the United States certainly defined much of professional practice as it exists today, a strong institutional tradition was in place considerably earlier. Further, some of the ideas associated with Modernism, its anti-eclecticism and belief that design had a mission to reform the excesses of industrialization, were

4. "Stereotyping and Electrotyping." Horace Greeley et al., *The Great Industries of the United States* (1871). General Collection, Library of Congress.

in evidence before 1900. Specialization within professional practice continued (and continues), but that does not detract from the professional's umbrella identification as a graphic designer. While maintaining different practices—type design, art direction, illustration, and the like—professional graphic designers recognized a common ground in one another's activities.[7] That is why they created bridging institutions: professional associations, schools, and journals dedicated to graphic design well before the middle of the twentieth century. Why and how that happened is the object of this inquiry.

The history of graphic design is a relatively new area of scholarship; it is studied most often by tracing the careers of major designers, by descriptions of styles, and, less frequently, by using semiotics to analyze individual works or categories of work. In contrast to these approaches, I explore the impact of new institutional structures, new technology, and the cooperative or social nature of professional practice on graphic design to answer questions about its emergence as a concept and as a profession. This book emphasizes the role of institutions: printers' and typographers' labor unions, advertising agencies, schools of art and design, and professional associations; the development of technologies, particularly those affecting the division of labor in the graphics industries; and the theories or aesthetic values expounded in contemporary books and periodicals, especially those of the Aesthetic movement and the Arts and Crafts movement.

To understand these aspects of cultural history, I have relied whenever possible on material written during the period: popular magazines and trade journals, school and association records and histories, newspaper reports, census data and economic surveys, instructional texts, and autobiographies. I have done this not because participants in the events necessarily understood them better but because the development of graphic design as a profession depended to some extent on how participants understood changes in their professional life and the ways they sought to control them.

Rather than follow a single narrative structure, I consider the same transformations from different perspectives: each chapter, in effect, represents a different aspect of this evolution. I begin with a discussion of the interconnection of technological and economic forces that encouraged graphic design activity. In chapter 2, I examine the issues and themes that shaped the beginnings of the profession as they appeared in trade literature. Chapter 3, "Career Transformations," traces the evolution of new occupations that occurred as a result of the

Introduction

separation of production from design and looks at the businesses that employed designers. In chapter 4, I describe how the late nineteenth-century phenomenon of professionalization and the formation of associations defined professional practice and brought different professional strands together. The emergence of graphic design coincided with a growing rift between high and low culture, popular and fine art. Chapter 5, "The Great Divide," describes these tensions as they were reflected in conflicting theories of art education, the curricula of art schools, and how graphic designers, particularly those in the advertising industry, responded to their ambivalent status by redefining the role of graphics in the visual arts. In chapter 6, I assess the contributions of women to graphic design, contrasting their absence from traditional histories with their presence in historical fact, as revealed by other kinds of historical documents.

Although early trade journals are an incredibly rich source of material for design historians, trade journals written for printers and advertisers are, quite literally, disintegrating. To underscore their value as primarily documents for graphic design history, an annotated list of relevant trade journals is included in Appendix 1. Appendix 2 contains W. A. Dwiggins's article of 1922, often cited but difficult to acquire. It is significant not only because it marks the first time the phrase "graphic design" appeared in print but because it recapitulates many of the developments examined in this study.

The current growth of professional literature, active professional associations, and annual meetings of designer-historians all attest to the keen interest of practicing graphic designers in understanding the roots of their profession. This work, it is hoped, will also interest historians of graphic design and popular culture and will be a useful contribution to research that approaches the study of design as a part of cultural history.

1. Contexts and Connections

Looking back to his youth in the 1890s, publisher Ralph Fletcher Seymour remembered it as a "time in which the nation was refitting itself with machinery and learning to manufacture everything by mass production, the graphic arts, in which field I hoped to find a career, were experiencing equal and revolutionary transformations. The art crafts which always had been an important feature in industry were developing into the most effective, available method for teaching everybody how to live the new life."[1]

Technology transformed how people worked and the meaning or value of their skills, their capacity to earn a living and the very quality of their working life. The graphic design profession emerged in this revolution out of a number of complex changes in which the mechanization of the printing process acted as a catalyst for the expansion of the publishing and advertising industry. The printing and advertising industry, in turn, encouraged further technological innovation. Exponents of new aesthetic theories either rejected or celebrated the results of mechanization. Seemingly unrelated though dramatic changes in the organization of manufacturing, transportation, and the postal service contributed to the development of graphic design.

As an activity, in contrast to a profession, graphic designing had been part of the colonial world; printing, advertising, and illustration were integrated into early settlement life. Colonists brought the graphic arts to America at the same time they brought commerce and law. Tradespeople informed passersby of their wares by hanging signs or symbols from their doors. These signs were made by artists who also painted portraits, designed coats of arms, and painted and decorated house interiors.[2] Legislative bodies issued printed decrees. Colonial printers imported type from Europe and composed pages according to their own tastes or the exigencies of the moment. Like Paul Revere, some printers were also skilled silversmiths. Early typographers (the first was Abel Buell of Connecticut) engraved maps and decorative designs. (Not so typically, Buell also minted coins, legally and illegally.)

Printers designed the business forms, handbills, tradecards, contracts and laws, maps, and books—in short, all the printed material needed by tradespeople and governing officials of the period. Outdoor advertising in the form of cigar store figures, barber poles, window signs, and painted signs on fences, barns, and boulders were common by the mid-nineteenth century. There were printers in every state and territory of the Union at the end of the Civil War. By 1900, the Bureau of the Census reported that the newspaper press, representing the printing industry, could be found "in almost every place which has passed the stage of the hamlet."[3] In addition the "job printer," a printer who undertook all work other than books and newspapers, was a significant presence at the beginning of the nineteenth century. With direction and advice from the client, the printer chose the type style and ornaments from a huge variety available and organized all the elements himself.

Quantitative statistical data before 1930 are frustratingly vague, but they do reveal some qualitative distinctions. The umbrella category of "printing and related professions," for example, included printers, typographers, compositors, and bindery workers. The category "engravers" covered those who worked on precious stones and metals, such as silversmiths, as well as those who copied illustrations onto metal plates for mechanical reproduction. The Bureau of the

9

Printing by hand,
Printing by steam,
Printing from type,
Or from blocks—by the
ream.

Printing in black,
Printing in white,
Printing in colors,
Of sombre or bright.

Printing for merchants,
And land-agents too;
Printing for any
Who've printing to do;

Printing for bankers,
Clerks, auctioneers,
Printing for druggists,
For dealers in wares.

Printing for drapers,
For grocers, for all
Who want printing done,
And will come, or say,
Call.

Printing of pamphlets,
Or bigger books, too;
In fact, there are few
things
But what we can do.

Printing of placards,
Printing of bills,
Printing of cart-notes
For stores or for mills;

Printing of labels,
All colors or use, sirs,
Especially fit for
Colonial producers.

Printing of forms—
All sorts you can get—
Legal, commercial,
Or House to be Let.

Printing done quickly,
Bold, stylish, or neat,
At ——— Printing-
office,
——— ——— Street.

5. "Jobber's Rhyming Advertisement," Luther J. Ringwalt, *American Encyclopaedia of Printing* (1871). Research Collection, Indiana University Library.

Census listed "designer" as a job category as early as 1890 without specifying in which industries the designer work. Enumerators were instructed to describe "designers" as professionals, along with dentists, clergymen, actors, and civil engineers. The designation obviously covered industrial designers, who were placed next to architects, engineers, and surveyors under "scientific professionals." Photoengravers and lithographers were considered craftsmen and listed in that general category. Only agents and copywriters are recorded as workers in the advertising industry. In 1910, however, designers were included as employees in "Printing and publishing establishments." They were distinguished from the engravers, engineers, machinists, compositors and typesetters, lithographers, and pressmen who were also listed under this heading.

According to these figures, there were 393,000 designers in printing and publishing: 355,000 men and 38,000 women. What exactly these "designers" did is not specified.[4]

As a result of technological advances made throughout this period, a series of dislocations and specializations transformed industrial processes. Unemployment was a frequent by-product. As change created greater opportunities, it presaged the end for many highly skilled craftworkers. Specialization often reduced skilled artisans who combined manual dexterity and a sense of design into automatons who worked on a small portion of production. For those with strong designing abilities, however, specialization increased opportunities. Linotype and monotype replaced the hand setting of compositors but gave type designers more scope. Layout (planning the design of the page), once included in the activities of printers and their assistants, became a discrete occupation. Photomechanical reproduction processes made the highly skilled wood engraver superfluous within a decade, while the demand for illustration expanded opportunities for those who had the requisite artistic talents.

The idea of "designing" as a separate activity from "making" characterizes the transition to a new profession. Historians who view graphic design as a part of printing history have often resorted to analogy in explaining the origins of the professional graphic designer. Clive Ashwin, emphasizing the role of technology in freeing printers from production, has compared the graphic designer to the orchestra conductor, "who by degrees forsook his place at the keyboard and his level with the rest of the orchestra, to acquire a level which was literally and metaphorically above the means of production—the orchestra—and a baton which was both the tool of his trade and an insignia of his office and authority." Ray Nash, stressing William Morris's influence, observed that "the designer could find a place to stand in the printing field analogous to that occupied by the architect in building."[5]

According to Joseph Blumenthal, the distinction between printer and designer first occurred at the Chiswick Press in England. He considers publisher William Pickering (1796–1854) the first designer because Pickering concentrated on the composition and illustration of books, in contrast to his partner, Charles Whittingham, who was concerned with the actual printing process. Blumenthal dated the general transformation of the field to the 1890s, with the activities of Bruce Rogers, "the first artist-typographer, and to the arrival of the free-lance graphic designers. These men were deeply involved in printing, but they were independent of shop ownership and maintenance."[6]

Technological advances in printing type and reproducing imagery were part of a larger development. The mechanization of paper manufacturing and printing, the invention and improvement of the rotary press, advances in ink chemistry, the use of wood pulp to replace rag in paper, at least partially, and the introduction of wood engraving occurred in the first half of the nineteenth century. At the end of the century the relation between design and production was recast. For the first time, letters and pictures, text and image, could be printed together.

IMAGE REPRODUCTION

By the end of eighteenth century, newspapers carried text advertisements sometimes accompanied by small illustrations, or "cuts," supplied by the printer. At first, the variety of cuts was limited; between 1726 and 1800, just eighty-four woodcuts were available for use in advertisements. By 1840, however, Clarry and Reilly, a New York printing company, owned $150,000 worth of inventory in these stock cuts. Newspapers sometimes refused to carry illustrated advertisements, apparently fearing they would lose the patronage of smaller businesses unable to afford them, yet by 1870, display advertising was common.[7]

Alexander Anderson (1775–1870) is usually identified as the first American commercial artist and certainly the first American wood engraver. He engraved illustrations for books and magazines, notably *Godey's* and *Graham's Magazine*, and designed cuts (for Binny and Ronaldson, an important typefoundry) and trade cards. Anderson began early in the century, about 1812; by 1840, there were perhaps twenty professionals in the United States and by 1870, more than four hundred. There is no accurate count of the illustrators employed in America, but their numbers escalated as the demand for their work exploded. By the mid-1880s, mass circulation magazines devoted 15 percent of their space to illustration. In 1893, the *Quarterly Illustrator* estimated that within a three-month period, the four leading illustrated magazines alone used 450 drawings, "not including initial letters, tailpieces, and maps." The twenty years between 1890 and 1910 are known as the Golden Age of Illustration because of the quantity and quality of illustrated material published during the period. Magazines, advertisements, all manner of printed ephemera, and many books required the work of professional illustrators. A few illustrators became public figures, the subject of intense interest and adulation, but many more earned a modest and precarious livelihood.[8]

New printing processes encouraged this growth. Early in the nineteenth century, a struggling German dramatist named Alois Senefelder, invented a new method of printing while searching for an inexpensive way to publish his plays. As he told it, one day while attempting to carve his text into limestone, he absentmindedly jotted down his mother's laundry list with a greasy crayon onto the stone's surface. When Senefelder etched his stone with acid, areas that were not covered by the greasy crayon became porous and able to hold water. Conversely, the surface covered by the greasy crayon repelled water but accepted an oil-based ink. To print, he rolled ink onto the damp stone and laid paper on top of it. Under pressure, the inked image was transferred to the paper. Unlike etching and engraving, lithography is a chemical process, based on the principle that oil and water do not mix. The surface of the limestone or plate remains flat; the image and non-image areas are separated chemically, not physically. Begun as an attempt to duplicate text, lithography dramatically expanded the possibilities of image reproduction. In 1818, Senefelder published a complete description of his invention, *Vollstaendiges Lehrbuch der Steindruckerei* (The complete manual of stone printing).

Commercial use of lithography in the United States began in 1828. Color lithography, or chromolithography, was developed eleven years later, in 1837, and arrived in Boston in 1840. It became a commercially viable process in 1846 with the invention of the rotary lithographic press (which used flexible metal sheets in place of stone). The growth of the American lithography industry was tremendous; in 1860 there were sixty firms and eight hundred employees, and this increased to seven hundred firms and eight thousand employees in 1890, with annual production valued at twenty million dollars. Of the many firms that produced prints, Currier and Ives of New York is perhaps the most famous today, but most of the company's designs were printed in black and white and then colored by hand. Printers who specialized in chromolithography began work in Boston in 1840 and were soon to be found across the country; none was more exuberant or successful than Louis Prang. Prang was a German printer who had emigrated to Boston in the aftermath of the failed revolution of 1848. In

1856 he founded a company that would produce tremendous numbers of prints, magazines, and eventually art-school texts and materials. Prang is also credited with introducing, in 1873, brilliantly colored advertising trade cards and with creating, two years later, the greeting card. In the 1880s, L. Prang and Company employed well over a hundred illustrators and graphic designers, including many women.[9]

Poster designers who worked in lithography were freed from the constraints of the strict horizontal-vertical format imposed by traditional printing methods, in which individual pieces of type had to be set in lines and locked into rigid rectangular cases. Working directly on a stone or a metal sheet, designers could draw letters of unlimited sizes and shapes and combine them with images in angles and irregular formats of their devising. The art of lettering and the creation of the lettering profession resulted in part from the freedom provided by lithography. The names of the early artists and letterers are not always known; their work was usually signed by the firm that employed them.

Early posters embodied the boisterous showmanship of the circuses, melo-dramas, and burlesque shows or nostrums they advertised. Until the 1880s, most posters were printed on letterpress, using engraved imagery and wood or metal type, but the spread of the lithographic process enabled printers to pro-duce very large color posters. Posters were initially made up of three sheets of paper; this expanded to eight sheets and then twelve, and by 1905, the sixteen-sheet poster was standard. "Artistic posters" produced in the 1890s combined new European styles with commercial interests in advertising. Signed by their artist-designers, they were smaller but widely admired and avidly collected. By 1905, other vehicles for advertising, especially magazines, replaced the poster in popularity, and not until the United States entered into World War I did the poster re-emerge as a powerful medium of persuasion. Once again, the leading designer-illustrators of the day participated in their creation.[10]

Nothing, however, shaped the future of the graphic arts as much as the development of photographic technology. The great historian of periodical liter-ature, Frank Luther Mott, labeled the use of photography in printing "a double revolution" because photography changed not only how images could be made but how they could be printed. Photography was both a means of creating imagery and was used to prepare other images for printing. In fact, the use of photomechanical processes for image reproduction preceded the actual use of photographs in magazines and advertisements.[11]

Photography was used to transfer drawn images onto a sensitized surface. By 1859, photolithography, the first photomechanical process used for illustrations in periodicals, was available in the United States; photoengraving arrived in the 1860s. Before these developments, the artist drew an image in the size it would appear. An engraver then cut the image into the metal or wood, in effect reinterpreting the original marks into printable form. Artist and engraver both contributed to the process, and their names appeared on the finished work. New photographic techniques freed the artist from working directly on the printing surface or in one size. The image could now be photographed and enlarged or reduced mechanically. The art director could adjust the size of the illustration to the requirements of the page, and the engraver now followed the photographed image rather than the original. This gave illustrators the oppor-

6. "Osborne's Copying Camera and Table." *Harper's New Monthly Magazine* (March 1875). Research Collection, Indiana University Library.

tunity to work in a greater range of media and directly from nature and allowed art directors more flexibility in composition. At the same time, the contribution of the engraver became problematic.[12]

It is difficult now to imagine the pace of change and the need to adapt to technological innovations during this period. Estelle Jussim has dramatized this evolution by tracking them in the career of one illustrator, Felix O. C. Darley (1822–88). Darley's drawings were reproduced by ten successive techniques over a period of fifty years: lithography, black-line facsimile wood engraving, black-line tonal wood engraving, black-line wood engraving with lithotint backgrounds (possibly photographed on the block), steel engraving, photogravure, photoetching, and phototype.[13]

None of the new photographic processes—including photogravure, photolithography, collotype, and woodburytype—could be printed with text in a single run through the press. A system was needed to recreate the image in relief so that it would stand above the body of the metal surface, on the same level as the type and could receive the ink in the same manner. With the invention of halftone printing, the integration of text and image in the printing process was finally realized.

Several inventors contributed to the development of the halftone process, beginning in Europe at midcentury. It was left to three Philadelphians, Frederick Ives and two brothers, Max and Louis Levy, to perfect the cross-line halftone screen and make it commercially feasible. The screen was composed of two pieces of glass, each with a series of parallel lines engraved by machine, running diagonally across it. The two pieces of glass were cemented together so that the lines were at right angles to each other. When a picture was photographed through the screen, the lines broke the surface of the image so that it read as dots. Areas where dots were largest and closest appeared darkest; where dots were smaller and farther apart, they appeared lightest. The distance between the lines determined the clarity of the printed image. The closer the lines, the finer the image, so that 175-line screens produced more precise tones than 60-line screens. The resulting photographic plate was then etched and "retouched" by hand to produce pure white areas and some delicate effects. The final image could produce gradations of tone unavailable in earlier processes and, as important, could be printed on the same press as the text. In her history of illustration, Susan Meyer has estimated that an engraver needed ten to twelve hours to

Contexts and Connections

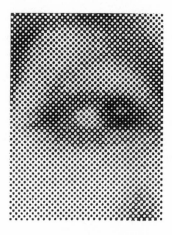

7. "Halftone Dots Enlarged."
Harry A. Maddox, *Printing: Its
History, Practice, and Progress*
(1923). Research Collection,
Indiana University Library.

engrave a four-by-five-inch woodblock and a week to complete a full-page illustration. In 1909, the *Pacific Printer* reported, "If everything goes well a picture
can now be ready for the press in thirty minutes after it has been turned into the
art department." No engraver, no matter how skilled, could hope to compete.[14]

Halftone revolutionized both photojournalism and advertising, especially in
newspapers and magazines. The New York *Graphic* began to use halftone illustrations in the 1870s. Halftone plates were ready for wider commercial use by
1883, and they appeared shortly after in mass circulation magazines. Even at the
time Louis Levy recognized the tremendous implications of halftone reproduction for mass communication: "The development of the half-tone process is mani-
festly destined to mark a more important era in the progress of the graphic arts
than any other method of graphic reproduction since the inception of photography itself. Its influence in the dissemination of intelligence is already making
itself felt in the pages of standard and current publication everywhere." Robert
Taft, writing fifty years later, went even farther: "In fact, the half-tone, more
than any other factor, has been held responsible for the tremendous circulation
of the modern periodical and newspaper. It has, indeed, revolutionized the me-

chanics of journalism, for it has completely changed methods of advertising, of paper and ink making, as well as of press construction and press work."[15]

By the end of the 1890s the halftone process, called "process engraving," was in wide use. Photography was also employed in conjunction with engraving to reduce and fix the original image on the plate, and it soon replaced most engraved work. With the development of good color reproduction in 1910, photography surpassed all other methods of image reproduction. Some years earlier, in 1883, the *Critic* predicted that the halftone would replace the work of the wood engraver, that magazines would soon feature "pictures without the intervention of an engraver's draughtsman." The personal dimension of this transformation is vividly recounted by Albin H. Hutchings, who began his career as a wood engraver in Buffalo, New York, but soon found himself in a dying profession: "Thousands of men had devoted their lives to its development, and then in four or five years the whole fabric of this work of man's brain and skill was swept away." Hutchings became a salesman for a time but ultimately returned to the world of graphics in a growing new profession, as an art director. By 1916 he was in charge of "a designer, an illustrator, a letterer, two retouchers, two photographers, and a layout man. In the engraving end he ha[d] expert color operators and etchers."[16]

As noted, the invention of photography in the 1820s did not immediately affect illustration. In large measure this was the result of technical problems, but historians agree that aesthetics also played a part: the public identified wood engraving with excellence in illustration. During the 1880s wood engravings were at their height of popularity, and not until the turn of the century would photographs begin to replace them. According to a study published in 1923, photographs only began to compete with other illustration media in magazine advertising in the 1920s.[17]

Photographs were first used in advertising to illustrate catalogs and business directories. Business associations, such as local chambers of commerce, published "booster books" with photographic views of their city along with business cards and advertisements. Railroad companies advertised their routes. Traveling salesmen carried photo albums depicting their wares, rather than actual samples, which one supposes lightened their baggage considerably.[18]

The success of halftone illustration—indeed, of mass communication as a whole—was possible only because of parallel advances in paper manufacture. As

18

early as 1856, Americans were using more paper per year than England and France combined, and developments in paper production were critical to meeting expanding needs. The replacement of rag paper with wood-pulp paper made paper stronger; it could now withstand the new rotary presses and it became significantly less expensive. Cost differentials were dramatic. Dard Hunter has found that by the early 1860s, 100 percent rag newsprint was sold at twenty-five cents per pound, whereas ground wood pulp was priced at fourteen cents a pound in 1869 and fell to two cents a pound in 1897. Boston newspapers began printing on wood-pulp paper in 1863, and New York City papers relied entirely on wood-pulp by 1880. Paper technology continued to match new reproduction methods; in 1881, Warren Mills began to manufacture a coated paper that produced a surface capable of reproducing halftone's fine tonal gradations.[19]

THE MECHANIZATION OF TYPESETTING

Although the new presses were much faster, setting pages of print remained a slow process that required appreciable skill. For every page that was composed, each letter had to be selected from cases of lead type, placed into a line of type (in reverse mirror image), and properly spaced with lead wedges. The lines were then locked into a block. This block, also called a case, had to remain absolutely rigid and level to print correctly. During the eighteenth century, printers devised a system of casting the block, known as stereotyping, that allowed them to work from a solid, uniform case. The mold was made initially of blotting and tissue paper, later of plaster, and by 1830 of papier-mâché. These molds could also be curved to fit the new cylindrical presses. In 1837, electrotyping, based on the well-understood system of electroplating, replaced these materials. A wax mold was made by pressing the case into wax. The mold was dusted with graphite powder to give it an electrically conductive surface. It was then lowered into a bath of copper salts, and the copper was deposited onto the surface by electroplating until it formed a solid, continuous layer. The resulting copper shell was then backed with metal to raise it to the proper printing height. Once the mold was produced (this was a separate process, done by specialists often outside the printshop) the case still had to be disassembled and the individual pieces of type redistributed to their proper compartments.

Contexts and Connections

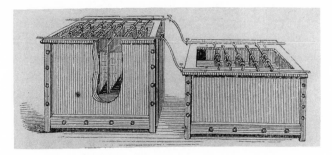

8. "Electrotyping Bath and Battery." *Harper's New Monthly Magazine* (March 1875). General Collection, Library of Congress.

Although stereotype increased efficiency, typesetting continued to slow production. The printer and historian Roger Levenson has observed that in the sixteenth century, printing establishments used three presses that required six pressmen and four compositors and that this proportion held until the advent of typesetting machines three centuries later.[20] Throughout the nineteenth century many attempts were made to mechanize the typesetting process. In the 1880s, Ottmar Mergenthaler and Tolbert Lanston devised two different hot-metal composing machines that could be used commercially.

Mergenthaler (1854–99), a German immigrant working as a mechanic in Baltimore, invented a machine in which a single operator at a keyboard assembled and spaced rows of individual matrixes (of type) and cast a completed line, or "a lin-o'-type." When the operator pressed the keyboard, the machine released small brass matrixes that fell in requisite order to the assembling point along with steel wedges that separated the words. The completed line was then conveyed upward to be justified and set in front of a container of molten metal. Once the metal cast, called a slug, was poured, the matrixes were elevated to the top of the machine and returned to their proper channels to be reused.[21]

The Linotype owed its success in part to the invention of a punch-cutting machine by Linn Boyd Benton of Milwaukee. Several matrixes were needed for each letter because letters usually occurred more than once in a line of type, and this required less expensive, uniform type that could be manufactured rapidly. Benton's pantograph, patented in 1885, engraved steel matrixes using a standard unit width. In producing indistinguishable units, the pantograph not only

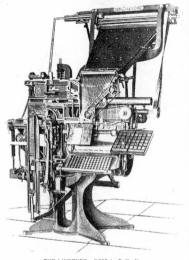
9. "The Linotype." *Inland Printer* (April 1902). Research Collection, Indiana University Library.

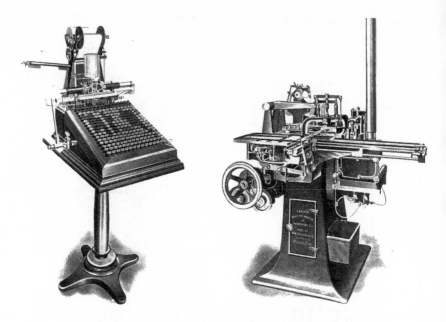

10. "The Lanston Monotype Machine." *Inland Printer* (June 1902).
Research Collection, Indiana University Library.

increased the production of typefoundries but made the use of composing machines economical. The Linotype (with Benton's type-cutter) effectively ended the commercial practice of hand-set typography. First used in 1886 by the *New York Tribune*, by the turn of the century the Linotype had replaced typesetting by hand in practically every newspaper room in the country.[22]

The other successful hot-metal composing machine, the Monotype, was introduced shortly after the Linotype. Devised by Tolbert Lanston (1844–1913) in 1889, by 1897 it was used in book publishing and advertising. The Monotype machine controlled the actual typesetting by means of a perforated pattern. The pattern was produced on a keyboard by one operator and then fed into a caster that was controlled by a second operator. In the caster, each piece of type was cast separately, letter by letter, and assembled in justified lines. The metal was later remelted and reused. Corrections were easier to make on Monotype because, unlike the Linotype slug, the entire line did not have to be reset.[23]

At the same time that the skills of compositors and type cutters were becoming obsolete, typefoundries themselves faced extinction. Extensive violations of type patents, lost battles with advertising agencies, and technological advances destroyed many. When typefoundries broke with their uniform price scale in 1885, the ensuing price wars bankrupted many more. In 1892, twenty-three of the remaining companies formed a consortium to standardize their prices. The American Type Founders Association originally included two large Boston foundries, one in New York, one in Philadelphia, two in Cincinnati, one in Saint Louis, one in Chicago, and twelve smaller firms. By 1919 all small typefoundries in America had been forced to join.

In spite of the rapid transformation, most observers and many participants looked on the myriad technological innovations in type production with satisfaction. Instead of focusing on the mechanics of type, they pointed to new opportunities in type design. In 1918, one writer asserted that "the field for the artistic development of type is inexhaustible, but it is difficult to imagine how type, as a mechanical product, can be improved beyond its present condition. The completeness and perfection of the system, the excellence of the machinery, and the skill in processes which have been developed make the product apparently perfect."[24]

That the origins of graphic design lie in the revolution in printing technology is indisputable. Related cultural changes that encouraged the mass production of printed matter, urbanization, and increasing literacy were also significant. In addition, advances in rail and ship transportation united the continent, while the advent of mass marketing spurred the growth of newspapers and magazines.

PUBLISHING FOR MASS CIRCULATION

In the second half of the nineteenth century, the number of magazines in America rose and fell with the economy but their total always increased. The Panic of 1857 reduced the 685 magazines published in 1850 to about 575 in 1860, but their numbers rebounded to 700 in 1865 and climbed to 1,200 by 1870. Production costs accounted for many failures as well as decreases in the circulation of the magazines that survived. Early census data do not distinguish between newspapers and magazines, but we do know that from 1830 to 1860 their combined total grew from 800 to 5,000. The best available calculations, all derived from Mott's research, show that the number of individual magazines grew steadily during this time (see table 1). Magazine mortality rates were high,

Contexts and Connections

TABLE 1

Number of Magazines Published in the United States

1865	700	1890	4,400
1870	1,200	1895	5,100
1880	2,600	1900	5,500
1885	3,300	1905	6,000

Data adapted from Mott, *History of American Magazines*

however. Individual magazines averaged only a four-year life span so that between 1865 and 1885, a total of 8,000 to 9,000 magazines were published, and between 1885 and 1905, half of the 7,500 that were started expired or merged with other publications. During this same period, 11,000 titles were published, although half of these ceased publication during these two decades. By 1919 there were 15,697 magazines and newspapers published in the United States. Circulation figures were notoriously inaccurate. Not until 1905, under pressure from advertisers, did magazine publishers agreed to make public true circulation numbers, and in 1914, the Audit Bureau of Circulations was established to ensure compliance.[25]

In 1800, Philadelphia, once the nation's capital, was the center of magazine publishing, with New York second and Boston third. By the 1880s, the center of publishing had shifted: New York was now home to two-thirds of the publishing industry, followed by Philadelphia and Boston. In the South, publishers established themselves in New Orleans, Atlanta, Baltimore, Richmond, and Louisville. Chicago continued to be the major publishing center in the Midwest with smaller centers in Saint Louis, Cincinnati, Kansas City, and Toledo. San Francisco was the most important publishing center in the West.[26]

To survive, magazines turned to advertising to supplement income from subscriptions. *Galaxy* (1868–70) was the first magazine to use advertising, and the Panic of 1873–78 encouraged other magazines to follow. By 1889, *Cosmopolitan* had as many as 103 pages of advertisements. At the beginning of the 1890s, *Youth's Companion* became the model for other mass circulation magazines: the publisher provided clients with a completed advertisement, used photographic illustrations, and published the first full-page color advertisement. According to data compiled in 1922, over 90 percent of advertisements used illustrations to

Contexts and Connections

TABLE 2
Amount Earned by Publishers from Advertising

1867	$9,609,326
1880	39,136,306
1890	71,243,361
1900	95,861,127
1909	202,527,925
1919	528,299,378

Data adapted from Presbrey, *History and Development of Advertising*

accompany the text. The kind of illustrations used in magazine advertisements also changed during this period. Advertisements with photography (or illustration combined with photography) increased, although studies conflict over the amount and the dates. At the same time, the number of pen-and-ink drawings, which earlier had accounted for nearly all advertising illustration, dropped precipitously. Color advertisements appeared in major magazines despite the additional costs they incurred. *Colliers Weekly* began using color in 1905; *Country Life* followed in 1907, *Ladies' Home Journal* in 1908, and *American Magazine* in 1913.[27]

The money received by all publishers from advertising grew steadily (see table 2). In 1919, the first year the Census Bureau published figures distinguishing newspapers from periodicals, newspapers earned $661,513,242 from advertising and periodicals earned $154,797,488.[28]

THE RISE OF THE ADVERTISING INDUSTRY

In 1883, the editor of *Chicago Printer* argued "that advertising is the essential sustaining power underneath all successful journalistic projects. Therefore it may be set down that the printing craft of the entire country owe to it, more than to any other one material cause, their own prosperity." Publishing, advertising, and printing technology were inextricably linked. Twenty years later, two leading advertising agents acknowledged this. "Real advertising," they wrote, "began when methods of printing had been so perfected as to make it

RELATIVE IMPORTANCE GAUGED
BY SUMS SPENT IN PUBLICITY.

1900
$95,861,127

1890
$71,243,361

1880
$39,136,306

THE RISE OF THE ADVERTISER.

11. "The Rise of the Advertiser." *Mahin's Magazine*
(September 1902). General Collection,
Library of Congress.

possible to multiply almost indefinitely the number of copies of a periodical which might be circulated."[29]

Advertising began inauspiciously as an enterprise to sell newspaper space and Volney Palmer is usually recognized as the first advertising agent.[30] Palmer started his business in 1841 in Philadelphia soliciting advertisements from sellers for newspapers on commission. That is, Palmer worked both for the newspaper, selling advertising space, and for the advertisers, to whom he sold the space. George P. Rowell, a successor in this new venture, expanded his profits by buying large amounts of space at wholesale prices and then selling them at retail prices to advertisers. To help his advertising clients reach target markets, Rowell compiled circulation statistics.

By the start of the Civil War there were twenty advertising agents in New York and ten in other cities. N. W. Ayer and Sons of Philadelphia was founded by F. Wayland Ayer and named after his father in 1869; J. Walter Thompson was founded in 1878. In 1908, the trade journal *Profitable Advertising* described fifteen large and five smaller agencies in Philadelphia alone.[31]

26

Contexts and Connections

During this time agencies assumed greater responsibility for planning and executing advertising campaigns. In 1898, N. W. Ayer and Sons became the first large advertising agency to hire an art director and establish a separate department devoted to the composition and design of advertisements. Art editors, who hired illustrators and supervised the layout of advertisements, were part of some agencies before the turn of the century and were common by 1910.

Outdoor advertising, used by the U.S. government during the Civil War to recruit volunteers for the Union army, also grew. In 1870, Bradbury and Houghteling started the first national outdoor advertising company. Contemporary estimates put the number of professional agencies at 275, each employing between two and twenty men to paste billboards or paint signs on buildings, rocks, barns—indeed any flat surface open to view. In 1891, the electric sign joined the display.[32]

Reliable figures on the amount and cost of advertising are not available until the 1930s. We know generally that in 1867, approximately fifty million dollars was spent on advertising in various media and that the total soared (see table 3).[33]

The interconnection of technology, manufacturing, and advertising design is encapsulated in the evolution of the trademark. New technology had transformed the manufacturing industry. Canning processes, refrigeration, and a relatively efficient transportation system encouraged mass production that in turn created the need for national advertising. Locally produced materials could

TABLE 3
Dollars Spent on Advertising in Various Media
(in millions)

1867	$50
1880	200
1890	363
1900	542
1909	1,142
1920	2,935

Adapted from U.S. Bureau of the Census, *Statistical History of the United States from Colonial Times to the Present*

Contexts and Connections

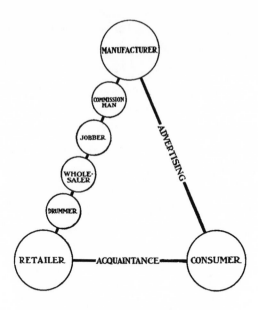

12. "The Business Triangle." Earnest Elmo
Calkins and Ralph Holdern, *The Art of Modern
Advertising* (1905). Science, Industry and Business Library, The New York Public Library,
Astor, Lenox and Tilden Foundations.

be sold simply by posting their availability in local markets, but once manufacturers wished to reach a larger audience, name recognition through advertising became a necessity. Canned and packaged goods, health remedies, ready-made clothing, and tools were important manufacturing products, and brand names became nationally significant: Ivory Soap, Quaker Oats, and Kodak are three familiar names from that era. As a consequence, trademarks became important tools in marketing and required protective copyrights. The first trademark was registered in 1870. Advertising agencies were hired to design not only the trademark but print campaigns that brought the product's name to public attention.

Manufactured items of all kinds began to replace handmade ones; though less expensive, they were usually less durable and, according to those who wrote on such topics, were poorly designed. The Philadelphia Centennial Exposition of 1876 is credited with educating public taste; many visitors to the fair expressed admiration for the well-designed objects produced abroad while regretting the inferior goods produced at home. During the exposition, Americans saw that the industrial products of other countries, especially those from England, could rise above shoddy uniformity. Manufacturers, who blamed the need to import designs on the lack of indigenous designers, were encouraged to raise American design standards and to support educational programs that would train designers. By the next great American exposition, Chicago's Columbian Exposition, held in 1893, public opprobrium was converted to national pride. Critics issued paeans to American achievements in applied and industrial design.[34]

The fate of magazine publishing and the advertising industry was inextricably tied to postal rates. When the advertising profession came into its own during the 1870s, postal rates were gradually falling and transportation and distribution problems were lessening. As I have noted, when business was conducted in person, little advertising was needed. However, once the retailer, the seed seller, the publisher, and, in the 1870s, the mail-order house attempted to reach consumers beyond their immediate community, postal regulations became an important aspect of a company's success. In 1847, the Post Office Department issued stamps for the first time, requiring senders to pay for their letters before they were mailed. In 1863, Congress established provisions for a mail carrier service so that customers no longer had to go to a central office or pay independent carriers to deliver the mail to private addresses. At first this system was in effect only in larger cities and served about a quarter of the population, but it gradually expanded to serve smaller communities. In 1869, Congress authorized the construction of a system of transcontinental rail lines, and by 1875, trains carried the mail from coast to coast. Other Post Office initiatives encouraged advertising agencies and magazine publishers. The Post Office issued the first penny postals in 1873 so that local retailers could notify at least a small number of customers about available goods. Privately printed post cards were allowed in 1898, and full-color picture cards were used in direct mailing. In 1879, the Second Class Postal Act provided favorable rates for magazines, and in 1885, Congress reduced rates further to one cent a pound for all second-class mail. For the next eight years, until the Panic of 1893, magazine publishing soared. Rural Free Delivery (RFD), a system of free delivery to individual farms, was begun in 1898, linking previously isolated regions with the larger mail delivery system. RFD began as a service by request only, but by 1906, it was available everywhere. Montgomery Wards had issued its first catalog in 1872. Other mail-order businesses, as well as newspaper and magazine advertisers, could now reach rural families, and catalog and mail-order magazine use increased dramatically.[35]

Catalogs were a significant advertising medium. Writing in 1892, one author observed:

> It is not simply a matter of personal taste that the catalogue publisher pays so much attention to the matters of convenience and attractiveness of the catalogue, but purely practical business grounds. In place of large pages, crowded with matter, and bound with limp paper covers, the modern catalogue is made in as convenient form as possible, with marked effort for legibility and durability. Some of the best catalogues are about 7 by 10 inches in size, securely bound with durable cloth or boardcovers. The use of initials and head and tailpieces is notable. Decorative work is found not only in the catalogues for promiscuous circulation, but among many of the largest machinery catalogues.

Remarking on the wide variety of reproduction processes used and their cost, he continued, "The large sums of money invested in catalogues are suggestive of the important part which they form in many branches of business." According to the writer, the Meridien Britannica Company of New York had spent $75,000 in publishing its latest catalog.[36]

The United States Post Office and its branches could be a thorn in the side of magazine publishers and advertisers, and they regularly applied political pressure to ensure that uniform codes and low prices prevailed. The indefatigable George Rowell often sparred with postal officials because of the "irregularity and uncertainty about post office usages." In one instance, he told his readers, he wanted to mail his *Advertiser's Gazette* unsolicited to "all the druggists in the United States, numbering many thousands," but the postmaster of New York ruled that this "was contrary to regulations" and held the copies up. Rowell sent an agent to Washington, D.C., got the opinion he wanted, and the journal went through.[37]

The composition of the American work force was also changing. With industrial expansion, women were increasingly employed outside the home. In 1900,

1.3 million women were at work; by 1920, there were 8.5 million. In both 1900 and 1920 they earned approximately half men's wages. Women's fight for suffrage and for economic equality spawned several important publications, printed by women and illustrated by the first generation of female cartoonists and illustrators; some of these women eventually found employment in the mainstream press.

Immigrants played a significant role in the changing work force. The failure of the revolutionary movement of 1848 in Germany forced many highly trained printers and typographers to emigrate, while greater economic opportunities drew others to the United States. Between 1880 and 1920, almost 24 million immigrants entered the United States. Many were skilled laborers who had worked in industrial settings and were familiar with the principles of trade unionism. German and Scots immigrants, trained in European printing traditions, were a significant presence in the American printing and typography industry. Immigrants made important contributions to graphic design as inventors, manufacturers, educators, writers, and artists. A few appear prominently in this history: Louis Rhead, Louis Prang, Ottmar Mergenthaler, Walter Smith, Fanny Palmer. There were many more.

This was also a period of increased enrollment in secondary schools. The Morrill Land-Grant College Act of 1862 encouraged the founding of state-supported institutions that prompted many more students to pursue advanced degrees. Art, printing, and design departments were part of these new state universities.

Trade union activity increased. Led by skilled workers, laborers agitated for higher wages, shorter working days, safe and sanitary working conditions, the end to child labor, the practice of collective bargaining, and compulsory arbitration. The United Typographical Union, founded in 1852, was in the forefront of this agitation and the United Typothetae of America, an association of printers, was formed in 1887 expressly to block the union's demands for a nine-hour day.

AESTHETIC REACTIONS

The Aesthetic movement and Arts and Crafts movement were impassioned responses to the working conditions and products created by the Industrial Revolution. These were broadly based crusades not specifically related to

31

graphic design, but their underlying concepts and characteristic styles were pivotal in the development of design. Both the changing quality of work in large factories and the changing quality of products produced in such factories generated intense reaction. This was especially true in England, where the effects of early industrialization were most pronounced. Design discourse of the period focused on the perceived dichotomy between handcrafted beauty and machine-made ugliness.

The English critic, art historian, and moral philosopher John Ruskin (1819–1900) deplored the conditions of industrial society and wrote eloquently about the damage caused by specialization in mass production. In response to Adam Smith's argument that mass production was more efficient when tasks were divided, Ruskin wrote:

We have much studied and perfected, of late, the great civilized invention of the division of labour; only we give it a false name. It is not truly speaking, the labour that is divided; but the men: divided into mere segments of men—broken into small fragments and crumbs of life; so that all the little piece of intelligence that is left in a man is not enough to make a pin, or a nail, but exhausts itself in making the point of a pin, or the head of a nail. Now it is a good and desirable thing, truly, to make many pins in a day; but if we could only see with what crystal sand their points were polished—sand of human soul, much to be magnified before it can be discerned for what it is—we should think there might be some loss in it also.[38]

Ruskin sought truth in "Art" and "Nature" to which he opposed mechanistic, machine-made "Society." At the same time, Ruskin insisted on the moral value of all forms of artistic endeavor, in both fine arts and applied arts, and he stimulated others to reevaluate the traditional hierarchy that scorned the applied arts as less conducive to spiritual experience. The American Aesthetic movement was inspired by Ruskin's belief that life could be made whole only when the beauty of nature and art infused everyday life and objects. The American magazines *Art Amateur*, *Art Interchange*, and *Crayon* carried his message. From the mid-1870s through the mid-1880s, middle- and upper-class Americans revived the practice of fine book design and appropriated ornamentation and patterns from past centuries and other cultures for decorating all manner of things, including books and journals.

The Arts and Crafts movement, stimulated in part by Ruskin and led by the designer, writer, and socialist reformer William Morris (1834–1896), had an even greater impact on graphic design. Morris emphasized honesty in craftsmanship and the integrity of materials; he rejected eclecticism and stressed the importance of integrating design with production. The power of Morris's aesthetic ideas and examples from his Kelmscott Press cannot be overstated. Commercial publishers, printers, type designers, and illustrators were enthusiastic converts. From 1891 through the first decade of the twentieth century, designers on both sides of the Atlantic claimed Morris as their inspiration. The private press movement in England found eager disciples in America, and a few Americans went to England to train at T. J. Cobden-Sanderson's Doves Press, a press dedicated to the highest standards of design and workmanship in the Arts and Crafts style. Many more joined Arts and Crafts societies founded in cities throughout the United States. Arts and Crafts–inspired work and activities were in evidence between the Chicago Exposition in 1893 and the onset of World War I. Educational theories based on Ruskin's and Morris's philosophy brought concrete changes in the art school curriculum, led to the creation of many new design schools, and increased opportunities for women in the arts.

Both Arts and Crafts societies and the private press movement ultimately used Morris's ideas to produce beautiful, often impractical, and almost always expensive objects. The societies became refuges from the industrialized world rather than an organized commitment to change the basic manufacturing institutions that deformed the lives of individual workers and created tawdry products. This inconsistency did not escape contemporary critics, such as the economist Thorstein Veblen, who wrote witty, scathing attacks on books produced with hand-set type at private presses and destined for the libraries of wealthy patrons.[39]

Beyond the intellectual elite and some who worked in the private press movement, Ruskin's and Morris's rejection of machine production made little headway in the United States. People who spent their working lives in the physically demanding and harsh conditions of earlier printshops were unlikely to despise the advantages of power presses and machine-set type. The romanticism of handicraft per se was not a compelling force. Morris's tremendous attraction for the graphic design community lay instead in the promise he held to reunite art and production, by his attention to the design of letters, of imagery, and of page composition, and in his commitment to standards of printing. American commercial printers recognized the challenge of assimilating new technology with fine design and the need to rethink older craft values in terms of new technology. The application of art to industry, a theme conspicuous in the trade magazines under the phrases "the art of printing" and "art in advertising," was a response to this challenge.

In the 1890s, other styles from Europe attracted American designers. Americans first saw examples of Art Nouveau in the pages of English magazines: the *Dial* (1889), the *Studio* (1893), the *Century Guild Hobby Horse* (1894), the *Yellow Book* (1894–95), and the *Savoy* (1896–98). Less conceptual and more visual, Art Nouveau inspired a new generation of artist-illustrators with unfamiliar decorative motifs from other times (especially ancient Celtic) and other cultures (especially Japanese) and a new, two-dimensional, "poster" style. Individual Art Nouveau artists may have embraced Ruskin's unity of art and life, but they, too, ignored his antimechanical rhetoric. Through posters and magazines, advertising artists, especially Jules Chéret and Aubrey Beardsley, inspired art directors and illustrators across the Atlantic.

Early advertisements gloried in Victorian eclecticism, using a wide variety of type fonts, cuts, and rules to enliven text. Beginning in the 1880s, artists experimented with European-influenced styles and formats and advertisers used fine art painting to give advertising status. At the same time, an alternate conceptual framework can been found in advertising literature that celebrated the joining of art and commerce. As the role of design in advertising changed from simple publicity to the creation of multidimensional campaigns, advertisers saw design as integral to the advertising message. In 1889, advertising was designed to notify the public that specific goods or services were available. Nathaniel Fowler, an indefatigable booster, admonished his readers that "an advertisement should be a public announcement of a fact."[40] But advertisers wanted designs that would persuade and entice as well as inform.

By the turn of the century, Walter Dill Scott, a professor of psychology at Northwestern University, advanced the idea that advertising should be approached scientifically, using data of marketing research and perceptual psychology. Following Scott's lead, Daniel Starch, Frank Parsons, George French,

Henry Forster Adams, and others advocated a change in the way advertising designers composed their work. Design was no longer simply a matter of adding decorative flourishes to enliven the text but a carefully planned scheme for persuasion based on the results of experiments in visual perception and "rules" derived from them. Or as Henry Forster Adams proclaimed, "The opinion may be ventured that it is possible to measure the development of any industry by the number of scientific laws which are applied by it." These men wrote text-books that explicated the psychology of persuasive composition and stressed the importance of combining text and images to convey a message as strongly and imaginatively as possible. It was in the context of advertising that writers sought to define the connection between graphic design and visual communication.[41]

When William Addison Dwiggins (1880–1956) first used the term "graphic design" in 1922, he was making a point about the significance of designers in the advertising industry. "Advertising design," he wrote, "is the only form of graphic design that gets home to everybody."[42] Implicit in this sentence, of course, was the idea that advertising design was one part of a larger entity called graphic design.

2. The Trade Journals

The multiplication of trade and class papers during the past ten years has been something enormous. Almost every line of industrial endeavor has one or more organs which represent, or misrepresent, its interests. They are for the most part handsome publications, rich in heavy paper, fine press work and tasteful typography, well edited. . . . They are pretty generally successful.

JOURNALIST, 1890

Every man who pretends to keep "up" in all the branches of his business subscribes to a trade journal. He knows it is for his best interests to do this.

PROFITABLE ADVERTISING, 1895

Trade Journals

Trade magazines function as professional communication networks, defining professions to themselves and to others. Over time, by their choice of subjects and presentation, they reveal either explicitly or implicitly the history of a profession, its changing practices and its relation to the larger culture. Although graphic design was recognized as a separate profession only in the early twentieth century, its antecedents are to be found in the journals of related professions.

The first inclusive graphic design magazine appeared in America in 1911. However, the designer's interests in typography, layout, and illustration were addressed much earlier in publications for less specialized and more diverse audiences. In addition, these earlier trade magazines provided graphic designers with a forum for defining themselves as the magazines evolved to reflect more specialized communities related by a shared interest in the printed page. Magazines devoted to printing, typography, advertising, and fine arts and, to a lesser degree, to book publishing and paper manufacture were all relevant to the interests of the graphic design community.[1]

The early magazines were the primary vehicles for information and communication within industries. They helped their readers assimilate relevant information on new inventions and technology that must at times have seemed overwhelming. They provided a historical perspective to many who lacked formal education. They were a forum for discussions of issues of the day that affected their readers and a source of news about others in the same professions. At the same time, the magazines played a significant part in inspiring professional identity and pride. As their audience became more specialized, they tried to define a broader communal viewpoint. In this sense, they were a mechanism of professional self-realization.

Issues and themes that shaped the beginnings of the graphic design profession are brought into focus in the editorial content of these early periodicals. Although many journals began as advertisers and forums for exchanging information, they evolved into vehicles for generating and transmitting professional ideals. Raising educational and craft standards, supporting workers' rights, monitoring and standardizing business practices, publicizing the importance of advertising to America's economy, and raising aesthetic standards were all important issues at different times and for different kinds of journals. The profound technological changes of the Industrial Revolution described in chapter 1 dramatically altered the practices of all the crafts and led to increased specialization. Printers, advertisers, and artist-illustrators sought to define their relationship to new concepts of applied art and design. English design theory and practice, British Art Nouveau, the Arts and Crafts movement, and William Morris's Kelmscott Press influenced both the ideas and the appearance of American trade publications. In particular, these movements reawakened an interest in typography and fine printing. By 1900, however, some of Morris's earliest admirers had adopted a lighter "classical" style. Both styles continued to inspire private press printers, as well as commercial jobbers and advertisers, into the second decade of this century. The two currents are reflected in the trade magazines.[2]

The earliest American trade publications were "price-currents," which, as their name implies, listed wholesale and retail prices for all manner of materials and goods. However, the first progenitors of contemporary graphic magazines are to be found in trade journals written for printers and typefounders.[3] These journals, like the ones for professionals in the sciences, law, and medicine, originated in the 1850s when such publications became economically feasible with the substantial drop in printing costs occasioned by advances in printing, paper, and graphics technology. By 1900 elaborate publications that exemplified the highest production values and included elegant samples of printed work served both the technical and aesthetic interests of the profession.

PRINTERS' AND TYPE FOUNDERS' TRADE JOURNALS

Journals for printers and typefounders began as advertisements produced by individual printer-publishers to display their type specimens and spot illustrations accompanied by relatively limited text. Following the Civil War, publications enlarged their mission to become true journals rather than advertisers by inserting brief articles often copied from other magazines. Most journals were distributed free to potential customers. Soon after, trade unions and professional associations published periodicals that reflected and encouraged the interests of their membership.

The *Typographic Advertiser* (Philadelphia, 1855–92) demonstrates the transition from a straightforward marketing device designed to merchandise the typefoundry's products to a publication with larger aspirations. The publisher's

13. "Cover," *Typographic Advertiser* (January 1859). General Collection, Library of Congress.

aim, stated in animated terms, appeared in the first issue. It was "to bring the Printer into more intimate relations with the Type Founder. . . . They may sometimes discover in our columns hints of no small value to the discerning printer, and ideas of typographic adornment which may tend to the beautifying of the products of their tasteful fingers, whether in the shape of the severely elegant book, the mercantile missive, the business card, the bill of fare, or the hymeneal token."[4]

In these early years the *Advertiser*'s editorials discussed the imposition of postal taxes, advocated funding for a memorial to Benjamin Franklin, and described employment conditions and more important current events, such as Lincoln's assassination. The *Advertiser* also included book reviews. Its pages showcased the company's type and illustrations and included directions for placing orders. Not incidently, issues were sent free to "every book, job, or newspaper printer in America." Advertisements for products or services of many publishers gradually faded from the front pages but continued on the inside pages of the *Advertiser*. This was true of many printing and advertising journals well into the twentieth century.

These publisher-editors took seriously their role in educating readers beyond daily technical concerns. In its first issue, the *Printer* (New York, 1859–75) defined its scope in these terms:

> The publishers of THE PRINTER will undertake to occupy this long unoccupied field, and they hope to fill it worthily. . . . The leading subject to which it will be devoted, will be typefounding, its history in its various stages of progress and improvements; the history and progress of stereotyping, electrotyping, copper facing, etc; the history and progress of papermaking in all its branches; the printing press, from its rude beginnings . . . down to the wonderful improvements of the modern "lightning press" throwing off its two hundred impressions a minute; a general history of printing and publishing, both in this country and in Europe, including periodicals, cheap literature, etc.; the history and progress of engraving, especially wood-engraving, which will be copiously illustrated in each number by some of the finest specimens of the art; and the manufacture of composition rollers, etc. These subjects, together with occasional papers on the fine arts generally, mechanics, new inventions, improvements, etc., it is believed will furnish material for a paper that shall not only be exceedingly desirable for all printers, publishers, and artists, but also a very welcome and cherished visitor in every family circle.[5]

Many more trade journals appeared after the Civil War. A good example is *Printers' Circular* (Philadelphia, 1866–90). It continued to combine immediate

No. 5038. $2.50

No. 5039. $4.00

COLLINS & M'LEESTER, PHILADELPHIA.

14. "Cuts for Sale by Collins and M'Leester, Philadelphia." *Proof-Sheet* (November 1867). General Collection, Library of Congress.

professional concerns, educational enrichment and entertainment: trade union news, obituaries, meetings, letters, news about foreign typographical journals and printers, jokes, historical articles, and a regular feature, "State of the Trade," that reported on business in major cities. One issue contained an extensive article on English master printers, a paragraph on Charles Dickens's income (about twenty thousand dollars a year), and short news items that gave insights into the state of the country as well as the profession. The *Circular* noted, for example, that "the people of Boston have elected a colored man, by the name of Mitchell, as representative to the Massachusetts legislature. He is a printer by trade, having worked in the office of the *Liberator*, Garrison's paper."[6]

The most distinguished magazine started during this period was the *Inland Printer*. Begun in Chicago in 1883, it soon became the acknowledged authority on typography, presswork, and printing stock. Although the *Inland Printer* later concentrated on printing issues, in its early years it addressed topics in design, layout, and illustration, particularly in historical and biographical articles. It was also a leader in magazine design and the first to change its cover design with each issue. This was done at the behest of a young Will Bradley (1868–1961), later to become a celebrated graphic designer, who suggested to the editor that instead of designing a permanent cover, "Why not do a series of covers—a change of design with each issue?"[7] The publisher agreed, and Bradley illustrated twelve cover designs for the magazine. Stylistically revolutionary in the United States, Bradley's work shows the strong influence of English Art Nouveau that he and other young Americans admired in imported magazines.

Just as Bradley's covers spurred the growth of magazine illustration, so the *Inland Printer* became an important vehicle for discussing the new ideas and technologies that were transforming all publications. At the turn of the century, it published a regular column called "Notes on Job Composition." Printers were asked to submit samples of their work for a critique on type choices and layout. Frank Holme, a Chicago newspaper artist, wrote a column on illustration and agreed to critique readers' efforts (up to five samples per reader). A section entitled "Advertising for Printers," with advice and examples for self-promotion, also appeared frequently.

Trade Journals

Two European printing publications, *Typographische Monatsblätter* (1882–present) and the *Process Work Yearbook—Penrose's Annual* (later *Penrose Annual;* London, 1895–present), were available in the United States. They included samples of actual work and addressed areas beyond their immediate trade interests (typography and printing). The Printing and Paper Union of Switzerland published *Typographische Monatsblätter,* "for the advancement of education in the profession." With editions in German, French, and English, it covered many aspects of printing, including printing techniques, the history of illustration, typefaces, and layout. The *Process Work Yearbook* concentrated initially on printing technology but gradually broadened its scope to include all aspects of printed graphics.

All these journals emphasized the importance of high standards and insisted that a broad education and good apprentice programs were required to attain them. But forces within the industry were beginning to overpower the idea of a self-sufficient printer, able to design and set type, cuts, and ornaments, to compose pages, and to cope with an expanding variety of printed matter. Specialization within printshops was evident and in the late 1880s evoked expressions of concern. In 1888, the *American Art Printer* (New York, 1885–90) contained the report of a British printer who had visited the United States. He noted:

Nobody can know everything, and the employees of large firms are individually possessed of very limited practical knowledge. "Comps." are "comps." and that only, nor do those of the press know their brethren of the job room. A pressman knows as much of setting type as does a cow of platoon drill. The "stone" man has no dealings with the "clicker" who takes charge of individual jobs, nor does the book-hand work in the same room as the poster printer. Half of the compositors who work on railway "folders" could not impose the matter set by them for a fortune—and so it goes.[8]

This was part of the transformation of the labor force, from generalists to specialists, from a producer-designer to a producer or designer in a limited sphere. Men who began their careers in general printing offices gradually found themselves in separate art departments of printing establishments or advertising agencies.

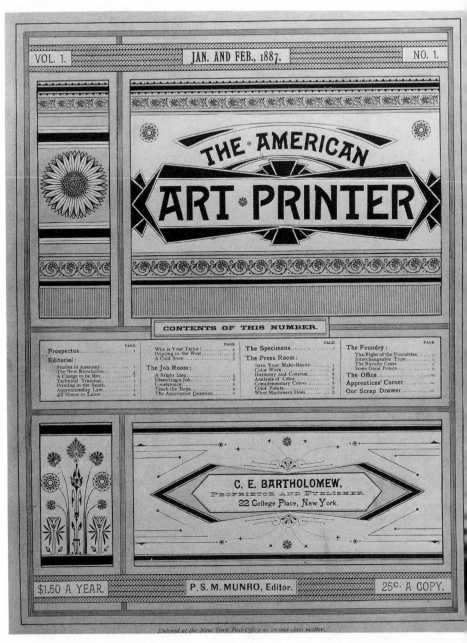

15. "Cover." *American Art Printer* (January–February 1887). General Collection, Library of Congress.

"THE ART OF PRINTING"

Faced with a variety of material and a more advanced technology it is not surprising that printers in the 1880s became interested in questions of aesthetics, or, as it was called, "the art of printing." This phrase served as a title for innumerable articles that appeared in printing magazines for several decades. To some, "artistic" simply meant employing generous amounts of ornament or elaborate decorative schemes. Others held that artistic composition signified a new attitude in designing. The *Artist Printer* (Saint Louis, 1889–93) railed against false "artistic printing" that it identified with the indiscriminate application of ornament embellished by unnecessary "slobs" and "daubs." "To produce a good job does not necessarily mean to besmear it with a lot of hieroglyphical nothings, which have no meaning or none of the attributes of an ornament, just because there is room for them," advised one writer. "The truly artistic printer is the one who possesses a natural taste for harmony, and who can make his white spaces and margins as effective as his type lines or his borders."[9] Artistic printing, however, had a more profound connection to design that writers attempted to define in the eighties and nineties.

Henry Lewis Johnson (1867–1937) began as a printer and newspaper editor. He was deeply influenced by the work of William Morris and later by his friendship with the Boston printing elite, including Will Bradley, William Addison Dwiggins, Daniel Berkeley Updike, and Carl Purington Rollins. Now virtually forgotten, he was a pioneer in graphic design journalism and a driving force behind the Society of Arts and Crafts of Boston (1897) and the Society of Printers (1905). Johnson's first attempt at magazine editing was for the *Engraver and Printer*, begun in 1885 as a house journal by the Boston Photogravure Company.[10] The *Engraver and Printer* was ambitious, going well beyond the immediate concerns of the company, and this was due in large measure to Johnson. As with many of his ventures, however, the journal was soon in financial difficulty, and within three years Johnson was replaced. Nevertheless, the experience marked the beginning of a passionate interest in design issues that he subsequently pursued in other publications, and it contains the first hint in the literature that the work of engravers and printers—heretofore separate spheres— was converging.

Trade Journals

In his premier issue, Johnson explained why these two disciplines now found common ground:

The increasing importance of engraving and its prominent part in book, periodical and commercial work, make a general knowledge of the attainments in the methods of reproduction necessary in many lines of business. This magazine is published for the purpose of showing the actual results in various departments of work, furnishing valuable information to all interested in the development of the engraving and printing arts. As the result of a wide spread use of illustration, the work of engravers and printers is becoming closely identified. This union of interest has become of great importance in all branches of work, and THE ENGRAVER AND PRINTER occupies a field of direct interest to a large portion of general business.[11]

From 1903 to 1910, Johnson edited the *Printing Art* (Cambridge, 1903–41), an illustrated monthly with a new attitude about mass-produced printing. Describing his new publication, Johnson wrote,

The technical side of printing is already admirably covered by the trade journals of the day. This Magazine will demonstrate by examples, bound in as inserts or upon mounts, rather than by explanation. These inserts will represent the actual work, printed upon its own paper, of the leading printers, both book and commercial, in America, and will consist of representative title-pages, interesting samples of attractive book-pages, engravings, color-work, general printing, etc., together with reproductions of fine binds and cover-designs. . . . It affords models and information as to processes and materials for those directly concerned, and suggestions as to styles and standards for the large number who, in all lines of business, must by necessity keep in touch with printing.[12]

The magazine featured beautiful color and black-and-white reproductions as well as samples of title pages, illustrations, page layouts, and different graphic reproduction techniques, including photography.

Johnson addressed a different audience than earlier journals. Many printers were aware of the debates surrounding better type design and printing quality. Johnson, therefore, emphasized aesthetic issues, in effect anticipating the arrival of a new professional. "There are numerous instances in which young men

Vol. XVI · No. 6   February · 1911   30 · Cents

FEB 9 1911

The Printing Art

Cambridge · Massachusetts · U·S·A

Foreign Agencies

London — S. H. Benson, Ltd., Kingsway Hall, W. C.
Leipzig — Gustav Ferd. Schloßi & Co.
Rome — Boatcher & Co. (Bretschneider & Regenberg)

Brussels — Maurice Sacré
Milan — U. Hoepli, Galleria de Cristoforis, 59
The Hague — Martinus Nijhoff

16. "Cover." *Printing Art* (February 1911). General Collection, Library of Congress.

of experience as designers, with some knowledge of color and pictorial effect, or of natural artistic temperament, have turned their attention to printing, and have brought to it a sense of proportion, harmony, and color which has resulted immediately in distinctive work. The more thorough the foundation in art, the higher are the standards attained."[13]

In its pages, the *Printing Art* mirrored the rise and fall of the Arts and Crafts movement as well as the continuing fight against Victorian eclecticism. During the 1880s and early 1890s, many American printers appreciated William Morris's densely ornamented style, but by the late 1890s there was a reaction. Writers in *Printing Art* favored a return to classic design principles with an emphasis on basic structure, symmetry, and harmony of style. They preferred layouts that were "tasteful," "appropriate," and "correct." They emphasized restraint in the use of ornaments and decorative borders, and advised that a single style produced more harmonious results. Will Bradley, who had been a leading exponent of Art Nouveau illustration and now served as art director for several important magazines, revised his stance in two articles he wrote on magazine design in 1911; the first article concerned typography, the second, layout. Here, Bradley preached consistency and flow in publication design in opposition to style changes from page to page. He warned against the use of "decorative design" and "elaborate ornament," advising that the basic arrangement of the type, the proportion of margins to text, and the relation of pictures to type were more fundamental to good design. "In the decorative arts," he wrote, "the only real beauty is that which is allied with utility, so there will be no ornament save where it can be structurally introduced." Bradley stressed the importance of coherence and consistency between image and type. He believed that the type used in letterpress printing, for example, should not be combined with heavy Arts and Crafts ornament: "This question of the quality of the line is of prime importance. The type itself has a heavy line and a light line, with intermediate gradation where the two are articulated at the points of contact. These characteristics must be closely copied and carefully conserved by the designer, if there is to be any harmony. Yet how many designers think of this? For most, a design is a design, and a William Morris pattern for the woodblock is of precisely the same value as the delicate work of the engraver's tool on copper. The lightness of the letterpress in the modern magazine strictly limits the choice of styles available."[14]

Trade Journals

By the second decade of the twentieth century, typography was the province no longer of the typefoundry owner but of the type designer. The prolific type designer Frederic W. Goudy (1865–1947), was responsible for both *Typographica* (Marlborough on the Hudson, N.Y., 1911–27) and *Ars Typographica* (New York, 1918–34). He presented these journals to a more sophisticated audience that was already familiar with the basics of type history and regarded themselves as professional designers. These magazines could concentrate on the finer details of typography, on assessments of modern type design, and on issues of design education and standards. (Goudy, characteristically, continued the early trade journals' tradition of self-promotion.)

In short, over approximately seventy years, from 1850 to 1920, printers' and typographers' advertising sheets were replaced by professional journals. In an attempt to educate their audience, editors published historical studies and sought to broaden their profession's interest beyond technological proficiency. Several of the journals that continued well into the twentieth century, such as the *Inland Printer*, stayed close to their base in printing. But specialization within the printing trade and a new interest in the aesthetics of printing inspired questions about art and design that magazines like *Printing Art* and *Typographica* addressed. These new topics transcended individual trades and crafts and found a ready audience.

ADVERTISING TRADE JOURNALS

The ability to mass produce printed material led, as we have seen, to an increase in newspaper circulation that in turn made advertising attractive to businesspeople. The advertising agents who sold newspaper space attracted buyers by convincing them of the value of their services. For this reason, the earliest advertising periodicals were directed as much at potential clients as at the advertising profession. They were often regional or focused on a particular field, such as the farm market, and employed an exuberant propagandist style. Along with a concern for their own professional enhancement they concentrated on effective marketing. Editors advised readers on good copy writing and on presentation, on the use of different type styles, and on choosing appropriate decorative devices and illustration.[15]

Trade Journals

The 1870s marked the beginning of conflicts among advertising agents, printers, typefounders, and editors. Agents demanded commissions of 25 to 40 percent from printers, arguing that they increased business for the printers. Agencies wanted rebates from typefounders on types created specifically for advertisements. Both advertising agents and printers called for an end to the protective tariff on imported type, threatening native typefoundries. In 1892 the periodical press reported tensions between advertisers and printers but urged the parties to remember their mutual interest in cooperation. Advertisers "consider the printer as a man on a lower scale than themselves, because they employ his services and pay him for them," whereas printers "regard the advertiser as a vexatious crank, who thinks he knows all about printing, but who actually is in a state of dense ignorance as to whether printing is done on a machine like a typewriter (in which, by the way, he would not be so very far out) or on an old-fashioned mangle."[16]

George P. Rowell (1838–1908), the dynamic advertising executive, was also responsible for several of the earliest magazines devoted to advertising. He began the first journal "to provide a medium of communication with persons likely to be interested" in lists of available newspaper space for advertising. *George P. Rowell and Company's American Newspaper Report and Advertiser's Gazette* (Boston, 1868–84) was a house organ for his agency. In 1869, he began *Rowell's American Newspaper Directory* modeled after an English publication but with a significant addition—a concerted effort to publish accurate circulation statistics. In 1877, Rowell sold his publication to W. H. Woodcock, owner of a printers' supply business, but eleven years later he felt the need for another publication to air his views on advertising. As he later wrote. "I had always an itching to have a mouth-piece through which I could speak to those whose interests were in lines parallel to mine." His new creation, *Printers' Ink* (New York, 1888–1967), would serve that function and many others. It became a major advertising journal and the model for many less successful magazines. (Rowell himself claimed there were at least two hundred copycat publications.)[17]

Much space in *Printers' Ink* was devoted to praising individual advertisers and assuring potential clients that the work of advertising in expanding the market economy was fundamental to the American way of life. *Printers' Ink* distinguished itself by providing, for the first time, relevant population statistics for those buying advertising space in newspapers, and it was instrumental in fighting for accurate circulation numbers. As publisher, Rowell helped found the American Association of Advertising Agencies and took part in controversies concerning food and drug legislation, "truth in advertising" campaigns, and in "making and keeping the manufacturers' advertising conscience." The integrity of the trademark registration system as well as postal rates were also areas of sustained editorial interest. Although it recorded the growing importance of layout design, illustration, and the contributions of photography, these were secondary considerations.[18]

Profitable Advertising (1891–1910), published in Boston, was originally modeled on *Printers' Ink* but developed its own personality and achieved the greatest circulation of all advertising journals of its day. Kate F. Griswold, its editor and by 1897 its publisher, was one of the best-known women in magazine publishing. The journal's motto was "We show you how to do it," and indeed its writers gave their readers practical, detailed, and highly opinionated advice on a variety of issues concerning copy and illustration. "Tips in Typography" was a regular feature. Also discussed was the propriety of advertisements showing a "pretty girl who stands perpetually posing . . . showing off the beauties of union undergarments."[19]

Readers sent in examples of their advertisements for design and marketing analysis. The editors could be blunt; witness their reply to a query from the manager of a stamp manufacturing plant:

"Who Cuts Your Brands" in bold handwriting is good. But it is not good enough to offset the general appearance of looseness and amateurishness that characterizes the typographical make-up of your advertisement and the bewildering ineffectiveness of that intricate cut.

A cut is valueless unless it tells a story to the point. Your cut is a picture of a stamp press with some sort of a border around it, a meaningless background, a semi-effective design in white on black and a spattering of words that tell only one thing—that you sell stamps, stencils, seals, etc.

You give no earthly reason why anyone should trade with you in preference to any other stamp concern.[20]

Such critical analysis was believed to improve standards in layout, typography, and illustration and thereby increase advertising business. The practice

17. "Cover." *Profitable Advertising* (December 1902). General Collection,
Library of Congress.

was so popular that for several years the advertising agent Charles Austin Bates published a magazine that contained only reviews. His *Charles Austin Bates Criticism* (New York, 1897–1902) provided entertaining assessments of advertisements submitted by individual businesses as well as analyses of major publications and advertising campaigns. Bates could be shattering. In disparaging an advertisement for stockings, Bates wrote:

From an artistic and anatomical standpoint, this ad. is remarkable. The two girls who are standing up could readily get a big salary in a Bowery museum. A full half of their height is from the waist-line to the knee. They are the longest girls in this respect that I ever saw.

The little girl in the left hand corner has evidently escaped from a hospital, where she was being treated for curvature of the spine. She is an object for pity rather than exhibition to a cold, unfeeling world. The ideas expressed in the letterpress are as badly distorted as the figures that accompany them.

Responded one subscriber, "There is a delightful sensation of uncertainty about submitting matter for criticism to the highest court of judgement. First we consider whether of two evils it is better for the office cat to get our offering, or ourselves get the devil." Bates never hesitated to remind readers that his own company would be willing to design advertisements for them.[21]

In the late 1890s, advertising journals, like their printing counterparts, railed against the overuse of decorative motifs, heavy type, crowded formats, and "grotesque" imagery. In attacking Arts and Crafts or Art Nouveau design, *Advertising Experience* praised a Pear's soap ad that reproduced a painting by the English artist John Millais as "striking, pleasing, dignified and lofty in sentiment. It associates the soap with the loftiest sentiments of the season."[22]

By 1912, however, the role of advertising art had changed. *Penrose Pictorial Annual*, the popular British publication, advised readers that the widespread use of picture advertising meant that every advertisement was in competition for the readers' attention, no matter what the product. Advertisements had to attract attention as before, but they also had to persuade: "Publicity announces or reminds. Advertising explains and sells." "The first business of every advertisement is to attract attention. Afterwards comes the real work of salesmanship; and remember! advertising is pure, unmixed salesmanship. To attract

18. "Louis Hermsdorf Dyer." *Charles Austin
Bates Criticism* (May 1898). General Collection,
Library of Congress.

attention without at the same time, or immediately afterwards, beginning to sell the goods is to leave the work half done."[23]

Theories of effective advertising art based on experiments in visual perception and market research appeared in the trade journals shortly after 1900. Walter Dill Scott, the pioneer advertising psychologist, contributed a series of articles on the theme to *Mahin's Magazine* (Chicago, 1902–4), a publication committed to "reducing advertising to an exact science." Frank Alvah Parsons, director of the New York School of Fine and Applied Art, wrote a series entitled "The Principles of Advertising Arrangement" for *Advertising and Selling*. He emphasized the importance of visual effectiveness—how advertising could best use typography, layout design, and color to communicate a message.[24]

Advertising journals continued to devote space to typography, illustration, and questions of style, but business and economic news gradually took precedence. Their original function was to convince business to use advertising and do so effectively. But when the agencies themselves began to design the advertisements in addition to selling them, the readership changed. Once the advertising industry gained a sense of legitimacy, magazines began to focus on the needs of advertising professionals, shaping and reflecting their attitudes. Advertising art appeared in all these magazines, though primarily as decoration. Only one publication, as we shall see, combined an interest in advertising art with other elements of graphic design. With the publication in 1922 of the first *Art Directors Annual* (New York), publications specializing in advertising design became part of graphic design literature.

ART JOURNALS

In the middle of the nineteenth century the distinction between illustration and fine art was still a fluid one, and many of the early art magazines provided an important showcase for illustrators and printmakers. The earliest art magazines were short-lived; many functioned as sources of illustrations to be removed for framing. In general, the early art journals are more valuable for their high production standards and their illustrations than for what they wrote about the graphic arts. Popular general circulation magazines, notably *Harper's Monthly* (New York, 1850–1939) and *Scribner's Monthly* (New York, 1870–1881; name changed to *Century Magazine*, 1881–1929), published beautiful examples of fine illustration and prints. Later, such magazines as *Harper's Weekly*, the *Nation*, *Scribner's Magazine* (New York, 1887–1939), and the *New Republic* carried debates about the dangers of using pictures as a substitute for text—did it exemplify social or intellectual deterioration?—as well as articles about individual illustrators. *Scribner's Monthly*, under the art editorship of Alexander W. Drake, published articles on American graphics, featured wood engravings, and sponsored illustration contests.[25]

19. "Cover." *Artist Printer* (August 1889). General Collection, Library of Congress.

Illustrators found a new and growing market in periodicals directed at the general public. John Sartain (1808–97), the English-born and trained mezzotint engraver, emigrated to Philadelphia in 1830. In his autobiography he wrote that when the first issue of *Graham's Magazine* appeared in 1841, "it had been an unusual thing for the monthlies to have new plates engraved expressly for them; they were content, when they had pictorial embellishments at all, to use old worn-out plates picked up at a trifling cost. . . . Graham decided to have a new plate engraved expressly for every number." Sartain believed that the magazine's success was attributable in part to these illustrations.[26]

The dramatic increase of magazines, books, and advertising displays created a growing need for illustrators. By the early nineties, the *Quarterly Illustrator* (New York, 1893–95) marveled at "the vast amount of work the artists and illustrators of New York turn out for the press." The *Quarterly* credited technological advances, such as the printing presses and photographic processes, as well as the lead taken by the major illustrated magazines, with allowing the illustrator and the writer to "stand on almost an equal footing as regards their reaching and influencing the public."[27] The magazine itself was crammed with illustrations taken from contemporary periodical literature and included profiles of individual illustrators and groups of illustrators as well as histories of magazines and art schools. It was used as a directory by publishers, editors, and others looking for illustrators and by aspiring illustrators to learn about the profession. More than any other publication it provides insight into the lives of professional illustrators of the 1890s.

At the same time, several art journals introduced American designers to new aesthetic movements. The editors of *Crayon: A Journal Devoted to the Graphic Arts* (New York, 1855–61) were disciples of John Ruskin (Ruskin himself contributed to its pages) and propounded the ideals of the Aesthetic movement. Gustav Stickley's *Craftsman* (Eastwood, N.Y., 1901–16), *Modern Art* (Indianapolis and Boston, 1893–97), the *Chap Book* (Chicago, 1894), *Brush and Pencil* (Chicago, 1897–1907), and *Handicraft* (Boston, 1902–4, 1910–12) championed the ideas of William Morris and the Arts and Crafts movement. Most interesting for tracing the emergence of graphic design was *Art Age* (New York, 1883–89).

The first issues of *Art Age* were devoted exclusively to "artistic printing," but Arthur B. Turnure, its co-publisher and editor, freely acknowledged his interest in all the decorative arts and Arts and Crafts aesthetics.

When the application of art to objects of common utility first presented itself as a new idea to Americans, five or six years ago, under the vague title of "decorative," there were few who regarded it as more than a freak of fashion. The ridicule that it encountered in such phrases as "aesthetic craze," "too-too," and "high art," was more general in fact than the serious consideration which it was accorded, and even now there are many persons of excellent good sense who sneer at art as something much overrated and of but little practical value. All this to the contrary notwithstanding, decorative art has continuously grown in importance since the first society for its promotion was organized in New York in 1877, and has been proved conclusively to be something more than a passing fancy.[28]

Within a few years the magazine had expanded in scope to become a lively, opinionated journal of literature, architecture, and the visual arts. Exuberantly eclectic, it incorporated many interests integral to graphic design. In a prospectus printed in the fourth volume, the editor wrote, "The *Art Age* aims to present examples of American art as they are produced by our professional artists, sculptors, architects, decorators, printers, and engravers. In each issue it expects to present one well executed, full-page illustration of the best recent work in pictorial art, in architecture, in interior decoration, and in fine printing or bookmaking." "Printers and Engravers" as well as "Painters and Sculptors" were regular columns. New printing and advertising techniques were noted, and fine examples of illustrations and advertisements that had appeared in other magazines were discussed in the same manner as paintings—that is, with rather breezy appreciation that was perhaps meant to be a sign of sophistication.[29]

European periodicals brought Art Nouveau to America. The English periodical the *Studio, an Illustrated Magazine of Fine and Applied Art* (London, 1893–1931) was a strong promoter. Its American edition, *International Studio* (New York, 1897–1921), introduced European poster design, book design, illustration, and photography to an American audience and demonstrated that the highest artistic values could be incorporated into a mass-produced work. Other British periodicals—the *Dial* (1889), the *Studio* (1893), the *Century Guild Hobby Horse* (1894), the *Yellow Book* (1894–95), and the *Savoy* (1896–98)—were also sources of Art Nouveau style. The German and Austrian magazines *Pan* (Berlin, 1895–1900), *Jugend* (Munich, 1896–1933), and *Ver Sacrum* (Vienna, 1898–1903) initiated Americans in Continental Art Nouveau. French Art Nouveau arrived primarily in the form of poster art. American graphic designers as diverse as Will

Bradley, Margaret Armstrong, and John Sloan began their own art education by copying illustrations from these foreign magazines.

THE GRAPHIC DESIGN PERIODICAL

A consistent theme in printing, advertising, and art journals was the incredible changes wrought by technology—in press design, in paper-making, and in text and image reproduction—and in the careers of those who worked in them. During a single lifetime those who had trained as typographers, printers, or engravers became art directors in advertising firms or publishing companies. Others worked for multiple clients and in many capacities. A few publications began to introduce other strands of the graphic design domain into their pages.

The *Graphic Arts* (Boston, 1911–15), Henry Lewis Johnson's third publishing venture, drew the strands together. The magazine's subtitle announced its focus: "A monthly magazine representing progressive developments in engraving, printing, publishing, and advertising." Neither the editor nor his contributors discussed this unique combination—a cause of some irritation for historians, to be sure—but apparently the new environment was so obvious to their contemporaries that it required no explicit comment. Johnson continued to pursue his passion for "the art of fine printing" into the realm of advertising, and he featured thoughtful articles on publication design and the adjustments required by new technology. He included profiles of individuals who had distinguished themselves in printing, typography, advertising, book making, lettering, and illustration along with beautifully reproduced examples of their work.

The range of subjects present in a single publication, *Graphic Arts*, proved that fashion illustrators, book designers, type designers, letterers, advertising art directors, and printers shared closely connected, if not overlapping, areas of interest. It was an acknowledgment, albeit an implicit one, that a new profession was coming of age.

3. Career Transformations

You are now learning to engrave tints on wood-blocks—under the erroneous impression that designers and illustrators engrave their own blocks.
WILL BRADLEY, "Notes Toward an Autobiography"

Every step in the labor process is divorced, so far as possible, from special knowledge and training and reduced to simple labor. Meanwhile, the relatively few persons for whom special knowledge and training are reserved are freed so far as possible from the obligations of simple labor.
HARRY BRAVERMAN, *Labor and Monopoly Capital*

Graphic design became a professional activity when the design of printing and advertising was divorced from its production. Most of the careers we now associate with graphic design were either created or redefined during a period

60

when machines and new production processes replaced the mechanical skills of the artisan. Printers, publishers, and advertisers were eager to exploit new technology and reach a greater audience, and they needed workers who could design graphic material. The act of designing, dissociated from manual labor, afforded new opportunities for those who had the skills to compete for them.

Job specialization was a fact of late nineteenth-century industrialization in the United States and in Europe, but it occurred in fits and starts as technology changed production and business opportunities expanded. When skilled artisans were replaced by machines and mechanical processes, most workers were retrained to operate machines that to a greater or lesser degree made their laboriously acquired skill obsolete. A few, however, concentrated on planning or design. Economists and philosophers alike have concentrated on the "deskilling" of workers and its implications for modern industrial society. Design historians have to address the other aspect of this transformation—how the separation of production from design created a different group of workers who were not involved in production but worked closely with people who were.

Driven by new technology, production was subdivided into discrete tasks that required skill but little opportunity for judgment. It was more economical in terms of time and money to reduce complex operations into several simple tasks and remove decision making altogether. As production was fractionated or mechanized, design became a separate responsibility. We can trace this transformation by looking at changing job categories, at the new or changed workplaces where designers worked, and at the careers of individual workers. Specialization within the printing and advertising industries changed the design process and created new occupations.

The names accorded particular activities changed considerably from 1870 to 1920 and have to a degree created a misreading of the history of graphic design and how contemporary designers view their predecessors. Current terminology does not completely reflect earlier professional practice, and modern definitions are, in any case, inexact in describing earlier categories. The ubiquitous term "commercial art" was used by the turn of the century to describe illustration for mass publication but was soon applied more broadly to any nonindustrial design or, more broadly still, to what W. A. Dwiggins would refer to as "graphic design." None of the definitions given by contemporaries are particularly helpful. Writing in 1916, one journalist explained, "We use the word 'Commercial Artist,

Commercial Designer or Commercial Illustrator' in describing men whose artistic talents have been developed and devoted to commercial purpose." The author went on to list professionals that fell within this designation. He included designers of furniture, lighting fixtures, textiles, and "advertising matter" and called them all "commercial artists." Three years later, another writer gave this definition: "The term 'Commercial Art' is very broad and covers a much wider field than 'illustration.' I would include within the scope of Commercial Art, the arrangement of advertising material, the type itself, and one could nearly consider type arrangement as illustration." In looking back, it is more useful to examine exactly what individuals did as designers rather than focus on their titles.[1]

Those caught up in this transformation were very much aware of how and why their lives were changing. Those just entering the field seem to have welcomed technological advances, or at least to have adjusted their career goals with relative ease. Obviously this was more difficult for their elders, who tended to downplay or deny the revolutionary character of these changes. By the 1890s the impossibility of mastering all aspects of printing was felt, although many writers advised individual workers to pursue additional education or training. The trade journals urged printshop workers to learn design: "There is a commercial value attached to good designing; it makes a workman of more use, and consequently, of more value to his employers. The man who can not only set up a job, but who can also design one, is the *coming man* in the letterpress business. The value of the designer has long been recognized in Germany, where in most of the large printers a man is engaged solely for this purpose." Others recommended that printers study illustration: "The successful job printer of the future must be a natural born illustrator. He must have the imagination and the taste to originate or adapt a design, and he must have a knack of making the same profitable to his patron and himself."[2]

Tensions caused by divisions appeared regularly in the trade press. One journalist admonished, "Forgetting the changes and improvements that have rapidly succeeded one another in printing, he [the artist] declares that the printer is 'merely a mechanic among machinery,' and points to what he calls 'an impassable gulf' between art and printing, ignoring the fact that the photoengraver has spanned that gulf, and that printer and artist stand hand in hand."

This writer suggested that at the very least the printer "must be prepared to select and procure illustrations for his work."[3]

As an interim solution, printers did hire "illustrators or decorators or architects" on commission. Bruce Rogers (1870–1957) was critical of these outsiders because they "tended toward picturesque treatment of both type and page, not always to the advantage of typography." The book designer did not exist in 1893. In 1943 Rogers noted ruefully, "Fifty years ago the form a new book was to take was a matter of consultations in the publishing office over specimen pages produced in the composing room, and usually modeled, with suitable alteration, on some preceding volume on the publisher's list. Sometimes when no one was especially pleased, the specimen pages were passed around the office for examination and votes, when even the office boy had a chance to air his opinion of them."[4]

SPECIALIZATION IN THE PRINTING INDUSTRY

It is hardly surprising that the dislocations and redefinitions taking place during this period caused concern, anger, and perhaps even despair for some but new opportunities for others. Workers in printing establishments had functioned within a highly organized craft culture in the printing industry. Its strongly held traditions and vocabulary, social values and organization, had been replaced by craft unions. As we have seen, compositors not only set individual characters but sometimes chose the font style and size, designed the general format, and added rules and borders; they were always expected to adjust spacing between characters and lines to create a harmonious, legible page. With the advent of the Linotype and Monotype machines compositors' work was reduced to mechanical motions. Studies conducted at the time show, however, that technological unemployment was temporary. The enormous growth of commercial printing and publishing houses gave hand typesetters employment as keyboard operators. Still, the intrusion of the designer was keenly felt by trade unionists: "Those interested in the welfare and advancement of our members, especially those engaged in job and ad composition, have been impressed by the invasion of the commercial artist or designer in the domain that once was exclusively the printer's. The tendency of this innovation has been to reduce the compositor to the position of a mere copyist."[5]

At the same time, however, a few compositors could concentrate on page design and become "layout men." In advising printers how to organize their shops efficiently, one author urged a clear separation between two functions: design (planning) and operation (doing). "The design function as far as it relates to the composing room is planned to be in the hands of one man and a stenographer assistant. Customers' specifications or suggestions from the salesman or superintendent as to style are given to this lay-out man. On him is placed the responsibility of laying-out the work in such a way that the resulting job has real design value. He makes his lay-out, prepares the copy for the job so completely that the man who sets the type and makes it up can do his work in but one possible way. *Absolutely nothing is left to the discretion of the compositor.*"[6]

Bruce Rogers epitomized the new kind of professional designer. Though he had a distinguished career in publishing as a book designer at the Riverside Press in Boston, Harvard University Press in Cambridge, and Cambridge University Press in England, Rogers had never trained as a printer. Rather, he had studied art at Purdue University and begun as a newspaper artist in Indianapolis. He worked for John Bowles on *Modern Art* magazine as an illustrator and developed an interest in design. When Rogers followed Bowles in his move to Boston, this interest evolved into a vocation. He worked closely with printers throughout his life but never as one of them.

Type designers no longer actually cut individual letters; the pantograph punch cutter replaced this finely honed skill. Again, a few workers benefited from this transformation. The printer Carl Purington Rollins (1880–1960) noted that "with the invention of the pantograph punch cutter, type design became an 'art' rather than a craft, and as might be expected the personality of the designer became for various reasons more important."[7]

In 1898 the *Inland Printer* began a series of articles by William E. Loy called "Designers and Engravers of Type." The columns profiled the lives and accomplishments of fifteen designers whose careers spanned the nineteenth century. The eldest was born in 1799, the youngest in 1861; five had died at the time the articles appeared. These men presumably reached the pinnacle of their field, so they cannot be considered representative, but the basic data provided by the sketches are nonetheless useful. Eight of the fifteen, more than half, were for-

20. "Gustav F. Schroeder, Designer of Type."
Inland Printer (December 1898). Research
Collection, Indiana University Library.

eign-born and trained; four emigrated from Scotland, an equal number from
Germany. All but two had served an apprenticeship in a typefoundry or punch-
cutting shop. All but one (who worked in San Francisco) lived in the East:
Boston, Philadelphia, and New York, in that order of popularity. All restricted
their professional activities to typeface design.[8] The generation of typographers
that followed broke with this pattern and followed significantly different career
paths.

After the invention of the pantograph, the job of cutting type matrices no
longer required design ability. Beatrice Warde made that abundantly clear in
her snide description of the position: "The operator, by the way, is likely to be a
young woman, as the work requires a combination of manual dexterity and
almost hypnotic concentration, to which any flash of creative, independent
thought would be a positive handicap."[9]

The type designers whose professional careers began in the 1890s were not
trained in an apprentice system; many were educated in art schools, and some

were self-taught. They worked outside the typefoundry as freelance designers. Most were initially influenced by Arts and Crafts aesthetics, and several of the most famous ran private presses. Many combined type design with advertising and magazine work or book design and practiced what the historian Robin Kinross has called, "designer typography," finding ways "of applying craft ideals to commercial work that used machine composition and powered printing." The typographers themselves were well aware of their break with the previous generation. Frederic Goudy observed:

> When I began my work as a type designer there were few who made type design except incidentally to some other allied avocation. In this country that sort of work was confined to artisans in type foundries, and their work seldom included the *creation* of a letter-form with an expression of its own; too often it meant merely the addition of a curlicue, or a change of weight in stem or hairline. Sometimes it meant dolling-up an old type which might then be newly advertised as a new one.

In contrast, Goudy asserted, "I really do believe that I am the first (in this country, at least) to attempt to draw letters for types as things artistic as well as useful, rather than to construct them as a mechanic might, without regard for any esthetic considerations."[10]

Without doubt Frederic Goudy was an exceptional man, but several features of his career were characteristic of his contemporaries. He did not study to be a type designer and indeed did not cut his first letter until age thirty. Trained as an accountant-bookkeeper, Goudy entered the world of graphic design in Chicago because of his fascination with printing presses and lettering. With other enthusiasts he established the Camelot Press, printed booklets, and modified and designed typefaces. He even combined bookkeeping with magazine layout for the Detroit publication *Michigan Farmer*. He soon returned to Chicago to find work as a letterer and type designer.

Goudy shared the intense interest many designers and publishers felt for Arts and Crafts aesthetics, and he worked for the leading avant-garde publication in Chicago, Stone and Kimball's *Chap Book*. He also showed an aptitude for printing and the design and production of type. Goudy and his wife, Bertha Sprinks Goudy, established the Village Press and moved it East in search of a sympathetic environment. For several years the Goudys lived in the Boston

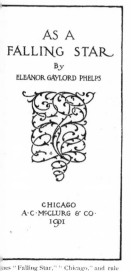

AS A
FALLING STAR
By
ELEANOR GAYLORD PHELPS

CHICAGO
A·C·MᶜCLURG & CO·
1901

nes "Falling Star," " Chicago," and rule
in red; balance in black.

RUGS
ORIENTAL AND OCCIDENTAL
ANTIQUE, AND MODERN
A *Handbook* for
Ready Reference
By
ROSA BELLE HOLT

CHICAGO
A·C·McClurg&Co·
1901

Word " Rugs," and line "A. C. McClurg & Co."
in red; balance in black.

THE
SCHOOL
OF ILLUS=
TRATION

1900-1
CHICAGO

Rule and the monogram in red; balance
in black.

21. "Suggestions for Title-page Arrangement by F. W. Goudy." *Inland Printer* (August 1902).
Research Collection, Indiana University Library

area, where they met leaders of the city's Arts and Crafts society and print
renaissance. In 1906, unable to support themselves, the Goudys moved their
press to New York. Here Frederic Goudy found work in advertising, printing,
and type design. From 1915 to 1924 he taught lettering at the Art Students
League. He designed types for the Lanston Monotype Company and in 1920
became its art director. Goudy wrote several books on type and was editor of
Typographica, Ars Typographica, and the first issues of the *American Institute
for Graphic Arts News-letter.* In spite of his late start, Goudy was incredibly
prolific; he designed approximately one hundred typefaces, was a printer, a
letterer, and a magazine and book designer, as well as a popular writer, teacher,
and lecturer.[11]

Foundries typically commissioned designers to create new typefaces for particular purposes. The Mergenthaler Type Company and the American Type
Founders were two of the largest purchasers. Oswald B. Cooper (1879–1940)
designed type as part of the activities of his design firm, Bertsch and Cooper in
Chicago. His most famous faces, Cooper Old Style (1919) and Cooper Black (1921),
were designed for the Barnhart Brothers and Spindler Foundry of Chicago.

As noted earlier, the lithographic process gave designers greater freedom to arrange letters and integrate lettering with illustrations. By the middle of the nineteenth century, men known as "letterers" worked in lithography shops, designing posters and sheet music covers. The outdoor sign industry also required proficient and imaginative letterers. Like type designers, many letterers seem to have been freelance designers who combined this skill with other accomplishments. Oswald Cooper, the typeface designer, was a well-known lettering man. Another Chicagoan, Elizabeth Colwell (b. 1881), designed department store advertisements and illustrated books that featured generous amounts of lettering. Colwell's Handletter (1916) and Colwell's Handletter Italic (1916), the two typefaces she designed for the American Type Founders, were based on her own hand lettering.[12]

THE NEW IMAGE MAKERS

The late nineteenth-century photography fad created a pool of would-be professionals, men and women who wanted to use the expertise gained as a hobby to earn a living. Work in portrait studios provided work for many, but opportunities in advertising expanded at the same time, spurred by improved halftone processes. Photography magazines encouraged this new interest. From October 1904 to June 1905, *Western Camera Notes* published a course in twenty lessons entitled "Commercial Photography and Its Adaptation to Modern Advertising." *Photo-Era* featured the work of Samuel L. Busha, who sold photographs to magazines for advertisements, calling him a "photographic designer" and referring to his work as "the art of camera designing." Although some advertising photographers began as illustrators and learned photography on their own, schools and colleges offered specialized training in photography. One writer even counseled women to enter the field because "photography is an art . . . that requires but a short apprenticeship as compared with designing [illustration]."[13]

By the end of the nineteenth century there were over ten thousand engravers and illustrators in New York City alone. Photography and the halftone altered the work of engravers, forcing them to merely copy or enhance photographically created images. In an editorial of 1879, *Scribner's* editor Richard W. Gilder explained to readers why the new methods were superior: they allowed the illustrator to work in a wide variety of media that the photograph could accurately capture. Previously the original artwork was pasted onto the wood surface and destroyed as the engraver transferred the image, cutting through the drawing. Now the engraver has "the original before him, not only as a guide, but as an inspirer." But Gilder, and Alexander W. Drake, his art director, knew that engraving as a career was doomed. Some engravers became illustrators, and some learned photoengraving; others left the field entirely. Yet many continued to deny the inevitable. William James Linton, the eminent English engraver, refused to recognize the demise of his profession and criticized the introduction of photography for reproduction as a lowering of standards. "If I object to photography on wood, it is because photographs even of drawings are not so good as the drawings themselves; because, also, photographs are never true." Joseph Pennell, the illustrator and author, argued that decline of wood engraving, though serious, was probably temporary. He attacked Drake for believing that "American engraving is about to disappear in process [halftone]—though of course there is not the slightest danger of anything of the sort happening—he is uttering premature wails over its disappearance, which is really not coming to pass at all." But it was.[14]

There was no clearly defined path to becoming an illustrator. No statistical studies exist, and anecdotal evidence is mixed. Will Bradley asserted that the best illustrators of his generation had aspired to become painters and "drifted into working for reproduction," in contrast to the next generation of "young men and women actuated less by a genuine interest in art than by the promise of large and prompt profits on graduation." He continued, "Thus illustration forms to-day merely a transition stage for most artists who practice it. And, instead of painters becoming illustrators as before, we have now the spectacle of the ablest men starting in to paint as soon as they are pecuniarily able to do so." Edward Penfield and Edwin Abbey fit this description to some degree, but the Leyendecker brothers, who started as commercial illustrators and then studied painting in Paris, returned to careers in advertising. And two highly successful illustrators were women who originally trained as engravers. Mary Hallock Foote (1847–1938) began as a prize pupil of William Linton at Cooper Union in New York but turned to illustration to support her family. Although she spent most of her adult life in remote areas of the West, where her husband was an unsuccessful mining engineer, Foote wrote and illustrated sixteen novels and regularly

22. "To See the Art Editor." Henry Dana Gibson, *Our Neighbors* (1905). General Research Division, New York Public Library, Astor, Lenox and Tilden Foundations.

contributed illustrations to popular magazines on Western subjects. Alice Barber Stephens (1858–1932) was another prolific illustrator whose work appeared in the major illustrated journals of the day. She had studied wood engraving with John Dalziel, an Englishman like Linton, at the Philadelphia School of Design for Women.[15]

Many illustrators began their careers as pictorial reporters. Felix O. C. Darley, Winslow Homer, and Thomas Nast worked for magazines, illustrating important events of the day, sometimes from written descriptions, sometimes as eye-witnesses. When newspaper artist-reporters were replaced by documentary photographers, these men turned to magazine, book, and advertising illustration. Homer eventually left that world for painting. Nast, of course, became the premier political cartoonist of his time. Another newspaper artist, John Sloan (1871–1951), abandoned his commercial work for painting and teaching.

Late nineteenth-century illustrators considered themselves to be part of a respected fine arts community. With the growth of commercial publishing and advertising, however, the relationship between illustrator and artists changed so that by 1920 illustrators were almost wholly absorbed into the advertising industry, losing their autonomy and status as independent artists. Yet their new situation, like that of the fine artist, lacked consistent employment opportunities and any form of economic security.[16]

John Sloan's autobiographical reminiscences dramatized the conflicts. Unable to continue his education beyond age sixteen, he went to work at a bookstore in Philadelphia, designing and selling handmade greeting cards to supplement his salary. He taught himself etching from books. Sloan worked for eighteen years at the *Philadelphia Press* and *Philadelphia Inquirer*. In these newspaper art departments, artists made spot illustrations, cartoons, illustrations for stories, decorative headings for regular departments and for feature articles, and advertisements. He specialized in "puzzle drawing," or "word charade" puzzles, a weekly feature that coupled words and images into phonetic puns. Sloan developed his "poster style" based on the Walter Crane illustrations he had discovered in magazines and on Japanese prints. Like Goudy, Sloan welcomed mechanical advances, even crediting new reproduction technology as an inspiration: "So the new photo-mechanical methods of reproducing original drawings were part of the industrial revolution, as it affected art. There was a kind of excitement in the air for those of us who were interested in drawing as a means of communicating ideas, when these new opportunities for mass production through publishing were opening up." Sloan drew eighty full-page colored works in "poster style" in the *Philadelphia Inquirer* beginning in February 1892 and continuing until 1903. He contributed to *Gil Blas, Moods, Echo,* and other small magazines devoted to the new style.[17]

Eventually Sloan left the newspaper art room to freelance. Encouraged by the painter Robert Henri, he enrolled at the Pennsylvania Academy and in 1896 began to work seriously as a painter. Although he did not sell a painting until he was forty-two, he supported himself illustrating books and magazines and teaching. In 1912 he became art editor of the *Masses,* an innovative journal of radical opinion. Sloan's diary, covering his early years in New York from 1906 to 1913, is filled with bitter passages recounting humiliating visits to art editors, portfolio in hand, seeking work and haggling over payment. In 1917 Adolph Dehn, an artist who studied with Sloan when he taught at the Art Students League, noted that Sloan disliked "the idea of commercial art—of making anything to sell. Don't believe in it. . . . Oh, how he rails against institutions; how he rails at commercial artists, portrait painters, etc.!"[18]

It is not altogether clear how many illustrators saw commercial work as degrading. Most distinguished between book and magazine illustration, or between those and advertising. Jessie Wilcox Smith apparently resented doing advertising illustration at the *Ladies' Home Journal* but found story and cover illustrating for the *Journal,* as well as for such publications as *Collier's* and *Century,* agreeable.[19]

THE ART DIRECTOR

Joseph Pennell implied that it was common in the United States, in contrast to England, for art directors to be drawn from the ranks of professional artists. He cited the example of Charles Parson, who began a twenty-six-year career as art editor for the Harper and Brothers publishing house in 1863. Previously, Parson had been a successful illustrator. Parson's success at Harper inspired other publishers to hire art directors. Alexander W. Drake was trained as an engraver at Cooper Union and the National Academy of Design and established his own wood-engraving business. When *Scribner's Monthly* began in 1870, its editor, Richard Watson Gilder, hired Drake as art director. Twenty years later, when Edward Penfield (1866–1925) finished his studies art at the Art Students League, he began immediately as art director for *Harper's Magazine,* then *Harper's Weekly* and *Harper's Bazaar,* but he continued his illustration. In a letter dated 1895, Penfield wrote, "My original intention was to be an illustrator, and I followed that branch for several years, making drawings in pen and ink and wash for various purposes. Lately, I have given my attention to decorative work, such as posters, bookcovers, &c. as I find it interests me most." Penfield resigned in 1901 to concentrate on painting and drawing. There was apparently no standard career path for art directors.[20]

During his tenure Parson ran what was later recognized as a combination art department, art school, and employment consulting firm. Parson was noted for his ability to identify untrained talent and nurture it. Under his direction, successful artists taught younger ones the technical skills needed to succeed professionally in a large market. Harper not only published mass circulation periodicals—*Harpers' Weekly* and *Harpers' Magazine*—but a tremendous number of books that required illustration. Six to eight artists worked on the payroll, and many others worked on commission. Prominent staffers included Edwin Austin Abbey, A. B. Frost, Edward Windsor Kemble, and Howard Pyle, Winslow Homer, Thomas Nast and later, Frederic Remington. (Homer was Harper's star illustrator-reporter, sending drawings back from Civil War battlefields.) The affection of his former illustrators for their editor is evident in later testimonials, providing a brief glimpse of a time when an art editor also acted as career counselor, teacher, and father figure. Similarly, in their reminiscences, Alexander Drake's contemporaries unanimously commented on his skill as a teacher and his charitable gifts to struggling illustrators and engravers, particularly to older engravers whose skills had become obsolete. The willingness of art directors to complete the technical and artistic training of young illustrators is characteristic of this transitional period. By 1920, however, the relationship between art director and illustrator was largely defined by contractual agreements.[21]

According to Presbrey, in the 1890s advertising agencies began to hire an "art manager," "art director," or "art editor" (the terms seem to have been interchangeable) to supervise design, in addition to editorial or production managers. Although many agencies continued to produce illustrated advertisements using halftone reproductions designed by a staff engraver, the use of art directors grew steadily. The need to coordinate large campaigns made them a necessity. By 1920 Richard Walsh, the first president of the Art Directors Club of New York, declared that the job of art director was *"a recognized profession,"* which he defined as "the highly specialized vocation of advising commerce in the use of art, and interpreting to art the requirements of commerce."[22]

THE EMPLOYERS

Geography was a significant factor in the formation of the profession. New York, Chicago, Philadelphia, and Boston and, to a lesser degree, St. Louis, Kansas City, and Cleveland, were centers of design activity in the East and Midwest. San Francisco was the leading publishing and advertising center in the West. Although Boston and Philadelphia were the most important publishing centers at the beginning of the nineteenth century, New York gradually overtook them. At the end of the century New York had the greatest number of book publishers, magazine publishers, and advertising agencies; Chicago had the second largest. The movement of students, teachers, tramp printers, and other professionals from one city to another is a recurring theme in autobiographies of the period. Many designers freelanced, while others worked as permanent employees on staff. Although designers during this period might not have done so, it is possible to distinguish five specific kinds of businesses that employed them: printing and engraving establishments, publishers, advertising agencies, lithography and poster houses, and commercial art studios.

Engraving houses, begun in Chicago in 1880, added internal art departments as a service to their customers. The Franklin Engraving and Electroplating Company of Chicago, for example, began as an electrotype foundry and expanded in scope as photoengraving processes became commercially viable. Its inventory included a vast array of "cuts," including "headings, borders, initials, ornaments and decorative illustrations in endless variety, their total number of different cuts amounting to nearly 10,000." The company trained its own workers. Three-quarters of the employees were apprentices. Customers either came with an idea or were assisted in developing an idea that was then given to the artist, first to sketch and later to create a finished image.[23]

When the publisher Ralph Fletcher Seymour arrived in Chicago at the beginning of his career, he started in the art department of this kind of engraving house. He described his co-workers as "artists who understood the requirements of commercial drawings." Seymour, with twenty others, was engaged in "drawing and lettering such ordinary objects as were needed in newspaper and general advertising." Their ambition was to become a "head line artist," like J. C. Leyendecker, who was admired because of his ability to "picturize" the wares of clothing manufacturers.[24]

Publishers of mass circulation magazines understood the importance of well-designed publications and used art directors, under a variety of titles, to oversee their creation. In describing the new facilities of the Curtis Publishing Company, publisher of the *Ladies' Home Journal* and *Saturday Evening Post*, a writer noted, "There is a well organized art department, which has charge of the layout for every page that has illustrations. The plates are all made according to a carefully studied formula. Nothing is left to chance, or the uninterested compositor." This approach, he believed, produced "magazines [that] are well balanced, consistent in typographic scheme, decorated harmoniously, and printed uniformly well."[25]

Though the author did not mention him by name, Drake was responsible for establishing the Curtis art department, where he served as art director for forty-three years. Drake conferred daily with printers, artists, engravers, and platemakers, and several memorial essayists described Drake's close working relationship with the printer, Theodore Low De Vinne. De Vinne is credited with painstaking efforts to ensure that the wood engravings, for which the magazine was famous, were printed correctly. He also installed the latest rotary presses, which by 1890 were capable of printing halftone illustrations from curved plates. Drake and De Vinne gave *Century Magazine* its international reputation for fine illustrations and high production values.[26]

Magazines competed for popular illustrators. In 1905, *Collier's* announced that henceforth seven artists would work "exclusively for *Collier's*." The seven under this exceptional arrangement, A. B. Frost, Maxfield Parrish, Charles Dana Gibson, Frederic Remington, E. W. Kemble, Jessie Wilcox Smith, and Frank X. Leyendecker, were leading artists of their day.[27]

The Curtis Publishing Company is about to erect the new building shown above on Independence and Washington Squares, Philadelphia, for the use exclusively of
THE LADIES' HOME JOURNAL   **THE SATURDAY EVENING POST**

23. "Curtis Publishing Company, Philadelphia." *Profitable Advertising* (October 1908). General Collection, Library of Congress.

Between 1870 and 1910, as the advertising agencies changed from space selling to full-service businesses, they began to orchestrate every phase of the advertiser's campaign. *Printers' Ink* credits the early advertising writers with initiating design services in addition to copywriting and placing advertisements. In 1896 Charles Austin Bates designed complete campaigns. He was followed in 1902 by Earnest Elmo Calkins and Ralph Holden. The Philadelphia agency N. W. Ayer and Sons created an in-house printing department in 1875 and in 1880 boasted: "The Composition, Illustration and Display of Newspaper Advertisements has so long been a study with us that we have become admittedly expert in preparing the best possible effects." It continued, "Having at command the services of an Artist, a Wood Engraver, and a number of Printers who have been for years engaged almost exclusively in this work under our direction, we possess entirely unequaled facilities for serving those who desire to entrust their business to our care." In 1888 Ayer purchased the Keystone Type Foundry to supply typefaces for its own use. By 1910 Ayer had an art director "who was primarily responsible for the design and illustration of all the advertisements turned out."[28]

Even smaller publishing companies required a variety of skills in their art departments. In 1916, addressing the art directors of farm journals, one writer described his ideal art department. He called for "an animal expert" capable of illustrating animal and bird life. He advised employing two letterers, one "a stylist in lettering to create unusual lettering, freak fonts for broadsides, trade-paper captions, folders, mailing cards and street-car cards, or poster assignments" and the second "an artistic letterer," "capable of rendering copper-plate style, French script for advertisements, brochure titles and catalog captions." Also essential were "decorative designers," those who "pull the design together," "who understand borders and composition and 'spotting' of the essential parts of a job." An airbrush retoucher was necessary, especially in catalog work, "to make dull uninteresting photographic subjects interesting." The art photographer had to master the technical side of camerawork but also "to paint with a camera." In addition, he suggested a specialist in automobile illustration, a colorist, and a layout man. The author admitted that few art directors could afford such a large workforce, but he insisted that all the skills represented in his ideal staff were necessary.[29]

Agencies like Ayer, J. Walter Thompson, and Lord and Thomas were in the

24. "The Mariner and Merchant Building, Home of the Ayer
Agency," *Profitable Advertising* (October 1908). General
Collection, Library of Congress.

forefront of this expansion, but other agencies followed. They began by hiring
staff artists shortly after 1895 and supplemented them with freelance workers.
As they became full-service agencies, sometime between 1901 and 1905, they
created completely separate art departments. Agencies hired printing employees "who showed unusual understanding of the special typographic requirements of an advertisement." They followed the same approach in hiring package
designers. As more businesses accepted the necessity of spending significant
amounts of money on advertising, agencies added staff artists, supplemented
with freelance photographers or illustrators. Presbrey, who ran a large and
successful agency and is our most detailed informant, argued that a permanent
art staff gave the agency the resources to plan a coherent campaign. Calkins's
description of a typical advertising agency of 1920 also emphasized the importance of the campaign plan that required individuals to work closely together.
"One of the charms of agency work," he claimed, "is the association, the interchange of ideas, the discussions, the constant novelty that renews the interest."
"The art director is an advertising man with a feeling for design." Although he

might manage a relatively small staff, he had to know the larger world of free-lance artists that specialized in particular styles of illustration or in lettering, trademark, and packaging design.[30]

From the end of the Civil War until the turn of the century, lithographer-publishers flourished. The great lithography houses, Louis Prang in Boston and Currier and Ives in New York, have already been mentioned. There were many others. They produced prints—sometimes of original works, sometimes copies of paintings—as well as all manner of business forms, sheet music, and posters and advertisements. Chromolithographs were one part of their business. Currier and Ives had two staff artists. Louis Maurer (1832–1932) was a German-born artist who had been apprenticed to a lithographer as a boy, studied mechanical drawing, and worked as a cabinetmaker before emigrating to the United States. Fanny Palmer (1812–76) was a well-educated woman who had studied literature and music as well as art in England. Maurer worked for Currier and Ives between 1852 and 1860; Palmer began somewhat earlier and continued until her death. Both artists worked in a variety of subjects and often reworked or added backgrounds for work done by others. At Currier and Ives, most illustrations were done on commission by freelance artists who specialized in different genres: Thomas Worth drew comics, including a series on African-American life called "the Darktowns," Arthur Fitzwilliam Tait depicted sporting and hunting events, George Henry Durrie specialized in rural New England scenes, James E. Butterworth was known for for marine landscapes, and Charles Parsons, later head of the art department at Harper and Brothers, drew marine landscapes and railroad scenes. Once purchased, their work was the property of the firm and could be changed, cannibalized, and used for any purpose; there was no system of royalties.[31]

Poster houses were a specialized branch of the lithography industry. They appeared in New York City about 1840 and the city remained an important base. In addition to compositors, pressmen, and engravers, these houses employed their own artists, usually one artist for three engravers, who specialized in this kind of work. Most worked in a realistic tradition favored by the patent medicine manufacturers and promoters of popular entertainment—circus, theater, and vaudeville—their principal clients. Although posters predating the 1890s were often unsigned, the artists were not necessarily unknown. H. C. Bunner, a champion of the artistic poster, believed that the better posters were done by

25. "One of the Ad Rooms, Lee Lash Company." *American
Advertiser* (September 1905). General Collection,
Library of Congress.

artists, not artisans, but claimed that "artists were ashamed to put their names
to the good work they did for the good money of the advertisers; and the advertisers fatuously congratulated themselves on the fact that good artists came a
few dollars cheaper anonymously than they did when they signed their
names."[33]

Artisans, often German immigrants or craftsmen of German descent, tran-
scribed the artists' original design onto stone or plates using a German system of
crayon stippling. It was an extremely sturdy technique, holding up after many
runs through the press, but Bunner argued that it produced a mechanical appearance with limited expressive possibilities. "The lithographic draughtsman
has very little use for Art and a profound contempt for the Artist," Bunner
sneered. "The spirit that inspired this perversity was the spirit that separates
the laborer from the artist. . . . he [the artisan] preferred to be a human machine
at a fixed rate of wages."[34]

The designers who created the "poster renaissance" of the 1890s were very
different from their predecessors. Never part of the artisan tradition, they came
from all over the United States, reflecting a wide variety of training and education (in commercial art, fine art, and architecture), and they included women in

26. "View of a Studio, Lee Lash Company." *American Advertiser* (September 1905). General Collection, Library of Congress.

27. "Hoke Process Sign Works." *American Advertiser* (July 1905). General Collection, Library of Congress.

their number. Photoreproduction technology and Art Nouveau aesthetics imported from Europe inspired their new style. Unlike the lithography shop artists, they were knowledgeable about Art Nouveau and scorned realism. By the end of the 1890s, a contemporary writer estimated that there were "twenty establishments which make posters alone their special production, and which show a capital invested of nearly $3,000,000. They provide employment for something like one hundred craftsmen and designers, and perhaps five hundred additional artists, who reproduce the originals of the former."[35]

An English visitor, Percy Bradshaw, provided a rare picture of a "commercial studio" at the beginning of the 1920s using Stanford Briggs, Inc., of New York as an example. It was, he admitted, larger than average, employing fifteen to twenty-five artists supervised by two art directors and an assistant art director, along with one full-time salesman. The directors planned campaigns and managed their progress, promoted sales, and dealt with clients. The artists were paid a regular salary, but four or five of the most prominent received 50 percent of the "proceeds." Bradshaw observed that American advertising artists were paid four times what their British counterparts earned and that once given an assignment they were allowed more freedom to interpret it. All the artists specialized. Apparently there was some kind of "research department," but Bradshaw did not elaborate. Ninety-five percent of the work was advertising illustration, most for magazines and some for newspapers. Clients were advertising agencies. "It is the contention of the organization that it can deliver any type of design or illustration within a very reasonable length of time and at a cost comparable to the price asked by free-lance artists doing the same character of work."[36]

INDIVIDUAL CAREERS

Although we know a great deal about a few individual designers and something about the historical changes that affected all designers, there is inadequate information about graphic designers as a group or even as specialists. Individual careers, nevertheless, provide some hints and bring into focus career choices available during this period. In addition, some designers wrote autobiographies or left substantial records of their life's work.

Career Transformations

The career of John Sartain (1808–1897) is a good example of the mid-nineteenth-century status of successful artists who worked for commerce. Sartain trained in England but emigrated to the United States in 1830, bringing with him the art of mezzotint engraving. He was a portrait engraver, magazine illustrator, publisher, educator, and leader of the Philadelphia art and social elite. He co-published *Sartain's Union Magazine* (1849–52) and managed its art department. Sartain conceived the idea for an art school that became the Pennsylvania Academy of the Fine Arts in 1870. By the turn of the century it would be difficult to find someone who would enjoy his social prestige while working in the graphic arts, but his range of interests would not have been unusual.

Rising through the world of publishing and advertising, John Adams Thayer (b. 1861) combined a series of skills in composing, advertising, and management that became qualifications for a career in graphic design. Thayer was trained in the composing room of a printing office in Boston. He worked as a typographer for newspapers and at the University Press in Cambridge, Massachusetts. Like other young men in his profession, he traveled west. With his union card he found work in Chicago, where he gained experience in more specialized kinds of typesetting and composition: letterheads, booklets, and invitations. When he decided to learn the business aspects of printing, he presented himself to his supervisor. "In a little speech, which I had carefully prepared beforehand, I told him that I had had wide experience in artistic job work and knew, if he would transfer me to his business department that, on account of my ability to sketch and plan, I could give ideas to customers which would increase orders." He failed in this application but returned to Boston, where he began soliciting advertising for newspapers. In 1892, Cyrus H. K. Curtis hired him as the advertising manager of the *Ladies' Home Journal,* where he designed advertisements, hired artists, wrote copy, and sold advertising space. Thayer is credited by contemporaries and later historians with substantial improvements in publication design. Presbrey declared that when Cyrus Curtis hired him as a typographer, "Thayer made up a set of rules for the *Ladies' Home Journal* advertising columns that changed them from the ugly black mess produced by the desire of every advertiser to outdo all others and gave them instead an appearance pleasing to the eye. Illustration was likewise censored into a more artistic appearance. The aspect of the whole periodical was changed. In a short time Thayer became advertising manager; here his expertise in typography was one of several abilities that resulted in the sale of prepared pages to advertisers." Thayer moved several more times. In Boston he worked for the *Boston Journal*. In New York he was "advertising director" at the *Delineator*. Eventually he became the publisher of *Everybody's Magazine*.[37]

Some individuals combined the practice of most graphic design forms, if not at the same point in their careers, at least serially, to such a degree that it is impossible to label them as simply illustrators, typographers, printers, or art directors. In the literature of printing they are identified as printers, and in the histories of illustration they are called illustrators. In Will Bradley's case, even the title "graphic designer" is inadequate. Bradley (1868–1962) was born shortly after the Civil War, and his professional activities span the period under discussion. In the course of his career we see, perhaps for the first time, a blend of all aspects of graphic design practice, serially and in combination.[38]

Bradley's earliest goal was to become an illustrator like his father, a newspaper artist who died young from injuries sustained in the Civil War. Instead, Bradley left school at age twelve to work at a small-town newspaper printshop, where he rose to the position of foreman. Not yet twenty, he saved enough money to go to Chicago, where he worked as a janitor in the art department of the Rand McNally publishing house in order to learn illustration. In the process, he also learned to engrave and design type. Unable to afford art school, Bradley turned to the pages of magazines and printed ephemera that he kept in a scrapbook. He was inspired by the work of William Morris, Walter Crane, Aubrey Beardsley, and Japanese printmakers, and his debt to them is clear in the series of covers and posters he designed for the *Inland Printer* and Chicago literary magazines. His illustrations and posters were the most celebrated examples of American Art Nouveau; with this success, he began work as a freelance designer.

In 1895, stimulated by the examples of William Morris's Kelmscott Press, of Stone and Kimball in Chicago, and of other Americans in the private press movement, Bradley decided to form a press of his own. He moved from Chicago to Springfield, Massachusetts, where he launched Wayside Press. He edited and published *Bradley: His Book*, a magazine of literature and art. Bradley rediscovered the beauty of Caslon type and used it to produce publicity for the

Strathmore Paper Company. Eventually the strain of publishing, editing, and printing took its toll on Bradley's health, and in 1898 he was forced to transfer Wayside to the University Press in Cambridge.

Bradley created "a campaign of type display and publicity" for American Type Founders, including a series of twelve booklets called *The American Chap-Book* (1904–5). He wrote a novel. By 1907, as art editor of *Colliers*, he redesigned the typography and layout. Between 1910 and 1915 he was art editor for *Good Housekeeping, Century*, and *Metropolitan* magazines and continued to write stories and undertake advertising assignments. Later, he became art editor for several other magazines: *Success, Pearson's*, and *National Weekly*. He contributed articles on publication design and the profession. In 1915 Bradley went to work exclusively for William Randolph Hearst's multiple enterprises, taking on "art and typographic assignments" and became art supervisor for a film. (In 1920 he wrote and directed his own movie.) He continued to redesign magazines and newspapers until his retirement in 1925. Pressman, illustrator, typographer, printer, advertising and publication designer, Bradley combined many of the skills and professions identified with graphic design.

Bradley's attitude is equally significant. He recognized and accepted the extra-artistic function of graphic design, not only in his work in advertising but in type design, illustration, and publication design. "At the age of twelve," he wrote many years later, "I had begun to learn that type display is primarily for the purpose of selling something. In 1889, as a free-lance artist in Chicago, I had discovered that to sell something was also the prime purpose of designs for book and magazine covers and for posters. Later I was to realize that salesmanship possessed the same importance in editorial headings and blurbs."[39]

Bradley was a member of several professional organizations: the Society of Arts and Crafts of Boston (he took part in their first exhibit), the Graphic Group, and the American Institute of Graphic Arts. As designers began to redefine themselves as professionals, Bradley, with many others, sought out men who shared his interests and understood his concerns. The part these associations played in defining graphic design is the subject of the next chapter.

4. Professionalization

A professional was definitely not a trade nor was it one of the mechanic
arts. A tradesman bought and sold merchandise and an artisan took on
manual labor. Neither was work befitting a gentleman. . . . The tradesmen
and artisans gave their customers what they wanted. The professional
gave his clients and patients what he thought was good for them.
SAMUEL HABER, *The Quest for Authority and Honor in the*
American Professions

The concept of graphic design as a distinctive endeavor and the emergence of
the graphic designer as a professional uniquely capable of pursuing it are part of
a general pattern in late nineteenth-century industrialization. More specialized
and educated workers distanced themselves from their craft or trade origins and
declared themselves members of an independent calling. Doctors, lawyers, engi-

neers, and architects followed this path. They created schools, ethical codes, and organizations and used their united power to force governmental recognition. Education via a system of apprenticeship continued, but it was judged inadequate to the task; formal schooling was required to master the knowledge and skills now needed for these vocations. The establishment of professional schools, a self-administered code of ethics, and the existence of strong professional associations were three significant institutional markers of professionalization.[1]

When graphic designers look back at their own history, however, its evolution in some of these areas is incomplete. The diversity of career opportunities in graphic design and the complexity of the market worked against a single career definition and path. It is because of its mixed heritage and the lack of agreement among practitioners in defining the core activities that constitute graphic design expertise that the profession remains problematic. At no time did designers agree on the qualifications or the basic education and training necessary for their profession, and they lacked the political strength and cohesion to define and impose a standard code of professional practice. Graphic designers did, however, create professional associations that helped define the common interests of their membership and gave them professional legitimacy.

Sociologists, in describing professionalization, have emphasized the importance of formal technical training required to make a person competent, some sort of demonstration that their skills meet a standard of excellence, and some institutional mechanism to control how these skills are to be applied. Having gained the recognition of their peers, professionals then shared in the economic rewards due their group. Unlike some professional groups, doctors or lawyers, for example, graphic designers could not enlarge their income through monopolistic practices. The authority and honor of medicine or law were not available to them, nor was the spiritual superiority claimed by the fine artist. Economic motives alone, however, do not account for the development of professions; prestige, rather than economic monopoly, often played a decisive role in fostering their development. A strong component of professionalism is its guild aspect, its appeal as an exclusive, organized community of people with shared interests. "Professions," concludes the sociologist Samuel Haber, "offer a way of life. This is the power of their attraction."[2]

The prestige associated with a profession is linked to demonstrated competence in an area that a society requires and values. This is what made graphic design so vulnerable: the ambivalence with which American culture viewed design activities. Even as other forces created graphic design by separating production from designing, designers had to convince their public—editors, publishers, and advertisers—that their work made a significant contribution to products and services. By joining in a variety of associations designers found a means to advance their professional aspirations.

Nineteenth-century Americans may have prided themselves on being individualists, but they were also enthusiastic joiners, and during this century they founded an extraordinary number of professional and extra-professional groups. Many organizations combined professional and social functions. Above all, associations and clubs provided a mechanism for sharing common interests, exchanging information, and creating networking opportunities. As the numbers of people employed in graphic work grew, so did the desire for professional legitimacy and a desire to communicate with others in their particular specialization or area of interest. Printers, typographers, advertisers, and illustrators joined many kinds of groups. The goals of the organizations and their memberships are of particular interest here because they show where individual professionals found their communal identities. The idealistic, high-sounding language that they used in describing their different societies was neither a sign of individual or group naïveté nor an act of cynicism. The sincerity of their convictions and the sense of dedication their language conveys rather speaks of a society that really believed in progress and the greatness of American cultural achievements. Like all professional organizations, graphic design associations were created from a mixture of motives and conditions, by individuals and groups not always in accord. It is also true that unlike, for example, architects, there were many more kinds of groups associated with graphic design and associations that included others besides graphic designers. It took several decades for purely graphic design associations to form, and like the trade magazines of the same era, they continued for some time to share interests and activities of others in addition to their own.

Class distinctions are reflected in these associations. Professionals sought out other men with whom they shared a common interest in printing, business, design, and theory. That they found these men in the same class is hardly surprising. Some printers and publishers ran large establishments and aligned themselves with other prosperous businessmen. Type designers identified with their own historical traditions, either as artisan-unionists or as disciples of William Morris. Advertising artists had no separate associations. They sought camaraderie either within the advertising industry or with illustrators. Illustrators in advertising and book publishing came from diverse backgrounds; some considered themselves artists rather than designers and found a community within artistic circles. The evolution of illustrators' clubs attest to their newfound prestige and affluence during the Golden Age of Illustration.

Into the twentieth century, graphic design professionals continued to maintain distinctions among different traditions. Members of the printing industry were very conscious of their heritage and looked back to Gutenberg, Caxton, and other predecessors for inspiration and for the reflected prestige it gave their work. At the same time technology and specialization destroyed the traditions of the artisan-printers and spurred the formation of new professions. Master printers and those inspired by William Morris's example as a printer-designer began to organize to share their enthusiasm. In contrast, designers in advertising lacked a tradition and operated in a system that initially valued text over image. Nevertheless, the need for commercial artists and art directors grew because there was simply so much work to be done. The advertising industry recognized the power of the visual statement and rewarded those who could contribute to creating effective messages. An expanding mass media reinforced these communities of interests and attracted other design professionals. The associations broadened their interests as the working lives of their members changed and as the distinctions in graphic design practice became less important than the issues that united them.[3]

For the most part, clubs and associations opened their doors only to those deemed completely acceptable through a system of nominating and electing new members. And these associations were not exempt from the racism and sexism that pervaded American culture. Women were excluded from most professional organizations either formally or by custom. Art and Crafts societies were the exception. Non-Caucasian groups were never acknowledged, much less banned, although we know that African-American and American Indian publishers and printers existed from colonial times. African Americans are not mentioned in the printing trade press, with the exception of one cause célèbre, the fight of Lewis H. Douglass to become a member of the Columbia Typographical Union. In 1869, Douglass, a typesetter at the Government Printing Office and the son of Frederick Douglass, attempted to join the union. He was rejected by local members, although the national union supported him. The ensuing imbroglio produced a good deal of documentation that shows how deeply racism penetrated the craft trades in spite of the number of nonwhite professionals engaged in them.[4]

In 1889, the *Inland Printer* acknowledged the increasing number of black printing establishments: "There is no denying the fact that the negroes have made great advances since their emancipation. . . . The printing business has proven attractive to many of these negroes, and a number of them have become proficient in 'the art preservative.' When it is remembered that they are entirely self-taught they will deserve the more credit." But with a patronizing tone and spurious racial theory, the editors dismissed them. If they wanted to gain recognition they must "learn to behave themselves, conform to the law and become peaceable and order-loving citizens, they will progress in the trades as far as their natural ability will allow. We do not think that they will ever become strong competitors in the better lines of work with the white race, who always lead in everything in this world, but the negroes will immeasurably benefit themselves and their posterity by the advance they are destined to make." Illustration was equally inhospitable to African Americans. In his autobiography, Joseph Pennell gleefully recounts how in 1881 he and his fellow students destroyed the academic career of the one young black man admitted to the Pennsylvania Academy of Art. Concluded Pennell, "Curiously, there never has been a great Negro or a great Jew artist in the history of the world."[5]

The success of Chinese-American printers caused intense anxiety in the West. In 1885, the *Pacific Printer* published an editorial about three Chinese-American printing offices that hired Caucasian men. Fearing that they would be underpriced, their competition recommended that "every printer in business refuse to allow a Chinaman to work in his office, and also refuse to give employment to any white man that has worked in a Chinese office. Form a club. Spot every man who patronizes a pigtail office, and let the entire fraternity withhold their trade from that man, and use their influence with others to the same end." The editor then commented, "The treatment is a little heroic, but then desperate cases require desperate remedies."[6]

Nonunion associations drew their membership from white males, usually professionals and businessmen in the middle and upper classes living in large metropolitan areas. The first associations followed the familiar division: fine printing, art-illustration, and advertising. What is significant is that as the work of graphic designers gradually changed, the associations expanded their base of interest and took on new roles. By the second decade of the twentieth century, their membership was beginning to lose readily definable borders.

Book clubs were created around an interest in the study of printing history, book production, and book collecting. The clubs published volumes in limited editions, organized exhibitions, established reference libraries, and rented or purchased rooms or buildings so that they would have a meeting place. The requirements for membership were explained in published constitutions. In addition to a demonstrated interest, most required that members be male and at least twenty-one. A system of nomination and election, with the backing of established members, was involved. Many of the early published histories invoked the influence of William Morris and the ideals of the private press movement.

The first book club, the Franklin Society of Chicago (1870–81), was founded by printers and others in related trades. Its statement of purpose spelled out the responsibilities these men felt that they, as professionals, owed to their craft:

Believing that "every man is a debtor to his profession, from the which as men do of course seek to receive countenance and profit, so ought they of duty to endeavour themselves, by way of amends, to be a help thereto"; and wishing to fulfil this obligation to our craft; for the cultivation of personal intercourse and greater harmony among the members of our guild; to aid each other in perfecting themselves in the practical portion of our work by reading and discussion; to found a library which shall be at once the professional companion and the instructor of each one of us; to collect and preserve the records of typography and kindred arts, so that those who come after us may know what our predecessors and we have done and are doing; and to advance this our common welfare as craftsmen and citizens, we organize and establish the Franklin Society.

Adolf Growoll, the prime source of information on this club, reported that the Franklin Club "numbered one life member, 103 active, and seven corresponding

Professionalization

members." Members created a library of books on printing, sponsored lectures, and published two books: *The Printer: What He Might Be* and *Early Newspapers in Illinois.* In 1870–71 they also produced seven issues of the *Printing Press.*[7]

Beginning in the 1880s, book clubs were organized in larger cities by men interested in fine printing: the Grolier Club (1884) in New York, the Club of Odd Volumes (1886) in Boston, the Rowfant Club (1892) in Cleveland, the Philobiblon Club (1893) in Philadelphia, the Caxton Club (1895) in Chicago, and the Book Club of California (1912) in San Francisco. The clubs shared many of the same characteristics; the Rowfant, for example, consciously modeled itself after the Grolier Club.

The Grolier Club, which continues today, was founded in New York by leading printers, publishers, as well as by men who collected books and incunabula.[8] Devoted to the aesthetics and the noncommercial aspects of publishing, the club sponsored exhibitions and issued elegant books in limited editions on subjects related to the art of the book. It met monthly. Its 50 original members were drawn from the elite of New York City. After fifteen months, membership expanded to allow for 150 resident members and 50 nonresidents. Among its early active members were: Theodore Low De Vinne, printer, scholar, and writer; Alexander W. Drake, art editor of *The Century,* Robert Hoe, Jr., press manufacturer and collector; Arthur B. Turnure, publisher; Walter Gilliss, printer; Edward S. Mead, publisher of Dodd, Mead, and Company; George H. Mifflin, publisher; Louis Comfort Tiffany, designer; and Cornelius Vanderbilt, financier and railroad tycoon. Serious book collectors and other lawyer-banker-collectors were also members.

These book clubs were not strictly professional organizations, but they involved many men whose professional lives were devoted to graphics, and most were motivated by William Morris's aesthetics, though certainly not his socialism. The clubs are important for the influence they exerted on graphic design: the high standards of their limited edition publications and exhibitions inspired professional designers.

Theodore Low De Vinne (1828–1914) was also a prime mover in the United Typothetae of America (1887), an association of master printers of the United States and Canada. This group prided itself on being the "first employers' organization" in the country. Printing establishments historically were small-scale operations, often one-man shops. Printshops were relatively easy to start, requiring a small capital investment by a journeyman printer who wanted to become his own boss; they also had a high rate of failure. Printshops could be found throughout the United States, although New York and Chicago accounted for 40 percent of them. The earliest master printers' associations were formed to set prices and work out mutually beneficial practices among competitors. The Typothetae of New York, for example, was begun in 1862 to deal with devalued currency and related problems caused by the Civil War. Leading firms in New York were all members, and De Vinne served as its secretary. Howard Lockwood, publisher of the *American Bookmaker*, advanced the association's views in his magazine. By 1887 associations had formed in Nashville, Louisville, Minneapolis, Detroit, Columbus, Omaha, Rochester, Richmond, Albany, and Boston.[9]

Local associations united in response to the International Typographical Union's demand for a nine-hour workday. The individual printer's relationship with the trade union movement, rather than its geographical location or size, seems to have accounted for the primary distinctions among the members. Newspaper and periodical printers faced a relatively large, stable, unionized workforce; commercial jobber-printers, in contrast, hired fewer full-time, long-term workers, and these workers were not easily organized by unions. During their initial meeting, the Typothetae members passed the first of many open-shop resolutions and discussed unfair competitive practices. Union demands and price wars were of concern to the printers, and both were addressed. Their written constitution, however, took a loftier tone. They united "with a view to developing a community of interests and a fraternal spirit among the master-printers of the United State and the Dominion of Canada, and for the purpose of exchanging information and assisting each other when necessary." A code of ethics, adopted at the fifth convention in 1891 included a pledge for "honorable competition" and defined proper behavior between colleagues, with customers, and with employees. In 1922 an amendment entitled "Printing Trade Customs" recommended procedures for reimbursing illustrators who did "experimental work performed on orders, such as sketches, drawings, composition, plates, [and] presswork" as well as the drawings, engravings, and electrotypes made from them. In other words, the amendment set accepted standards for dealing with work on commission and reproduction rights within the profession.[10]

28. "New York Delegation to the Golden Jubilee Convention, International Typographical Union." *Inland Printer* (September 1902). Research Collection, Indiana University Library.

In 1888 under De Vinne, first president of the United Typothetae of America, members discussed the perennial problems of the apprenticeship system and the need for an international copyright law. Soon other professional concerns and interests came into play. At the fourth convention members adopted a resolution condemning "the craze for grotesque and so-called fancy job types as an unnecessary expense to the composing room, and inconsistent with good typographical taste." In later annual conventions, De Vinne presented papers on other noneconomic matters, such as "Uniformity in the Bodies of Type," "New Fixtures for the Composing Room," and the correct organization of specimen books. In 1892, at the sixth convention, De Vinne talked about "Masculine Printing," referring to William Morris's Kelmscott printing style, which had made such a tremendous impression on the American printing world that year.[11]

Unlike the United Typothetae, which was composed primarily of commercial printers interested in practical ideas and economic problems, the Society of Printers (1904–present) consisted of men who were not only inspired by

29. "National Executive Committee, United Typothetae of America." *Inland Printer* (July 1902). Research Collection, Indiana University Library.

Morris's aesthetic program but were actively engaged in the private press movement and in what is now regarded as a typographic renaissance. A series of lectures on "The History and Art of Printing" given at the Boston Public Library at the behest of the librarian, Lindsay Swift, was the impetus for forming the society. It is worth noting the topics because they reveal the broad interests of its leaders and their emphasis on design issues.[12]

The first series, presented during the winter of 1904–5, included four lectures:

"Type Display in Modern Printing," by Will Bradley

"Typographical Evolution," by William Dana Orcutt

"The Making of Books," by J. Horace McFarland

"Symbolism of Form and Color," by Henry Turner Bailey

A second series was held in 1906:

"What Constitutes Style in Printing," by C. Howard Walker

"Benjamin Franklin: The Printer," by Lindsay Swift

"Illumination and Its Relation to Book Decoration," by William Dana Orcutt

"Influences for the Advancement of Printing," by Henry Turner Bailey

"Decorative Printing," by Henry Lewis Johnson

The third series was presented in 1907:

"Modern Printing Establishments and Their Output," by

    Henry Lewis Johnson

"Distinctive Types of American Illustration," by Charles H. Caffin

"Design and Color in Printing," by Henry Turner Bailey

Encouraged by the success of the first series, Henry Lewis Johnson urged the formation of a permanent organization. Interested parties met in January 1905 and announced the founding of the Society of Printers.

The society was run by a nine-man council of printer-publishers: Henry Turner Bailey, George French, Carl H. Heintzemann, Henry Lewis Johnson, Frederick D. Nichols, William Dana Orcutt, Bruce Rogers, Daniel Berkeley Updike, and C. Howard Walker. Activities were designed to further the society's aim, "to advance professional standards and support trade schools to teach the Society's ideas." Members traveled to Providence, Worcester, Salem, New York City, the Newark Free Library, and the American Type Founders Company in Jersey City. They visited public and private collections, spoke with their counterparts in other cities, and added members to their group. The society sponsored a visit by T. J. Cobden-Sanderson of Doves Press in England to speak in Boston. It also actively supported the founding of the American Institute of Graphic Arts. In addition, society members convinced the dean of the Harvard Graduate School of Business Administration to offer a two-year program in printing. Called "An Introduction to the Technique of Printing," the curriculum included internships, laboratory work, and most important, a lecture series on the history of printing delivered by Updike. These lectures became the basis for Updike's classic work *Printing Types: Their History, Forms, and Use; A Study in Survivals* (1922). (The course was discontinued at the beginning of World War I.)

In New York City, another group of professionals based in printing but concerned with a broader view of the graphic arts met at the National Arts Club during the winter of 1911–12. They called themselves the Graphic Group. Their aims were sevenfold: to advance the graphic arts, to establish standards of achievement, to stimulate investigation and research, to act as a clearinghouse for ideas, to show examples of individual effort, to hold annual exhibitions, and to cultivate friendships. In the course of defining their organization the group listed occupations it associated with the graphic arts: "Our membership was made up of men engaged in various activities in the Graphic Arts, such as Design, Engraving, Printing, Photography, Illustration, Typography, Lithography, Publishing, Advertising, Paper, and Electrotyping."[13]

The group met for lunch and a lecture every two weeks at the National Arts Club. Although the membership was heavily weighted toward printers and publishers, the luncheon topics also show the range of interests those activities now included: color use and color printing, plate-making, photography, advertising campaigns, and layout. Their speakers formed a distinguished cross-section of the academic, scientific, and professional community. Topics were sometimes technical: the photographer Arnold Genthe spoke on autochrome plates, Harry P. Carruth, an industrial papermaker, on new paper-making processes, A. H. Munsell on color, and Frederick E. Ives on the history of plate-making. Others speakers talked about their own work: Alfred Stieglitz lectured on photography, Frederic Goudy on type and fine printing, Max Weber on poster design, and Earnest Elmo Calkins on advertising.[14]

The Graphic Group was a prototype for the American Institute of Graphic Arts; members of the Graphic Group all joined the AIGA and the new organization continued to pursue the group's range of interests. Indeed, many members served in leadership positions in the new AIGA, or as one member later wrote, "Eventually this group joined the American Institute of Graphic Arts and in time took over the conduct of its affairs."[15]

During a lunch meeting in 1914, leading members of the National Arts Club discussed the need for an association able to represent the nation at an international book fair held every year in Leipzig. The National Arts Club itself had for several years sponsored an annual exhibition called "The Fifty Books of the Year" to encourage higher standards in design and printing. It was felt, however, that a different kind of organization was needed. Members then called a larger meeting to authorize the formation of a committee to draft a constitution for such an association. Charles DeKay, a magazine editor and art critic, wrote the constitution with help from newspaper publisher William B. Howland, Joseph H. Chapin, art director of *Scribner's Magazine,* Alexander W. Drake, art director of the *Century Magazine,* and others. The Leipzig Book Fair was temporarily forgotten.[16]

On November 13, 1913, the *New York Times* reported that John G. Agar, president of the National Arts Club, had delivered a speech at the eighth annual Fifty Books of the Year Exhibition in which he announced the founding of a new society, the American Institute of Graphic Arts. "The institute will include engravers, etchers, the Typothetae, lithographers, illustrators, panel painters, mural painters, and generally, *all arts and crafts intended to make ideas visible.*"[17]

The broad-based appeal continued in a subsequent membership drive directed at "those interested in the graphic arts throughout the United States, including artists, printers, publishers, etchers, engravers, photographers, lithographers and electrotypers." The goals of the institute were

> To stimulate and encourage those engaged in the graphic arts; to form a center for intercourse and for exchange of views of all interested in these arts; to publish books and periodicals, to hold exhibitions in the United States and to participate as far as possible in the exhibitions held in foreign countries relating to the graphic arts; to invite exhibitions of foreign works; to stimulate the public taste by school exhibitions, lectures and printed matter; promote the higher education in these arts, and generally to do all things which will raise the standard and aid the extension and development of the graphic arts in the United States.[18]

Although commercial printers and typographers dominated the AIGA's early offices and printers composed half its membership, other interests were represented. Beginning in 1920, the AIGA Medal was awarded annually to individuals for contributions to the graphic arts. Among the first ten recipients were a photoengraver, an advertising executive, an advertising designer, an artist–wood engraver, and a museum executive. In 1925 the *News-letter* defended the institute on charges that it favored typography and printing at the expense of pictorial arts. Wrote the editor, "The Institute membership is composed largely of men of three different callings; men who work with type; men who make pictures; men who reproduce pictures for printing—in other words, printers, artists and engravers or lithographers."[19] The AIGA continued to sponsor the

"Fifty Books" exhibition, expanding the number of cities on its itinerary but adding exhibitions of illustrations and posters.

ASSOCIATIONS BASED ON ILLUSTRATION

As opportunities grew, aspiring illustrators flocked to large cities, notably New York and Chicago. In New York they studied at Cooper Union, the National Academy of Design, or, later, at the Art Students League. They also formed or joined clubs. In New York City alone, the following clubs welcomed illustrators: the Century Club, the Lotus Club, the Grolier Club, the Society of Illustrators, the Salmagundi Club, the Tile Club, and the New York Etching Club.[20]

The Salmagundi Sketch Class (1871) was founded in New York by five young illustrators: Will Low, F. S. Church, J. Scott Hartley, Joseph Hartley, and William Henry Shelton. Shelton was its chronicler. He later wrote that the original club was limited to twenty men: illustrators, painters, sculptors, engravers, art students, and "laymen." They met one night a week in the dingy studio of a sculptor to critique each other's work, eat sausages, drink coffee, sing, and engage in friendly boxing and fencing matches that raised clouds of plaster dust. Most of the group pursued careers in illustration and spent other evenings at the National Academy of Design "in the cast room or in the life class" or at Cooper Union. At the beginning of each session the group selected a subject for illustration, and "on the following Saturday evening a half-dozen sketches would be displayed on the Studio easel for mutual admiration and friendly criticism." Shelton recorded some of the topics: "Weirdness," "Happy as a King," "Conviviality," "Silence," "Wind," "Hell," "A Frosty Morning," and "Extremes Meet."[21]

The club changed its name to The Black and White Society in 1879, when it began to hold annual exhibitions of its members' work. By then many successful illustrators, including Howard Pyle, W. W. Denslow, and F. S. Church, had joined. Now fully employed professionals, members had neither the time nor interest in maintaining a sketching program, and in 1887 the club, having three years earlier changed its name to the Salmagundi Club, officially became a social organization. It had moved to elegant quarters on Fifth Avenue complete with chandeliers, a cook, alcoholic refreshments, and other refinements. The change

Professionalization

30. "Boxing in Hartley's Studio by Will H. Low." William
Henry Shelton, *The Salmagundi Club* (1918). General
Collection, Library of Congress.

in address merely affirmed that illustrators, at least some of them, were flourishing in the world of New York advertising and publishing.

There were other clubs. The Tile Club (1886), for example, counted A. B. Frost and Edwin Austin Abbey, two of the most noted male illustrators of the day, among its members. But most of these organizations included successful professionals in other arts—sculptors, painters, musicians, architects—and so are less relevant here.

The Society of Illustrators was founded on February 1, 1901, by nine illustrators and a businessman adviser. Its ostensible aim was "to promote generally the art of illustration and to hold exhibitions from time to time." In fact, the motivations for its inception were more complex. Historians suggest that illustrators wanted to reassure potential employers of their "professional"—that is, probusiness, antiunion—stance, and saw the society as a nonthreatening arena for gatherings. Its monthly dinners and other activities brought together illustrators, editors, and publishers so that it became a congenial meeting place for the exchange of professional information and employment opportunities. Within a short period the leading illustrators of the day had joined, including Abbey, Pyle, Remington, Gibson, the Leyendecker brothers, and Penfield. Many of these men were employed in advertising and had professional ties with other organizations. John Sloan, at least, felt it necessary to join though he was repelled by its emphasis on elaborate, raucous entertainment.[22]

THE ARTS AND CRAFTS SOCIETIES

Unlike the printing and illustration societies, Arts and Crafts club members worked in a wide range of media and were joined by a shared belief in the universal need for art, the nobility of labor, and the moral value of craftsmanship and handcrafted products.[23] Although the first society was founded in Boston, within the year similar groups began in Chicago and New York. There were active societies throughout the country in small as well as large cities, representing varying degrees of professionalism. They included women, sometimes in positions of leadership.

On January 4, 1897, at the Museum of Fine Arts "prominent Bostonians" listened to a lecture by Henry Lewis Johnson on the importance of a formal Arts and Crafts organization. He apparently convinced them. The early organizers began with an exhibition in Copley Hall in April 1897 with Johnson as director. It included four hundred exhibits "by over 100 exhibitors, at least half of whom were women." Sarah Wyman Whitman (the society's vice-president) was cited for her work in decorative book binding. There were book covers, bookplates, and illustrations by Amy M. Sacker; pen-and-ink designs by Theodore Brown Hapgood, Jr., and Harry Goodhue; an "Altar Book, with type, initials and borders designed by Bertram Grosvenor Goodhue"; and carpet designs by William Morris, "to whom this and all the arts and crafts exhibitions owe their existence more than to any other man." Daniel Berkeley Updike and Will Bradley also participated. In addition to graphics, miniature painting, pottery, stained glass, decorated china, oil painting, and watercolor painting were represented.[24]

The Society of Arts and Crafts of Boston was formally incorporated in June 1897 with a membership of twenty-four, including three women. Charles Eliot Norton, the society's first president wrote that "The Society of Arts and Crafts is incorporated for the purpose of promoting artistic work in all branches of handicraft. It hopes to bring designers and workmen into mutually helpful relations, and to encourage workmen to execute designs of their own. It endeavors to stimulate in workmen an appreciation of the dignity and value of good design."

Professionalization

The society continued to organize juried exhibitions, maintained a salesroom and reference library, and published a journal, *Handicraft* (1902–4; 1910–12). In 1907, on the occasion of the society's tenth-anniversary exhibit, twenty-three Arts and Crafts societies from around the country formed the National League of Handicraft Societies.[25]

To the extent that the Arts and Crafts movement sought to reunite artisan and artist, it worked against professionalization, blurring the lines between production and design, amateur and professional. To the extent that it celebrated handicraft over machine production, it ignored economic reality. Within the societies, there were tensions between designers and artists and between those committed to Morris's medievalism and others who felt a greater affinity with French or Japanese decorative design, those interested in reforming industrial production and those who wanted to raise popular taste. As historian Eileen Boris notes, the handicraft shop and the consumer, rather than the industrial workshop and the worker, often became the focus of interest. Nevertheless, these societies directed public attention to design issues in printing and bookmaking and encouraged commercial printers and designers to rethink design choices and strive for higher standards.[26]

ADVERTISERS' ASSOCIATIONS

Unlike printers and illustrators, who organized, at least in part, to celebrate and publicize their shared tradition, advertising professionals had no tradition.[27] They founded clubs to socialize, to discuss common concerns, and to gain a measure of professional respect. The earliest advertising clubs were formed by copywriters in retail advertising; the Business Writers Association was founded in Detroit in 1890, the Agate Club in Chicago in 1894. Men in the outdoor advertising businesses formed associations to regulate posting sites. The Associated Billposters and Distributors of the United States and Canada was founded in Chicago in 1891. In 1914, the Painted Display Advertising Association became the Outdoor Advertising Association; it merged in 1925 with the Poster Advertising Association to form the Outdoor Advertising Association of America. Their trade journal, *Advertising Outdoors*, showcased advertising campaigns, included a feature entitled "Outdoor Advertising: The Art Gallery of the People," and in later years published an "Annual Poster Design Number: Advertising Outdoors; Best Poster of the Year" and "The Best Canadian Posters of the Year."

In 1896 the heads of the leading advertising agencies formed a club in New York called the Sphinx Club because members vowed to keep quiet about what went on during meetings. At odds with this pledge, their object was "to acquire and disseminate, through the interchange of ideas, a clearer understanding of the problems of advertising and the betterment of advertising." Many of their lectures were reported verbatim in the trade press. The Sphinx included a diversity of interests in advertising. John Adams Thayer, George Rowell, Artemas Ward, Frank Presbrey, Condé Nast, other book and magazine publishers, heads of major advertising companies, and heads of art departments in these companies, were members—or, as the club's literature accurately boasted, "The leading advertising men and other business men of New York City and other cities throughout the United States."[28]

Although these clubs began in New York and Chicago, by 1906, *Printers' Ink* noted, "there was at least one advertising club in each of fifteen cities," including the Pacific Coast Advertising Men's Association, Periodical Publishers' Association, Advertising Club of Western New York, Banking Publicity Association, and American Gulf Association of Advertising Interests. In 1899 the American Advertisers Association, composed of national advertisers, was formed in New York and the American Society of National Advertisers began in the West; eventually they merged with the American Advertisers Association. The Advertising Clubs of America, formed in 1906, became the Associated Advertising Clubs of America in 1911, and the Associated Advertising Clubs of the World in 1914.[29]

Advertising organizations were not particularly concerned with advertising art, but some of their members were. In 1908 the National Arts Club in New York sponsored the first annual exhibition of advertising art. Initiated by Earnest Elmo Calkins, its intent was to demonstrate that advertising art could be both effective advertising and of great artistic merit. According to Peirce Johnson, a founding member and president, the Art Directors Club of New York was created partially because of the tremendous interest in the annual exhibits. Additionally, Johnson pointed to the Armory Show of 1913, which demonstrated the enormous potential of graphics to young art directors. "It offered hope for experimentation in their own vocation." Finally, Johnson credited the effects of

World War I on advertising, giving the industry a newfound legitimacy and economic opportunities.[30]

The Art Directors Club began in New York in 1920 with fifty-three charter members. Characterized by Johnson as "practical idealists," members fell into two groups: "salaried people . . . who were engaged in the direction and production of illustration and design for agencies, publications, and art services" and "those who operated chiefly as individuals, such as typographers and free-lance artists."[31] Men who owned or worked in advertising agencies dominated the association's officer roster. In its charter the group pledged to raise professional standards, "improve conditions in the field," and participate in public affairs "to promote the best interest of art, applied art and advertising." An Ethics Committee and an Exhibition Committee were immediately established. The annual exhibitions that had preceded the club's official founding remained an important aspect of its work. In his foreword to the first annual catalog, Egbert G. Jacobson asserted that "from the beginning, usefulness has been the criteria of vitality in art." Unlike past cultures, "in the United States, where encouragement from government, religion and private wealth is infrequent, the need and wealth of commerce have empowered it to assume the patronage of art." He continued, "This book is a catalog of an exhibition of paintings and drawings not only prescribed by commerce but made for the purpose of stimulating commerce."[32]

The jurors themselves represented the leading figures of the day: painter Robert Henri, illustrator Charles Dana Gibson, painter E. H. Blashfield, educator and painter Arthur Wesley Dow, and illustrator and writer Joseph Pennell. Reporting on its selection for the first show after the club's founding, the jurors observed that "the awards have been made only with regard to the merit of the subjects as paintings or drawings and without attempting to judge their value as advertisements. The fact that they have been used for advertising has necessarily been accepted by the Jury as prima facie evidence of their advertising value." And, indeed, the annual contained both original art and art as it appeared in the advertisement. Significantly, jurors regretted that they had to award original works as submitted, without seeing them as advertisements, and "strongly recommended" that future exhibitions "show not merely the illustration but the advertisement in which it appeared." This suggests that the exhibition of original art may not have been an attempt to give the show a more artistic air, as some historians have argued.[33]

Professionalization

The club reached out to the advertising art community and beyond to other graphic designers. Shortly after the establishment of the New York club, Chicago art directors began their own club and exhibitions, and art directors in other centers of advertising followed. The New York club ran a placement service, sketch classes for members, and a luncheon lecture series that featured Frederic Goudy and Fred Cooper, members of the AIGA, and editors and advertising agency luminaries. Ernest Elmo Calkins and other Art Directors Club leaders were active members of the AIGA. Interdisciplinary networking, clearly, was routine. By 1920 members of graphic design associations had achieved a sense of professional solidarity and pride, but they continued to grapple with problems of status. Graphic design, like other applied and popular arts, held an ambiguous place in the American cultural hierarchy.

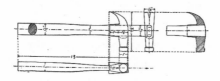

5. The Great Divide

The "artists" in the engraving house art departments bent over their desks, working like beavers, so engrossed that they could not spare time to even talk about the work of the "great artists." That art was as unmeaning to them as to the average man. They were deeply interested in formulating their own new mode of graphic art and it was based on usefulness.
RALPH FLETCHER SEYMOUR, *Some Went This Way*

By separating art from the practical we erect a barrier, the "Great Divide."
CHARLES CAFFIN, *Art for Life's Sake*

That the United States Commissioner of Labor Carroll D. Wright contributed an article entitled "The Practical Value of Art" to a popular magazine does not seem unusual or worthy of comment. To espouse the cause of vocational education in the form of applied arts would be entirely appropriate, but Wright did not stop at urging the prosaic advantages of such a curriculum; he claimed far more. "Every work of creative art," he wrote, "is a revelation of divine beauty; hence it is of deepest significance to religion, and to every element of social well being. Even the lowest forms of artistic expression, so long as they embody art ideas at all, are beneficial."[1]

The defense of popular art as an educational, moral, even spiritual force is no longer taken for granted, but at the end of the last century when Wright advocated such ideas, it was a common, if not unchallenged creed. Wright then linked the power of the applied arts to the nation's economic health:

> But industry flourishes because it is not limited to the production of things that are needed for food, raiment, and shelter. It is because art has come in to increase the wants of the race that trade and commerce flourish. Art carries industry beyond our actual wants, and calls upon it to supply those things which make for social progress. The future expansion of industry and of commerce, the future elevation in the character of the employment of all classes, the increase of their earning capacity, the opportunity of increasing the standard of their environment—all depend upon the cultivation of the industrial arts.[2]

In Wright's view, the applied arts not only shared in the spirituality of the so-called fine arts but ensured the economic well-being of the nation. How did such enormous claims come to be made?

In a period when hierarchies of artistic value were recodified and the distinction between elite and popular taste intensified, many professionals took part in a public debate about the place of applied arts and design education in a democracy and the increasing use of art in advertising. The applied arts—and graphic design was considered to be in that category—were scorned by an intellectual elite that elevated some arts, notably oil painting and sculpture, to a place outside popular comprehension. Among their adversaries were leaders in the industrial arts movement and in the advertising community who were determined to gain recognition and prestige for their profession. In their response to the attacks of their critics and to the uneasy relation between advertising management and the artistic community, advocates of applied art began to define a new aesthetic position.

At the beginning of the nineteenth century, Americans of all classes attended public performances of instrumental music, opera, and theater; Americans participated in a "shared public culture." By the second half of the century, however, more educated and generally wealthier Americans demanded a more refined entertainment insulated from the noisy crowd. In the visual arts they sought a refuge from what they perceived as vulgarity and rampant materialism. They celebrated a spiritual, transcendent encounter that the less educated could not understand. Their appreciation of the arts, as well as of the natural world, was identified with spiritual or religious experiences. Popular arts could satisfy only crude taste, whereas the fine arts appealed to cultivated sensibilities. By the end of the century, the rift between fine and popular art was deep. The historian Lawrence Levine calls this evolution "the sacralization of art."[3]

At the same time, late nineteenth-century America was also an age of good works, of great reformers, muckrakers, and crusading social workers. Many with wealth and education recognized an obligation to educate the lower classes, to bring to the slums of cities and the wasteland of Main Street the beauty found in the arts. Art was their refuge, but it could also be a moral crusade, because they believed with Commissioner Wright that the recognition of beauty in art, as well as in nature, led to a higher spirituality. To appreciate the arts required aesthetic and spiritual training. The reformers, at least some of them, felt they had an ethical responsibility to raise the level of public taste by teaching the masses. In short, two conflicting impulses appealed to the guardians of high culture: to erect a barrier against the philistinism of popular culture and to educate those less fortunate. The tension between withdrawing to a citadel of purity and reaching out to the hoi polloi would not be easily resolved. Both impulses were at work by the last third of the century, and both had roots in English aesthetic theory.

The English experience of rapid industrialization, and the reaction to it beginning in midcentury, was an important influence. The Aesthetic movement, particularly as it was defined by John Ruskin, attempted to unite the search for beauty with lofty social and moral ends. Books, periodicals, and traveling lecturers spread the new message. Important figures in the British art movements made well-publicized tours of the United States, most notably Oscar Wilde in 1882 and Walter Crane in 1890. The Philadelphia Centennial Exposition of 1876 presented the ideas as well as the objects of the British Aesthetic movement to

Americans. The exposition was seen by many as proof that English industrial arts education had dramatically raised the standards of commercial products.

Schooling has, of course, always been a matter of intense public debate in the United States, but no more so than during an era when new skills are needed to enter the workplace. Even before the Civil War, the old apprenticeship system was unable to cope with an industrializing economy. In the 1850s, with the tremendous increase in manufacturing and a boom in new technologies, a concerted effort was made to introduce drawing into the public school curriculum. The men Peter Marzio calls "the art crusaders" emphasized the practical, utilitarian aspects of art. In particular, they believed that drawing instruction could raise design standards in manufacturing. Workers needed training in drafting and in understanding technical drawings for construction, for machinery and industrial processes, for printing textiles and wallpaper, and for the manufacture of other household items. They justified industrial art education on purely utilitarian grounds. Workers would be more productive, and manufacturers would no longer rely on imported European designs. Courses in drawing could ultimately advance American products in the marketplace.[4]

Complementing this idea was the belief championed by William Minifie, head of the newly founded Maryland Institute College of Art that "all persons who can learn to write, can also learn to draw."

> I would not be understood to say, that all can learn to draw equally well; or, that all may become Artists: very far from it; all who learn to write do not become good penmen, although its practice is generally commenced in early childhood and continued through the whole course of education.
>
> But I do mean to say, that every person, male or female, may acquire sufficient facility in the use of the pencil, to render its practice agreeable as well as profitable.

Minifie promoted drawing not as "among the superfluities of life" but as a necessity to any "engaged in any of the industrial arts of life. . . . How can a manufacturer give intelligent instruction to a machinist for some new arrangement of his machinery without a diagram?" Workers who could read working drawings were more valuable. Drawing was an essential skill for engineers, architects, mechanical draftsman, and surveyors, as well as for those who produced patterns for shoemakers and tailors. Drawings were needed to file for patents and for recording crime scenes and great events of the day; manufacturers used drawings for textiles and wallpaper design.[5]

Just as the industrial drawing movement was beginning to find support, however, two books by John Ruskin, *Modern Painters* (1850) and *Elements of Drawing* (1857), were published in the United States. Ruskin attacked the art crusaders in no uncertain terms. He railed against industrialization, materialism, and the development of soulless culture. "It seems to me," he observed, "that we are all too much in the habit of confusing art as *applied* to manufacture, with manufacture itself." From Ruskin's doctrine of the unity of art, nature, and spiritual experience grew the conviction that art instruction had to be part of a moral education, not professional training.[6]

Ruskin's vision of art as a path to transcendent experience appealed to many American intellectuals. Its implications for design education were, of course, significant. Ruskin despised the connection of art and commerce, though he did not link design (which he considered an art) with utility. Instead he wrote, "The tap-root of all this mischief is in the endeavour to produce some ability in the student to make money by designing for manufacture. No student who makes this his primary object will ever be able to design at all; and the very words 'School of Design' involve the profoundest of Art fallacies. Drawing may be taught by tutors: but Design only by Heaven; and to every scholar who thinks to sell his inspiration, Heaven refuses its help." Unlike the industrial art educators, Ruskin emphasized appreciation over skill. "I would rather teach drawing that my pupils may learn to love Nature, than teach the looking at Nature that they may learn to draw. It is surely also a more important thing, for young people and unprofessional students, to know how to appreciate the art of others, than to gain much power in art themselves." Yet in Ruskin's philosophy, appreciation was not a passive act but one that required great effort. The development of good taste was part of a student's moral education.[7]

The battle over the art curriculum in public education was by no means decided. English design schools were established in 1836 by English manufacturers to train skilled designers for industry. Only in the 1870s did Americans follow suit. Massachusetts made industrial drawing a public school requirement and hired Walter Smith (1836–86), a British-born and -trained artist, as state director of art education and director of drawing for Boston's public schools.[8]

Walter Smith was not part of the art crusade tradition, but the earlier commitment to industrial education found a receptive audience in William Morris's disciple. The Arts and Crafts tradition was based on the craft workshop, and Smith wanted to transferred the ideals of the workshop into a public school classroom. Similarly, he advocated the unity of manual and artistic effort and refused to denigrate the applied arts. He contested the growing split between high and low culture: "In many places the idea prevails that, if a man or woman has not skill or imagination enough to become an artist, it is better to become a designer; in other words, that the weaker vessels of either sex, who cannot pass through the fine-art furnace, should be prepared, as coarser clay at a lower temperature, for the more ignoble occupation of pattern-drawers for the factories." Instead, Smith emphasized the importance of training all children. "It has been this senseless estimate of art which, ignoring its capabilities for ministering to the highest requirements and capacities of men, and looking upon it as an exceptional characteristic of a few eccentric persons,—this false judgment has alone been responsible for the absence of opportunities for its development into usefulness, and its elevation into the position of an element in all education."[9]

Smith treated drawing as part of general manual training. In the manner of the earlier art crusaders, he created a graded system of teaching that began in elementary school. Drawing was a language, a vehicle of expression in the study of other subjects with practical application. "Perhaps the most practically important view of the subject of art education is its value commercially. In an essentially utilitarian age, things are judged by the standard of usefulness, rather than sentiment; and wherever we find great success following the experiment of introducing art education, it is where business men have forwarded and developed it as a question of dollars and cents."[10]

For a time, Smith prevailed. In May 1879 the state of Massachusetts required public schools in all cities with a population of ten thousand and over to teach drawing. Smith, in collaboration with Louis Prang, produced appropriate textbooks and art instruction manuals to supplement his curriculum.

The message of Arts and Crafts, interpreted in the United States by Smith and others, was replete with mixed signals and contending goals. To some extent, the Arts and Crafts artisanal tradition conflicted with Ruskin's spirituality. At the same time, the Arts and Crafts movement itself owed much to Ruskin's revulsion at industrial dehumanization and his insistence on the artistic value of the decorative and craft traditions. Although William Morris had rejected ma-

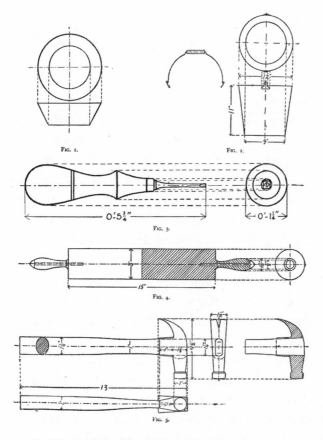

31. "Construction." *Prang Elementary Course in Art Instruction, no. 7* (1898). Research Collection, Indiana University Library.

chine-produced materials, this part of Morris's teaching was generally ignored, allowing Smith to avoid at least one obstacle. Yet Smith and other proponents of the Arts and Crafts movement failed to grapple with the very real issues of class divisions implicit in the industrial education curriculum. The movement faced two sources of criticism. The first came from those who insisted that it kept working-class students from following a college preparatory curriculum, a warning that resonated with parents who had higher aspirations for their children. The second came from those who regarded art instruction, in any form, as superfluous. Smith disputed the accusation that his curriculum was class-based, but he lost public support. His dismissal from his post in Massachusetts in 1880 marked a rejection of the industrial drawing curriculum, though not the end of industrial education.[11]

Late nineteenth-century theoretical disputes were much more complex than a simple dialectic between the utilitarian-industrial drawing movement and the fine arts curriculum, and it is not possible here to do more than summarize them. Nevertheless, these two were significant to graphic designers because they determined to a considerable degree the character of art institutions created during the second half of the nineteenth century and affected how educated Americans interpreted the role of design in the arts and in society.

American educational institutions adopted various approaches in teaching art. Some schools combined art with a traditional liberal education curriculum, while others were dedicated specifically to fine or applied arts. When the major museums east of the Rocky Mountains were founded, many of them between the end of the Civil War and 1900, they often established art academies as part of their mission. Other schools originated at the behest of local manufacturers. Some state and private institutions, like Harvard University, based their courses on Ruskin's philosophy and established strong programs in art history and connoisseurship. Others, such as Yale University and Syracuse University, created professional schools in fine and industrial arts.[12]

Small schools with perhaps only part-time faculty seem to have been important, although they were short-lived. Little is known about the curriculum of these institutions, but figures of importance to graphic design were involved with them. The Frank Holme School of Illustration, for example, was located in the Athenaeum Building in Chicago. It was begun in 1898 by Ida Van Dyke Holme with help from her husband, who worked as an illustrator for the *Chicago Chronicle*. Frederic Goudy taught at the school around the turn of the century, and it was there William Addison Dwiggins, Oswald Cooper, and Will Ransom studied lettering with him. Correspondence courses were a significant part of the school's activities. Ralph Fletcher Seymour described Smith's Academy, another popular Chicago school, as "a sort of co-operative institution where students divided the weekly maintenance costs and the poor ones paid for their tuition by doing janitor service. After class sessions teachers, students, models and janitors gathered in some room to drink beer, eat sandwiches, sing and relax." Boston was home to the Cowles School, where poster artist Ethel Reed

32. "The Day Class at the Art Academy, Chicago." *Brush and Pencil* (February 1898). General Collection, Library of Congress.

studied for a time, and the Eric Pape School of Art, where book decorator Marion Peabody taught. These were small professional schools, teaching students a specific form of applied art. Yet even finishing schools for upper-class young women offered courses in "advertising design" and illustration.[13]

The Clarence H. White School of Photography shows the conjunction of educational theory with new professional opportunities. Like many photographers, White began as an amateur dedicated to artistic photography. When he became a professional he was torn between the need to earn a living in the world of advertising and retaining his status as an artist. White met Arthur Wesley Dow (1857–1922), a professor at Columbia University Teachers College, and Dow offered him a way of reconciling the two worlds. A landscape painter as well as an educator, Dow developed a popular and influential theory of design education based on his understanding of principles of Japanese art and admiration for the work of James Abbott McNeill Whistler. Dow focused on the formal elements of

33. "The Men's Night Class at the Art Academy, Chicago." *Brush and Pencil*
(February 1898). General Collection, Library of Congress.

visual art (line, color, mass) and their combination based on five principles:
opposition, transition, variation, repetition, and symmetry. In contrast to earlier
methods that predetermined the ideal solution to every lesson, Dow encouraged
students to find their own solutions. Dow's curriculum included projects in textiles, mosaics, graphics, and photography. He staunchly championed applied
arts and the idea that everyone was capable of artistic expression.[14]

Dow's theory offered White a philosophy that encouraged would-be professional photographers to learn the technical aspects of their craft and gave them
an vision of photography grounded in fundamental principles of art. Under
Dow's sponsorship, White taught at Columbia Teachers College and began the
Seguinland School of Photography in Georgetown, Maine. In 1914, with the
painter Max Weber, he founded the Clarence H. White School of Photography in
New York City. In describing his school, White wrote, "This is a professional

institution for the training of men and women for the vocation of photography. It treats photography not only as a fine art with an established technique, but also as a practical art, indispensable to modern commerce and industry." White's curriculum gave student photographers the tools to earn a living in the commercial world that did not sacrifice their claim to photography as a valid artistic medium. Margaret Bourke-White, Anton Bruehl, Paul Outerbridge, and Ralph Steiner, first-generation students at the school, were leading advertising photographers in the 1920s.[15]

Home-study courses were popular with would-be designers. In Minneapolis, the Federal School of Commercial Designing (established in 1916) and the Federal School of Applied Cartooning (established a year later) offered a wide range of courses taught by some of the most successful designers in the country. Like other correspondence schools, it promised fortunes to successful graduates. The Federal School blandly assured prospective students that "Commercial Artists are the highest paid men in this country today." And the Meyer Booth College of Commercial Art in Chicago boasted that its students could earn thirty-five dollars a week immediately after graduation and that some earned fifty thousand dollars a year, a veritable fortune for the day. The course offerings show that what once had been considered separate areas of accomplishment now comprised a single course of study. A Meyer Booth College brochure of 1919 offered the following classes in its one-year curriculum: drawing, photo retouching, fashion illustration, color, lettering, composition and perspective, and the mechanics of reproduction. The program was planned to prepare students for careers in advertising. The brochure described the profession this way:

> Commercial Art speaks a universal language. It tells its story at a glance, it has power to cheer and charm, educate and edify, to inform myriad minds or transform prejudice. It is the magic wand that builds prestige and conjures up good-will—that greatest of merchandizing assets. It enters every home, rich or poor, every business large or small. It is before all the people, all the time, everywhere and is silently, surely and persistently elevating the masses to a higher plane of art appreciation who otherwise would not have the time, money or inclination to develop their esthetic sense.[16]

115

Many graduates of design schools did find employment, if not fortunes. Yet in spite of the proliferation of job opportunities in the mass media, the work itself was often attacked in intellectual journals. What made graphic design so threatening? When the *Nation* published an article excoriating all that was tawdry, unauthentic, and mediocre in American society, it entitled the piece "Chromo Civilization," a label that struck a chord among the cultural elite. Chromolithography, once hailed as the medium that brought Art to Everyman had come to mean everything cheap and degraded. In a telling point, Marzio notes that the changing status of reproductive illustration can be measured in its fate between the two great world's fairs. During the Philadelphia Centennial of 1876, lithographs were shown with the fine arts along with sculpture, painting, and engraving. By 1893, at Chicago's Columbian Exposition, they were reclassified as part of the commercial or industrial arts.[17]

Four aspects of popular graphics seem to have offended the intellectual community: its creation by mechanical reproduction, the weight it gave to images at the expense of text, its lack of a single artistic vision, and its connection with the world of commerce.

The critic Walter Benjamin characterized this new era of popular art "the age of mechanical reproduction." The duplication of text and imagery by means other than by the human hand had been a part of the Industrial Revolution. But, as Benjamin argued, the fact of reproducibility by machine had implications beyond the brute fact of technological change. Unlike the hand-pulled print and the hand-set text, this new amalgam had no historical precedent, no revered tradition, and none of the prestige associated with handcrafted work. Prints and fine books were printed in limited editions for those who could afford them; the new machine-produced images proliferated in unimaginable numbers and could not be avoided. They were invasive; they changed the very character of public as well as private space.[18]

Mechanical reproduction was also suspect because it raised questions about the role of the artist. Arts and Crafts purists agreed that artists must control and shape the artistic object. Oscar Lovell Triggs spoke for many when he thundered: "If beauty did not require the expression of the human soul, if beauty were simply a matter of the material, if beauty were merely a form, then the

116

machine might populate the earth with objects of beauty. But the fact remains, that to have beauty in an object the human hand must touch the materials into shape, and the closer the object is to the soul the more beautiful it becomes in its ultimate form."[19]

The intense arguments that raged over engraving and photography—could art be created in these media?—were important aspects of this conflict. At question was the ability of mechanically reproduced art to communicate a personal vision, an individual voice, that the intelligentsia identified with authentic artistry. Students trained in the fine art tradition entered a field previously dominated by artisans and felt the pressure to adjust not only to technological constraints but to a loss of a spiritual fulfillment. Louis Levy, writing about the early 1880s, confirmed this view. "The mechanical draftsmen of those days, who had been taken mostly from architects' offices or machine works and trained to make drawings for reproduction in imitation of woodcuts and even of steel engravings, then began to be supplemented by students from the art academies and schools of design. These novices usually had to be weaned from the transcendentals of their art."[20]

Second, the use of pictures to enhance or even replace text challenged the supremacy of the written word and, by extension, intellectual authority. In magazines like the *Nation*, writers attacked the increasing use of illustrations in books and magazines by attacking the images themselves as inaccurate, misrepresenting either the facts or the writer's imagination and distorting reality. Realistic images, whether created by the engraver or by the photographer, were equated with soulless materiality.[21]

Third, the arts that were created indirectly by reproduction involved a group effort, potentially reducing the role of the artist-designer to a talented but unimaginative cog. The historian of advertising, Ralph Hower, has described the advertising artist's work as "essentially to finish a rough sketch prepared by the agency's art director and layout man after numerous conferences with the client's advertising manager, the agency's account representatives, and the copywriter."[22]

In spite of these negative attitudes, graphic design might still have escaped the wrath of the guardians of high culture. The great value Ruskin placed on the decorative arts and Morris's workshop artisanal tradition, ideals upheld by many American printers and respected critics like Charles Caffin, had gone

34. "C. S. Houghtaling, Signs." *Profitable Advertising* (1894). General Collection, Library of Congress.

some way to showing that mechanical reproduction could produce beautiful objects and designs. It was graphic design's relation to commerce that the advocates of high culture found appalling.

Advertising graphics had created a dramatically new visual environment that some took as a assault. Flamboyant (or grotesque, depending on your point of view) advertising tradecards were collected, advertisements were displayed on trains and buses, huge posters overwhelmed the sides of buildings, and magazines and newspapers were increasingly filled with large advertisements that made outrageous claims.

With the appearance of artistic posters, based on a Japanese-inspired "flat" style imported from Europe, it seemed for a time that the demands of commerce and the aspirations of fine art could work in harmony. Some contemporary observers believed that the popularity of the art poster in the 1890s demonstrated the possibility of a reconciliation between high and low culture. The tension between art and commerce, the artist and the artisan, and issues of art and morality all came to the surface in the debate about poster advertising. Posters were, as has been noted, a traditional advertising medium that art critics, such as H. C. Bunner, regarded as "pictorial horrors." Bunner concluded that posters were loved by Americans of "all types and classes" because "the untaught native taste will accept pretty nearly anything in the general line of graphic art."[23]

Posters in a new style, smaller in size and intensely colored, became the preferred advertising medium for the burgeoning magazine industry, book publishers, the Sunday supplements of newspapers, the new bicycle industry, and manufacturers of health products. The *Inland Printer* used the work of poster artists to promote itself as well as to champion individual artists and their work. Will Bradley's covers began in April 1894, and the magazine profiled him in 1895. Percy Pollard's "Poster Lore and the Newer Movements," a regular feature in the magazine, celebrated the work of individual designers and reported on exhibitions and campaigns. Stone and Kimball, publishers of the *Chap Book*, used illustrations and cover designs by Bradley, John Sloan, Frank Hazenplug, and Edward Penfield in their publications, as well as posters by the same artists to advertise the journal. Ethel Reed was admired for posters advertising books published by Lamson, Wolff and Company of Boston. Printing ink manufacturers, for example, Ault and Wiborg Company of Cincinnati, commissioned

35. "Across the Continent." Printed by the Strobridge Lithography Company.
Bunner's caption read, "An example of the primitive and confused theatrical poster."
H. C. Bunner, "American Posters, Past and Present." *Modern Poster* (1895).
Fine Arts Library, Indiana University.

36. "'Carnival Time' for the *Chicago Sunday Tribune* by Will Bradley." *Modern Poster* (1895). Fine Arts Library, Indiana University.

promotional posters by Bradley and another highly regarded poster artist, Louis Rhead.[24]

The new posters were valued beyond, or in spite of, their commercial message and were seriously collected. Individual poster artists signed their work, and the art press reviewed them with respect. Critics, including Bunner, hailed the advent of the new style. Poster publishing was becoming a small but significant industry. The *New York Times* took note: "The United States has to-day something like twenty establishments which make posters alone their special production and which show a capital invested of nearly $3,000,000. They provide employment for something like 1000 draughtsmen and designers and perhaps 500 additional artists who reproduce the originals of the former. . . . In addition to this, they give commissions continually to no inconsiderable number of painters who draw for the illustration of the magazines."[25]

For a time, the "poster craze" convinced some in commerce that it was possible to unite fine and applied art. *Profitable Advertising* went so far as to declare high and low art a single entity. "But who shall draw the line between art, pure and simple, and art as applied to and in connection with advertising? Perhaps it is not necessary to draw the line. It is more than possible that individual artists are doing this for us, right along, or it is quite probable that the art, as an art, will adjust itself." The illustrator and critic Francis Hopkinson Smith, speaking at a meeting of the New York Typothetae, declaimed: "The artist-printer, he who will use his types as a painter uses his pigment, will live in history, and his book will live, and will be a record of good taste and of the period which sustained him. In Paris, a year ago, a man named Cherrie [Chéret] made an illustration for a circus poster. All Paris stopped and admired. Two weeks later he drew the design of a danseuse at the Comique, and everybody threw up their hats. The next month the government pinned the decoration of the Legion of Honor at his button-hole, not because he was a good designer, but because he was a great artist, and because, even on a billboard on the boulevard, he had exhibited the same qualities that Barye had in his bronze, or Millet on his canvas."[26]

Not everyone embraced the new "poster style" that younger artists promoted, and a significant number of American advertisers distrusted this avant-garde fashion to generate sales of their products. One businessman, speaking for many, said, "To our mind the realistic poster, rather than the eccentric, will attract and secure more demands for the articles which it is intended to advertise. There is the temptation, which many artists cannot resist, to press the point of 'high art' (so 'high' that the common people do not appreciate it!) beyond the boundary of good taste, and thus the announcement loses its force along the particular lines in which it is supposed to be unusually strong." Most businessmen continued to use printers rather than artists to design their posters and preferred a straightforward, realistic image of their product.[27]

The educational function of poster art was often cited in trade and mass-circulation journals. One extremely popular theme was the role of art posters as educators of the masses. Posters brought art into the street, to the people who would never go to a museum. They functioned as "a liberal education in Art and as a stimulator of good taste." The city itself would become "the poor man's picture gallery," and posters could share the sacred calling of the fine arts by elevating public morality. In an article entitled "The Moral Aspect of the Artistic Poster," Louis Rhead combined his support for the new decorative style with moral exhortations. In a wonderful example of conflating art with ethics, Rhead defined the good poster as "a creative invention designed to be beautiful and to ennoble while yet it pleases and attracts attention." He praised the work of Eugene Grasset because "he is pre-eminent as a designer pure and simple, and one who understands perfectly the spacing and lettering, as well as a fine draughtsman, cherishing always *ideal*, noble sentiments." Rhead then attacked Jules Chéret: "he has not a particle of design; his compositions are bad and he takes the lowest and lewdest type of womanhood for his ideals." Rhead summed up his argument: "No, the moral aspect of the artistic poster, then, is that it may be, if done well, an important factor in the community, and it is best to begin aright, with high ideals and aims, to educate, ennoble, and make men and women think of life not as a silly dream, but as earnest and sublime."[28]

Amid all of this moral uplift, the critic S. de Soissons took a more acerbic view of commercial motives. "In spite of their lack of taste," he wrote, "business men were obliged to trust the sale of their patent medicines to the masterpieces. For the sake of money-making they were forced to employ the artist to make posters for them. Destiny sometimes maliciously obliges stupidity to pay homage to talent."[29]

By the late 1890s, most advertisers had lost interest in the poster as a advertising medium and had turned to magazines and newspapers because improvements in color halftones made advertisements more attractive. Publications increased their use of full-page, full-color advertisements on the back and inside covers, and advertising opportunities expanded.

At the end of the nineteenth century most advertising combined images with text. The advertising advocate Nathaniel Fowler observed:

> There are few catalogues without illustrations. There are hardly any periodicals that are not illustrated. Half of the advertisements, classified advertisements excepted, are illustrated. If the proof of the good of illustration is in the use of it, engraving is necessary to the economy and conduct of business. Some things can be described by words better than by a picture. Some things can be shown by illustration better than by words. Most things can be represented better by both illustration and text.[30]

Even before "scientific" advertising, those in the profession recognized the importance of graphically connecting the product and the advertisement in a meaningful way. With the advent of psychological theory, however, the persuasive power of advertising became the focus of attention. In his writing, Walter Dill Scott, the Northwestern University professor of psychology and originator of this movement, emphasized the huge cost of advertising and asserted that "seventy-five per cent. of all this is unprofitable." He advised advertisers to follow a "scientific" program rather than rely on instinct, to use marketing survey techniques to "know his customers' wants—what will catch their attention, what will impress them and lead them to buy." Advertising design had to engage the potential customer and forcefully convey an idea.[31]

Designers were obliged to learn to use rules of composition, layout, and color to create compelling advertising, not merely to decorate a message. In an unsigned article in the *Inland Printer,* one writer criticized the prevailing use of art:

> Many of the pictures which accompany advertisements have really no logical connection with the advertisement, being used apparently only to attract attention, in the same plane with the "ad. writer" who writes "catchy ads."
>
> The designer and illustrator's chief claim for consideration is *perceptiveness.* To thoroughly understand the impression an advertiser desires

to make and to work out the idea strongly, gracefully, artistically, and yet with a captivating originality—is the qualification of a successful designer and illustrator.

Another writer reminded the designer that good advertisements had "tremendous sales power that resides in their construction and appearance alone." In *Advertising and Selling,* still another admonished designers that "those who know how to combine type rightly with pictures, borders and ornaments—who understand structure as well as art and typography, are able to accomplish really wonderful results. Their ads tell a story before a word is read, and, after seeing them, to pass them by without reading is almost impossible." For these writers good commercial art could be distinguished from fine art by its ability to communicate. A. Rowden King, for example, argued that neither the impressionist nor realist style of his time was appropriate because impressionistic images were imprecise and lacked a clear message, whereas the realist image lavished the same attention on the unessentials as on the object to be sold. All criticized "idea-less ads," advertisements that used either pleasing or surprising imagery and were ultimately ineffective as sales makers.[32]

Earnest Elmo Calkins, the indefatigable advertising agent, writer, and promoter, discouraged the use of "art paintings," such as the widely praised "Bubbles," by the English painter John Millais, that appeared in an advertisement for Pears' Soap. Calkins argued that it was simply an ineffectual symbol of high art and called for art created especially for advertisements. These art paintings were "good genre pictures used by the advertiser in place of advertising. They were not great advertisements." He contended that fine artists were incapable of producing good advertising art and instead praised advertising artists, whose "secret ambition is to paint a great advertising design."[33]

Some of these arguments were addressed to the art community, especially to professional illustrators, who continued to regard advertising assignments as degrading. Designers who worked in the commercial world often combined advertising work with what they considered more acceptable jobs in book illustration and magazine cover design and illustration. Nevertheless, the advertiser, or the advertising agent, expected the commercial artist to be able to work effectively with the limitations imposed by the client and the agency. In an unsigned article in *Fame,* one writer observed that "the world of art-illustrators, painters and magazine artists has some very pointed views upon this matter of art in advertising pictures. While the illustrator looks upon the engraving house artist as a member of the guild of the brush, he considers it a calamity to have to come to the making of advertising pictures." At the same time advertisers admitted that artist-illustrators were well paid for work in magazines, and given greater freedom as well as prestige not available in advertising.[34]

How much freedom did the illustrator have? There are repeated notices in the literature to the effect that very few artists were able to establish their own identities. For the most part they were asked to copy successful ads, not to use their own ideas. The stars were exceptions.

During the early 1900s the advertising community sent mixed messages to artists. Some exhorted talented artists to join the profession, arguing that they would enhance the field. A writer in *Profitable Advertising* argued that advertising standards were higher than formerly:

> This improvement is due, without doubt, to the employment of a higher grade of artists to paint and draw the original, men and women who were trained as artists, and have now come into the advertising field in response to the call for better work. These artists are to be sharply distinguished from the advertising draftsmen who were previously depended upon to turn out commercial "art" work. They have brought along with them a thoro knowledge of the principles of art and have become able to so apply them as to give force, attractive power, and vitality to the advertising motive.

Others complained of undisciplined egotism. An article published in 1911 began with the story of an advertising manager who was tired of yet another dramatic display of "artistic temperament" by a well-known unnamed artist. Rather than placate the artist, the manager devised his own layout and gave orders to an artist "who does not sign his work and whose name is unknown" to provide a finished design. The result, he reported, was "a much more successful ad than any of the so-called 'artistic' ads." The writer argued that the basic idea, layout, and text should all have been decided by advertising experts before the artist is brought in so that " when the instructions finally reach the artist they should be so explicit that *his* work should be almost entirely work of *execution* as opposed

"THE SECRET"
JESSIE WILLCOX SMITH

"GOING HOME TO SEE THE FOLKS"
A. B. FROST

"THE CIRCUS"
FRANK X. LEYENDECKER

"THE VULTURES' ROOST"
E. W. KEMBLE

"RECIPROCITY"
CHARLES DANA GIBSON

"EXCLUSIVELY FOR Collier's"

With the addition of A.B. Frost, whose drawings will henceforward appear only in Collier's, the art staff of The National Weekly is now complete.

The following artists are now under contract to draw exclusively for Collier's:

**A.B. FROST
MAXFIELD PARRISH
CHARLES DANA GIBSON**
(COLLIER'S AND LIFE)
**FREDERIC REMINGTON
E. W. KEMBLE
JESSIE WILCOX SMITH
FRANK X. LEYENDECKER**

To draw "exclusively for Collier's" means to an artist the opportunity to do less work and better work, to be free from the grind of magazine illustration, to have a freer hand, a larger space, a more important subject.

Thus, every reader of The National Weekly will receive every week during the year examples in black and white or in color of the best work of the foremost American artists.

In its art, as in its editorials and short stories, Collier's aim will be to print nothing but the best.

In the "Editorial Bulletin" this week will be found a more detailed statement of the Art Department's plans.

"THE TRAMP'S THANKSGIVING"
MAXFIELD PARRISH

"THE EXPLORERS"
FREDERIC REMINGTON

"Exclusively for Colliers." *Colliers* (1905). Research Collection, Indiana University Library.

to work of *creation*." This was necessary because the "artistic temperament" was interested in beauty, whereas the advertiser-businessman was interested in "sales." In this instance, production was to be separated from design, but the artist was not to be the designer.[35]

Advertisers added moral inducements to attract artists to advertising. Unlike the fine artist with a necessarily small audience, commercial artists could form public taste in the vast readership of the mass circulation magazines. In an address to the Sphinx Club, R. C. Ogden dismissed the "snobocracy of art" and chastised those who believe in "art for art's sake. . . . I have no doubt that the high priest of art would sneer at the statement that art in advertising is art for humanity's sake, but, nevertheless, such is the case." In concluding his lecture, Ogden made one final point: "Be sure that your artist accepts his limitations. His art must be your servant. If otherwise, you will fail of results." The editors of *Fame* distinguished between uninspired fine art, which they called "art commercialized" and produced "by the yard," and commercial art, an art created to order. Several writers drew a parallel between advertising commissions and fifteenth-century Renaissance patronage. Furthermore, they argued, applied artists were educating the masses, who were not likely to enter museums but were confronted with outdoor posters and magazine advertisements every day.[36]

Max Wineburgh launched a boisterous attack in the populist mode before the Sphinx Club in 1905. He defended subway placards from criticism: "A poster that tells [people] where they can save a quarter on a hat or a half-dollar on a suit of clothes is a million times more interesting than a Whistler creation or Tissot masterpiece." He continued,

> The gentlemen of artistic temperaments, who are so familiar with the harmony of colors, who talk with such discriminating niceness of the "style" and "spirit" and "atmosphere" of a painting, are not familiar with either the times or the people who make them. . . . .
>
> They hang in their parlors and in museums nude pictures that our friend Artemas Ward would not permit an instant on the Subway walls, and neither would the public.
>
> The real question is this:
>
> Shall a few gentlemen of leisure be permitted to substitute art for

128

commercialism, or shall commercialism, backed by the plain people, brush
these meddlesome busybodies aside as common scolds?

Advertising is greater than Art.

Advertising [is] the greatest influence that the brain of man has
evolved. . . .

Art is great and has its place, but the world will not grant it a dictator-
ship over its people or the doings of those people.[37]

Did Wineburgh bring the audience to its feet? Were those who attacked the
fine art tradition merely apologists for cynical business interests? Were appeals
to populism sheer demagoguery? Pathetic self-delusions? As crude as some of
the statements now appear, they were delivered in response to attacks by the
art press that now seem equally outrageous. Writers in fine art periodicals of
the time endlessly debated opening museums on Sundays because it might encourage less desirable visitors (who would be at work the other six days). They
applauded the Metropolitan Museum of Art's refusal to allow a plumber and his
family to enter its hallowed precincts. Other defenders of high art wanted to
charge for seats in New York's Central Park to keep out unsuitable members of
the public. The head of the Thomas and Lake advertising agency, Alfred Lasker,
recalled that in 1898, bankers refused to lend businessmen money if they revealed that it would be used for advertising. "Any man was an unreliable manufacturer who advertised; he was putting himself in the patent medicine class; it
just wasn't ethical, it wasn't being done, it was socially barred with very few
exceptions." The defenders of advertising art did not shrink from retaliatory
assaults.[38]

CREATING A NEW AESTHETIC

During the early decades of the twentieth century, advertising artists began
the search for alternate aesthetics. As the chasm between fine art and popular
graphics widened, two events outside the immediate profession reshaped the
vision of graphic designers and modified this rift: the Armory Show of 1913 and
World War I. The Armory Show presaged a new relation between the fine and
advertising arts, and World War I brought the advertising industry a new
measure of respect. The Armory Show introduced an American audience to the
vocabulary of the European avant-garde. It not only inspired American artists

129

and critics but appealed to designers, too. The exhibition showed that the relation between fine art and graphic art could be symbiotic. European painters incorporated examples of type used in newspapers and imagery from advertisements into their paintings and collages—that is, they appropriated visual elements and ideas from the popular media. In the following decades this relation would become reciprocal and more complex; the curators of the Museum of Modern Art exhibition "High and Low" characterized it in 1990 as "a permanent circuit" between high art and popular culture.[39]

The status of the advertising industry also underwent a change. During the war, George Creel's Committee on Public Information (CPI) brought advertising agencies into the government's effort to create public support for the war. The Division of Advertising and the Division of Pictorial Publicity ran campaigns for war-saving stamps and Liberty Loan bonds as well as appeals for fuel conservation and warnings about spies. The Division of Advertising coordinated advertising efforts and designed the campaigns; the Division of Pictorial Publicity found the artists to produce the work. This was a massive undertaking, and most American advertising agencies and associations participated in the effort. In fact, the Division of Pictorial Publicity was founded by members of the Society of Illustrators, led by its president, the popular illustrator Charles Dana Gibson. Prominent painters, illustrators, and designers joined, including Cecilia Beaux and Childe Hassam, as well as Will Low, Maxfield Parrish, and Joseph Pennell. Advertisers were strongly encouraged, and strongly encouraged others, to link advertising with community service, sacrifice, and patriotism. In return, advertisers could associate their businesses with these same virtues. Creel exalted in the effect that participation with the CPI had on advertising; he concluded his remembrance of the Division of Advertising by writing, "Had the Committee done nothing else, its existence would have been justified by the decision that gave advertising the dignity of a profession and incorporated its dynamic abilities in American team-play."[40]

The tension between the demands of art high and low, pure and commercial, remains unresolved, of course. The intensity of feeling it engenders may be greater at different periods, but the criteria for judging "commercial art" work began to change in the first decade of the twentieth century. It was not a prostitution of "real art" for mass consumption, nor was it simply the addition of pictures and ornamental type to advertising copy or magazine covers. By 1920

38. "The Spirit of America—Join." *Western Advertising* (November 1919). Science, Industry and Business Library, New York Public Library, Astor, Lenox and Tilden Foundations.

there were those who argued that advertising designers were engaged in a new kind of work that distinguished them from the fine artists and a body of opinion that welcomed their work as a new kind of visual experience.

Whether advertisements are symbolic of a civilization devoted to greed, materialism, and superficial beauty continues to be debated. The concept of an art that could communicate visually what could not be transmitted by words alone, that might be accessible and understandable to a large public, and that could be appealing and even entertaining, validated graphic design as a profession. Rather than accept the standards set by connoisseurs of the fine arts, the advertising designer, as a graphic designer, sought a new role.

6. Women in Graphic

Design History

*Wage-earning women stressed the contradiction between social ideas
about women and the actual reality of their own lives.*
SARAH EISENSTEIN, *Give Us Bread But Give Us Roses*

When Linda Nochlin's article "Why Have There Been No Great Women
Artists?" appeared in 1971, it generated enormous interest in neglected work by
women artists. Nochlin challenged art historians to analyze the institutional and
ideological structures that distort what women have accomplished or have been
unable to accomplish. She warned that women must "face up to the reality of their
history and of their present situation, without making excuses or puffing medi-

ocrity. Disadvantage may indeed be an excuse; it is not, however, an intellectual position." Since then feminist historians have explored the limitations placed on women who pursued careers in the arts and on the representation of those women who did succeed in the literature of art history. Only recently, however, have historians of graphic design faced the biases in their own field and begun to identify individual women and document their position in graphic design history.[1]

Martha Scotford Lange began this process by showing that the major texts used to teach graphic design concentrate on the work of a limited number of "great men" and that, consciously or unconsciously, graphic design historians have created an unacknowledged canon that excludes women. She suggested that cultural history, rather than art history, would provide a better model for historians to follow.[2]

A reading of the basic texts of graphic design history leads one to assume that women were marginal if not absent in the transformation of the field. Even feminist art historians, when they include illustrators in their histories, are inclined to ignore the commercial aspects of the artists' work. Art historical models are often based on the great artists and their masterpieces and so fail to go beyond narrations of lives, assessments of influence, and progressions of styles.[3] In describing women's experiences in the printing industry, the advertising industry, and commercial illustration, one can show, however briefly, not only where women participated in graphic design but how their experience reveals the profession's ties to other aspects of American culture.

In a pioneering article, Cheryl Buckley argued that women's role in all fields of design has been defined by "the sexual division of labor, assumptions about femininity, and the hierarchy that exists in design." Preliminary research confirms that this is true in graphic design. During the second half of the nineteenth century many women worked in the printing industry, but in limited, gender-based capacities. Women were gradually forced out of the printing trades because male-dominated unions argued that the work was too physically demanding even as it became less so. Women worked in the advertising industry but are absent from the histories because they were unable to reach the higher levels of management, where their names would be associated with particular campaigns. At the same time, the women's movement, identified with the fight for voting rights, grew in power and forced the nation to confront "the woman question." The number of schools and colleges, including schools of fine and applied art open to women, increased dramatically. This was in part a result of the Aesthetic and Arts and Crafts movements. Changing attitudes toward the applied arts and women's education gave female illustrators new opportunities, but it encouraged them to work on domestic subjects and in a decorative style.[4]

The changing definition of gender appropriate work is an important aspect of this story. In her encyclopedia on *The Employments of Women* (1863), Virginia Perry listed career options for women to consider. Like her contemporaries, Perry defined some work as masculine and some as feminine, but she argued that many male-dominated professions were essentially "feminine" and that women should be able to pursue these vocations. For example, Perry considered copperplate engraving (the production of business cards, calling cards, and invitations) to be a feminine occupation that was dominated by men. "The patience and careful attention to details requisite, and the sedentary nature of engraving, render it a more suitable occupation for women than men," she wrote.[5]

This attitude was shared by John Durand, editor of the *Crayon*. In an editorial of 1861 entitled "Woman's Position in Art," he declared that lithography and wood engraving were, or ought to be, feminine occupations.

Man is not made for sedentary life; woman, on the contrary, conforms to it without inconvenience; she better maintains that close, unceasing attention, that motionless activity which the engraver's pursuit demands. Her nimble fingers, accustomed to wield the needle, lend themselves more easily to minute operations, to the use of small instruments, to the almost imperceptible shades of manipulation that wood-engraving exact. Cutting on copper and steel demands also a patience and minutia much more compatible with the nature of woman than with that of man. It is only in *womanizing* himself, in some degree, that man succeeds in obtaining the development of these faculties so contrary to his physical constitution, and always at the expense of his natural force.[6]

At the same time, real working women were ignored in the literature. A good example of this is the case of Frances Flora Bond Palmer, known as Fanny Palmer. Palmer was one of two full-time lithographers at Currier and Ives. Although Palmer was all but forgotten after her death, modern feminist art historians have revived her memory. Born and trained in England, she emigrated to New York in the 1840s. At Currier and Ives, Palmer was responsible for more than two hundred lithographs, making the original drawings and transferring them to the stone. She worked in a tremendous range of subjects: landscapes, cityscapes, hunting scenes, and still-lifes, as well as prints of trains, steamships, and buildings, and dramatic Civil War scenes. These were not defined as "feminine" subjects (ironically, Palmer was thought to be weakest in rendering the human figure). Her "Rocky Mountains, Emigrants Crossing the Plains" (1866), was one of the company's most popular prints and could be found in homes throughout the country. Palmer also contributed to the technical aspects of commercial lithography: she developed a method of printing a background tone and, with Charles Currier, improved lithographic crayons. Although she was unusually gifted and productive, her historical fate was nonetheless typical. Palmer was an employee, so her work was not recognized as that of an individual in her own right but subsumed under the Currier and Ives imprint. She supported an alcoholic husband and their children, yet her obituary identifies her only as her husband's wife, in the less than felicitous terms of that

39. "Fanny Palmer, 'The Rocky Mountains: Emigrants Crossing the Plains.'" (1866).
Prints and Photographs Division, Library of Congress.

day: "a relict of Edmund S. Palmer of Leicester, England." Palmer was mentioned only in passing, as a part of Currier and Ives history, until feminist art historians became interested in her work.[7]

DOCUMENTATION

To understand the positions women found in graphic design, we must turn to documentary sources that provide a broader picture of the profession and the era when it began. The relation between the struggling printers' unions and women who worked in the printing trade was discussed in union journals and the popular press of the period. Workers in the printing industry regarded themselves as a highly skilled and close fraternity, and their trade unionism developed early. The ambivalence union members felt toward female workers explains as much about the situation women faced in entering the design profession as it does about the precarious situation of trade unionism itself.[8]

Histories of the women's movement, whether by participants or by modern feminist writers, are excellent sources because many suffragettes published and edited newspapers and magazines as part of their activities. Susan B. Anthony and Amelia Jenks Bloomer were allied with women trying to find jobs in the printing trades, and their confrontations with local and national printing unions are well documented.[9]

Many of the art and design schools that opened throughout the country in the second half of the nineteenth century accepted women students. The published histories, original charters, and early annual reports of these institutions describe the ideological basis for education in the applied arts and explain why women were encouraged to pursue careers in design.

If women's presence in the workplace generated heated arguments about trade unionism and women's rights, it also attracted the attention of statisticians and economists. Statistical studies describe the position of female workers in the larger picture of economic development.[10]

Trade magazines for printers, typographers, and advertisers reflect the prevailing attitudes of their professions toward women and only unintentionally reveal women's participation. Unfortunately, as we shall see, these journals often preferred to ignore women and so are eloquent, if not informative, by their silence.

Women in Graphic Design History

Histories of art, particularly of American graphics and illustration, and biographies of American women artists contain information on women who worked as illustrators for magazines, books, and posters. They continue to emphasize painters, sculptors, and "fine" printmakers untainted by commercialism, although women art historians have written about individual female illustrators. By concentrating on broader cultural issues rather than individual artists, a few art historians have shown how particular artistic movements have influenced educational and professional opportunities for women. Roger B. Stein argued that promoters of the Aesthetic theory encouraged upper-class women to pursue artistic interests, thereby diverting them from radical political activity. Even the Arts and Crafts movement, as Anthea Callen has demonstrated, reinforced patriarchal ideology as it opened opportunities for women in the arts.[11]

WOMEN IN THE PRINTING TRADES

A number of men associated with the beginnings of graphic design began their careers in printing establishments, and so it is logical to look for women there as well. Indeed, from the colonial period on, women were well represented in the American printing industry. Several presses, including the first press in North America, were run by women. It is often argued that women became printers only when it was their family's trade, but to the extent that this was true, it held equally for male printers. Girls, however, were generally trained in the printshop at home, in contrast to boys, who often learned their craft during an apprenticeship. The issue of apprenticeship, as we shall see, became a critical one for women.[12]

There is no doubt that some female printers attained the respect of their profession. The *Typographic Advertiser* carried an obituary for Lydia R. Bailey, a widow, who took over her husband's printing establishment. It noted that from 1808 to 1861 "her office was one of the largest in Philadelphia. She instructed forty-two boys into the mysteries of typography; and some of our present prosperous master-printers served their apprenticeship under her. For a considerable period she was elected City Printer by the Councils; and her imprint was well known. She had great energy and decision of character." Bailey's achievement, moreover, was placed in the wider context of political and economic rights: "Of late days we hear much talk about women's rights. Something may probably come of it to women's advantage: how we may not forecast. There is certainly room enough for improvement in the condition of many women; but will the privilege of suffrage bring it about?"[13]

Women not linked by family ties to printing were nevertheless interested in the printing trades because they were relatively open to them and offered higher wages than the other industries where they found employment, notably in textiles, clothing, tobacco, and papermaking. Yet women who worked in printshops earned considerably less than their male counterparts. In Boston in 1831, for example, men were paid three times as much as women and boys: the 687 men in printing earned $1.50 a day, whereas the 395 women and 215 boys in printing earned just 50¢ a day. In 1860, women in the printing trades earned on average $18.65 a month, more than women in any other branch of manufacturing. By 1880 in Boston the average weekly earnings for women in all trades was $6.03, whereas women in printing and publishing earned $6.61, an additional 9 percent.[14]

In 1853 the suffragette and social reformer Amelia Jenks Bloomer began publication of the *Lily: A Ladies' Journal Devoted to Temperance and Literature*. When, a year later, she tried to hire a woman apprentice, the printers refused to work and went on strike against both her publication and one produced by her husband. Bloomer persisted and finally found three women and three men to publish both papers; she paid them equal wages, although at less than union rates.

By the end of the Civil War, more women had entered the profession. In 1868, for example, there were two hundred women typesetters in New York City, approximately 15–20 percent of printing trade workers. And the printing trades attracted an increasingly larger percentage of women workers (see table 4). In 1870, 3.7 percent of compositors were women, in 1880, 4.7 percent, in 1890, 9.9 percent, and in 1900, 10.3 percent. Despite the introduction of new technology that raised worker productivity, an increase in demand for printed matter allowed the total number of workers in printing to expand.[15]

Composition sometimes required a high degree of skill and a strong sense of design. On "straight matter" the compositor might simply be required to follow a standard format with a limited number of fonts; other material demanded considerably more judgment. Advertisements, for example, appeared in a variety of media: trade cards, posters, and stationery, as well as newspapers and periodi-

T A B L E 4
Number and Percentage Distribution of Female Gainful Workers in
Printing, and Allied Industries, 1870–1930

	1870	1880	1890	1900	1910	1920
Printing and allied industries	4,233	8,947	23,771	31,613	45,090	45,274
Women workers (%)	40.8	39.1	51.6	53.8	59.4	55.8
Engravers	29	103	303	453	538	561
Women workers (%)	0.3	0.4	0.7	0.8	0.7	0.7

Adapted from H. Dewey Anderson and Percy E. Davidson, *Occupational Trends in
the United States* (Palo Alto: Stanford University Press, 1940), 300–301

cals. In general, men underwent an extended apprenticeship and became skilled
at a variety of work. Women, in contrast, were taught for six weeks without pay
and then put to work setting plain matter and redistributing type.[16]

As noted, printing professions were practiced in two very different environ-
ments: newspaper and periodical printers and the book and job trades. Few

40. "Composing Room, Riverside Press." *Paper World* (December 1880).
General Collection, Library of Congress.

women were employed at large city newspapers, and even in smaller cities, where they often did set straight matter, they did not design layouts or advertisements. In 1900 newspapers and periodicals employed 73,653 men earning $45 million ($610 per month) and 14,815 women earning $4.6 million ($310 per month). There are no comparable figures for women in book and job offices, but they represented, respectively, two-thirds and half the total number of workers. Of 9,045 linotype machine workers, just 520 were women.[17]

Local printing unions, which had existed in a variety of forms during the first half of the century, formed a national organization, the United Typographical Union, in 1852. In contrast to their progressive tradition, these all-male organizations were highly ambivalent about unionizing female workers. Many printers hired women at lower wages under the guise of giving them an opportunity to learn the trade, and women often worked as scab labor during strikes. The unions had two options: either fight for equal wages and unionize women or ban them from the industry. They tried both tactics. The editorial positions of the *Inland Printer* reflected the contradictions. In 1884, the editor wrote:

> The printers employed on the *Evening Wisconsin*, of Milwaukee, twenty-three in number, are on a strike because the manager of that sheet insisted, after several remonstrances, on paying the female compositors, members of the Cream City Typographical Union, twenty-eight cents instead of thirty-three cents per thousand ems—the union scale—as paid to the male compositors; and this, too, in the face of the admission that the women did better work than a majority of the men.
>
> The action of the union in making the cause of the girls its own is worthy of all commendation. Of course, no protective organization could tolerate, for a moment, a *sliding scale* arrangement, all its members, irrespective of sex, age, or nationality, being required to observe the *minimum* rate of wages. Any other policy would be suicidal. The standard raised—"equal pay for equal work"—is one which will command the sympathy of every right-minded citizen; and it is needless to add that those now engaged in this struggle have our warmest wishes for their success.[18]

In spite of these sentiments, this same editor advocated barring female students from trade schools and accused any woman who wanted such training—or indeed worked in the trades—of selfishly taking jobs away from men with families to support. Although they did not all subscribe to the idea that women were incapable of performing the tasks or less hard-working, contributors to the journal argued that the printing trades required a greater amount of time to develop skills and that many female workers left as soon as they married. Some arguments appeared in the form of patriarchal sermons on the need to protect women from the dangers of the work: their exposure to materials dangerous to health, their supposed frailty and inability to carry heavy type forms, and their potential contact with "unsuitable" printed matter. Others argued that women lacked training, that they were incapable of doing anything but the most straightforward jobs because few had served an apprenticeship. Women, indeed, accounted for only 9.7 percent of all apprentice typesetters. But the most troubling issue, and the primary focus of the opposition, was that women worked for lower wages and were used by employers to fight unionization. And it was on this issue that the suffragette leader Susan B. Anthony entered the fray.[19]

Anthony encouraged women to learn typesetting by taking jobs they were offered by printers, even during strikes. It is unclear if she really lacked an understanding of the need for worker solidarity, as some writers charge, or if she, unlike female unionists, considered male workers so unsympathetic that they would never voluntarily integrate their shops. In a report of her fight for admittance to a union convention, printed in the *Workingman's Advocate* in August 1869, Anthony said she represented:

> a class of women that had no husbands, and who were on the street penniless, homeless and without shelter. Now, I ask you what we are to do with these girls? Shall we tell them to starve in the garrets because the printers, by their own necessities, open their doors and give a slight training to a few girls for a few weeks? Shall I say to the girls, "Do not go in, but starve?" or shall I say, "Go in, and get a little skill into your hands, and fit yourselves to work side by side with men?" I want to ask the Co-operative Union of New York how many girls they have taken to learn the typesetting business? How many women have you ordered each department or establishment to take as apprentices, and to train in the art of typesetting?[20]

Union leader Augusta Lewis clashed with Anthony over these tactics. Lewis (c. 1848–1920), a journalist and typesetter, believed that by preserving union solidarity, by foregoing the immediate advantage of work, women would eventually find an equal place in union shops. Lewis had founded the Women's Typographical Union No. 1 (WTU) in October 8, 1868, and she urged women members not to accept nonunion work. A year later, in 1869, the United Typographical Union became the first national union in the country to admit women, and in 1870 Lewis herself was elected corresponding secretary of the national organization.

Yet Lewis was soon disillusioned by the union's treatment of its female members. "[We] have never obtained a situation that we could not have obtained had we never heard of a union. We refuse to take the men's situations when they are on strike, and when there is no strike if we ask for work in union offices we are told by union foremen 'that there are no conveniences for us.' We are ostracized in many offices because we are members of the union; and although the principle is right, disadvantages are so many that we cannot much longer hold together."[21]

When women did succeed, they were derided as unfeminine and grotesque. In describing an itinerant printer he had met in western Ohio, one writer claimed, "She was dressed plainly but neatly in what might be called a cross between a traveling and office suit of brown color. The toughened expression on her face indicated that she was familiar with the tricks of the profession, versed in the study of vulgarity. No tender, trusting female was she, but a hardened, suspicious, masculine woman."[22] When they were not questioning women's abilities, the journals ignored them. They were quick to take umbrage at similar treatment from women, however. The *Inland Printer* reprinted an article from a British trade journal reporting that women compositors in Boston published a journal called *Elle:* "This paper is a veritable man-hater; not the slightest mention of man in any shape or form is to be found in its columns, neither is the *genus homo* allowed to hawk it!" The notice is doubly significant. *Elle* does not appear in any of the standard sources on magazine literature, and it is possible that no copies have survived. We know of its existence now only because it irritated the editors of a mainstream journal.[23]

The introduction of new technology, particularly the Mergenthaler Linotype beginning in the 1880s, might have increased opportunities for women. The typographer's union admitted that women learned to work with the system more quickly but also charged that they lacked endurance. In the end the union insisted that only fully qualified—that is, male—printers should be allowed to operate the machines. In typesetting, the one printing profession in which women significantly competed for work, they had lost ground. By 1900 only 8 percent of women belonged to unions, compared with 32 percent of men, and that number decreased rapidly. Only 10 percent of compositors were women, while only approximately 700 of 12,000, or just 5.8 percent, operated typesetting machines. Barred from the apprentice system and trade schools and betrayed by the trade unions that ostensibly represented them, working-class women rarely followed men who made the transition from the printshop into the design of printed material.[24]

The private press movement inspired American printers and designers from Boston to San Francisco, but women are excluded almost completely from its history. Fragmentary records indicate, however, that these presses existed and that some women took part in the movement. In 1873 two sisters, trained designers and wood engravers, founded the Crane and Curtis Company in San Francisco. Women ran the Chemith Press in 1902 in Minneapolis and the Butterfly Press from 1907 to 1909 in Philadelphia. Bertha Sprinks Goudy, who operated the Village Press with her husband, Frederic Goudy, is fulsomely praised for her work, but only in studies of her husband's life and career.[25]

Artist-designed bookbinding was a significant field before the advent of the book jacket both in the private press movement and in commercial publishing during the 1890s. Most of the women book designers who gained recognition for their work came from upper-class backgrounds; Margaret Neilson Armstrong (1867–1944) was one of the first and one of the most prolific. Armstrong was born into a socially prominent, wealthy New York family, and both she and her sister, Helen, made their careers out of choice rather than economic necessity. By 1913 she had designed more than 250 book covers, working as a freelance artist, although Scribners was her most important client. Sarah Wyman Whitman, an important member of Boston society, was a leader of the Arts and Crafts Society as well as a successful designer. Ellen Gates Starr (1860–1940), a colleague of Jane Addams, was also a disciple of William Morris; she shared his beliefs on art and his commitment to socialism and studied book design in England with T. J. Cobden-Sanderson at the Doves Press. Starr returned to Chicago to establish a bookbindery in the 1890s. Unlike others in the movement, Starr recognized the contradiction between fundamental social reform and the handicraft tradition. She eventually abandoned design for political activism, writing, "If I had thought it through, I would have realized that I would be using my hands to create books that only the rich could buy."[26]

Modern historians may explain the relatively large number of successful women in book design and binding in terms of the receptivity of the Arts and Crafts movement to their participation. Contemporary observers and participants, however, ascribed it to gender-specific skills. Cobden-Sanderson, Starr's teacher, is quoted as having said, "Women ought to do the best work in bookbinding, for they possess all the essential qualifications of success: patience for detail, lightness of touch, and dexterous fingers." These views were not held by men alone. Alice C. Morse, herself an accomplished book-cover designer, claimed that women had an inherent ability: "Women seem to have a remarkable faculty for designing. Their intuitive sense of decoration, their feeling for beauty of line and harmony of color, insures them a high degree of success."[27]

It is no coincidence that the Arts and Crafts societies begun in 1897 were among the few clubs to include women or that when the prestigious Society of Printers was founded in 1905 in Boston, no women were admitted. In fact, women were not admitted until 1974, after a prolonged and acrimonious battle. Women were not allowed to become members of the Grolier Club until 1976, although the club exhibited their work much earlier. The Art Directors Club also showed women's work but refused women membership until 1948, admitting Cipe Pineles (1908–75) only because her husband, William Golden, refused to join without her. Fifteen years passed before the second female member was admitted. The Graphic Group was exclusively male, as was the American Institute of Graphic Arts in its early years. In 1926, after a change in its charter, the *News-letter* proudly announced that Frances Atwater, a typographer at the *New York Times*, and Florence N. Levy, director of the Baltimore Museum of Art, "share the distinction of being the first women members."[28]

ADVERTISING ARTISTS

Although women were immediately recognized as important targets for advertisers' messages, they were rarely mentioned in the early advertising journals as practitioners and are absent from advertising histories until the 1920s. Information about women in the advertising industry appears fortuitously in advertising trade journals, which were unsympathetic to them in general but which intermittently championed the work of individual women. More frustrating are the published reports of design contests in which women's names appear regularly as winners, suggesting that there must have been a significant number of trained and employed women in the field.

With its first issue in 1891, *Profitable Advertising* sounded the derisive note that it sustained throughout its years of publication. The ridicule and warning, though somewhat incoherent, were impossible to ignore:

The Boston *Globe* is encouraging women to become "writers on business," female "Powers," as it were; scientific experts, etc. O, General Taylor, this is too much. And offering prizes for advertisements, too, written by women! Great guns! there are about 6,946 male scientific advertising experts in the United States who will soon with Othello raise the very devil about their flown occupation. The result will be more disastrous than the female typewriter craze. Of course the women will cut rates. Boys, get together, formulate a union and boycott *The Globe*. Or start the women off on writing advertisements for pants. Would they succeed? Well, *would* they? They would find virtues in pants us poor males never dreamt of.[29]

Women's participation on the editorial staff of any trade journal was extremely rare and, given prevailing attitudes, even when they were present, editorial policy was not enlightened. Kate E. Griswold began at *Profitable Advertising* as manager and became editor in October 1893. Earlier that year, in June, an article appeared that she may have written. Signed "Miss Progress," it was a diatribe against uniform wage scales. The writer acknowledged that women have been limited in their professional opportunities in the past "but that day has gone. Oh, no, we are not ranting 'women's righters' in the common acceptance of the term. We have no fondness for women who disgust men, as well as members of their own sex, by their arbitrary methods of attempting to secure what they are pleased to sum up as their 'rights.'"[30]

Even when their work was noticed, women's achievements were attributed to their femininity. *Advertising Experience*'s issue of February 1898 featured advertising photographers Beatrice Tonnesen and her sister, Clara Tonnesen Kirkpatrick. In praising their work, the editors claimed that "the fact that the Tonnesens are women photographers has no doubt made it possible for them to secure a better class and a larger selection of models than could be secured by a male photographer." Years later, *Printers' Ink* acknowledged that Beatrice Tonnesen was the first photographer to use "live models." She had organized a register of models from which to draw so that "when she received an advertising order, she first created an idea and then selected a model best suited for its expression." Evidently, the "Tonnesen Models" were nationally known.[31]

Photography may have provided an entry for some women into advertising, although little research has been done in this area. Women participated in the photography fad in the 1890s, but many preferred to remain "amateurs" devoted to personal artistic expression. We know of some who did become professionals and worked in portraiture and photojournalism. In an study from a feminist perspective, C. Jane Gover shows that from 1890 to 1920 photography was a profession adopted by economically secure women who found in it a measure of personal freedom and yet remained firmly tied to Victorian gender definitions by upholding "the domestic ideal and woman's place as nurturer" in their work. Unfortunately, Gover, like most historians of photography, does not include advertising photographers in her study, although she does mention Beatrice Tonnesen in other contexts.[32]

Advertising posters provided work for many illustrators, including a significant number of women. Jacquelyn Server argues that because poster design was a new field, without the usual prejudices, women were relatively successful. The numbers of women involved, however, should be put in perspective. In an exhibition of work by prominent poster designers held in 1896, of the eighty-three designers whose works were shown, just seven were women. Some women poster designers continued in graphic design. Blanche McManus (Mrs. Francis Milton Mansfield) (b. 1870) designed posters and illustrations for books and magazines and in 1911 became art editor of *American Motorist*. Helen Dryden (b. 1887) designed posters and stage scenery, illustrated for magazines, and worked as an industrial designer. (She was involved in designing the 1937 Studebaker.)[33]

Ethel Reed (b. 1876) was the most famous female poster artist of her day. For a short period she designed book posters for the publisher Lamson, Wolffe and Company of Boston, and she was the only women profiled in the *Poster*. The author began with a lengthy dissertation on womens' limited abilities in general and women artists' lack of artistry in particular. He then praised Reed, because she "knows well the marvelous secret of design and colours, and while she

41. "Ethel Reed, 'Folly or Saintliness.'" (1895). Prints and Photographs Division, Library of Congress.

executes pictures with clever hands, she sees with her own and not masculine eyes; her work has feminine qualities, one sees in it a woman, full of sweetness and delicacy, and this is the greatest praise one can bestow upon a woman."[34]

Will Bradley also profiled Reed in "The Womans' Number" of *Bradley: His Book*. He tackled the issue of nature versus nurture directly: "The so-called 'poster movement' has brought into first prominence but one woman designer. Whether this is due to a defect in the ordinary course of training for artistic purposes, from which young women students too seldom have the courage to break away, or is owing altogether to the lack of original inventiveness which women themselves evince, it would be hard to say. Probably both conventional training and inherent incapacity that mar making ventures into new fields of work are to blame for the undeniable fact that thus far men hold the honors in this new branch of art production, with the single exception, it may be, of Miss Ethel Reed of Boston."[35]

Advertising art was rarely signed, and it is unusual to be able to identify the artist. Jessie Wilcox Smith was an exception; Smith's name appeared prominently on all her work. She produced advertisements throughout her career for Campbell's Soup, Eastman Kodak, and Ivory Soap. Very popular male artists, such as J. C. Leyendecker and Charles Dana Gibson, also signed their advertising work.

In 1913, Elizabeth Colwell (b. 1881) became the only woman ever featured in *Graphic Arts* (1911–15), a magazine that regularly profiled leading printers, designers, and advertising artists. A Chicago designer, Colwell did publicity for Marshall Field and for Cowan Company. She designed bookplates and was known for her lettering and book designs. The editor of *Graphic Arts*, Henry Lewis Johnson, acknowledged in a note preceding this article that "it has been an axiom among designers, although just why it is hard to say, that women cannot do good lettering. Miss Colwell with many other women designers, offers direct proof to the contrary."[36]

An Art Directors Club exhibition held in 1921 at the National Arts Club in New York included the work of a significant number of women. Reviewing the exhibition, *Arts and Decoration* reported that women "have attained real distinction in the field" and were responsible for "some of the most interesting and arresting exhibits on the walls." Yet women faced overt sexism that cut both ways. The author of an article in the *American Advertiser* criticized one agency director who refused to hire a female assistant because he doubted she would be

A — Another newspaper advertisement by Miss Colwell. B — One of her numerous and interesting book plates. C — Three examples of decorative initials

42. "The Work of Elizabeth Colwell." *Graphic Arts* (March 1913). General Collection, Library of Congress.

as capable as a man. The author argued, however, that because so much advertising was directed at the female consumer, female advertisers, with their unique "insight," would create more persuasive campaigns. Like their male advertising counterparts, only women in executive positions earned substantial salaries, and in 1905 just a dozen women had reached this level.[37]

Women in Graphic Design History

In her autobiography, *Through Many Windows*, Helen Rosen Woodward, a pioneer in advertising, describes advertising practices as well as the atmosphere of the workplace: the sexism and anti-Semitism encountered by workers at the turn of the century. When Woodward began in New York in 1903, agents were expected not only to plan campaigns but to design advertisements, write copy, and hire and direct illustrators. At that time female agents earned eighteen dollars a week, men twenty-five dollars. In 1926, Woodward reported, "The difference between the pay of men and women for the same work has largely disappeared in the advertising business but it is still hard for women to get positions where the bigger money lies."[38]

This was corroborated by Taylor Adams, who began his advertising career in the 1920s. According to Adams, "Women began flowering in the creative departments of agencies in the '20s, but you could hardly have said they were prevalent. With a single outstanding exception, they were either temporary tokenists hired for specific tasks (such as 'influencing' decision makers of client or prospect) or more often anonymous foot-sloggers who rarely made it to title or stockholder."[39]

Of course, the work of most advertising artists, male and female, was unsigned and ephemeral. The heads of advertising agencies took credit for successful campaigns, and women remained part of anonymous teams. And although trade magazines encouraged higher standards of composition, drawing, and typography, little was written about the people who designed advertising.

ILLUSTRATORS

To the degree that the proponents of the Aesthetic and Arts and Crafts movements broke down barriers between fine and applied art, they gave many of the crafts traditionally associated with women a new legitimacy. They also encouraged the establishment of schools to train women in the arts, although their motives here were not straightforward. Walter Smith, the English Arts and Crafts advocate who became director of art education for Massachusetts, saw the arts as a way to divert women from their struggle to gain political power. "We have a fancy," he wrote, "that our lack of art schools and other institutions where women can learn to employ themselves usefully and profitably at work which is in itself interesting and beautiful, is one of the causes which

43. "Frank Holme, 'Miss B. Ostertag.'" *Brush and Pen* (December 1897). General
Collection, Library of Congress. Blanche Ostertag was acclaimed as a young and
talented designer at the turn of the century. Little is known of her life or career,
only that she was born in St. Louis and studied in Europe before coming to
Chicago, where she designed posters and advertisements for leading businesses.

drives them to so unsex themselves as to seek to engage in men's affairs. Give
our American women the same art facilities as their European sisters, and they
will flock to the studios and let the ballot-box alone."[40]

In the United States the first applied art school for women began in Philadelphia at the behest of Sarah Peter, a wealthy philanthropist, under the aus-
pices of the Franklin Institute. The School of Design for Women opened on
December 3, 1850, with a class of ninety-four students and expanded rapidly.
The arguments for its establishment, found in the Franklin Institute proceedings, reflect the ideology of the Aesthetic movement: the legitimacy of the applied arts and women's contribution to them, the development of women's "natural" ability as it related to their domestic life, and the nonthreatening nature of
women's work. Peter was explicit; she wanted "to enlarge the sphere of female
occupation" without endangering male employment or upsetting women's tradi-

tion sphere: "I selected this department of industry, not only because it presents a wide field, as yet unoccupied by our countrymen, but also because these arts can be practiced *at home*, without materially interfering with the routine of domestic duty, which is the peculiar province of women." The chairman of the Franklin Institute expanded Peter's argument: "Women are especially adept at decoration and this would not cause an economic problem: their quick perceptions of form and their delicacy of hand very especially fit them; while even should they, in these and similar branches of labor, finally supplant men entirely, no evil could occur, especially in a country like ours, where such broad fields for male labor lie entirely unoccupied."[41]

The number of art schools for women or open to them increased in the 1870s. The earliest, begun in the East, separated the sexes; Western schools were generally coeducational. The Lowell Institute in Boston, begun in 1850, followed the Eastern pattern. During the 1871–72 academic year the school enrolled 124 male and 127 female students; classes for women were held in the afternoon, those for men in the evening. Similarly, in 1856, when Peter Cooper endowed an Academy of Design for Women, "in which the art of engraving and designing will constantly be taught," women studied during the day and men at night.[42]

Most women and men who trained in design schools found careers in textile design, mechanical drawing (including drawing for the U.S. Patent Office), architectural drawing, and wood engraving. New York, with its publishing businesses, was the center of wood engraving but women also worked in Chicago, Boston, Saint Louis, and Cleveland. Apparently pay equity varied considerably: female wood engravers earned half the rate of their male counterparts in engraving offices, although they could earn the same rate as men by freelancing. The few women who engaged in mechanical drawing were also paid at the same rate as men.[43]

Many of the early women cartoonists began their careers in the suffrage movement. Taking advantage of new educational opportunities, they trained as illustrators and then used their skills in the battle for the vote. Edwina Dumm, Rose O'Neill, May Wilson Preston, and Lou Rogers were among them. Often they combined cartooning with illustration for books and magazines and advertising work.[44]

Although women were allowed greater access to an art education, they were still blocked from membership in artist clubs. As we have seen, many clubs began as informal sessions for sharing work and evolved into social occasions for editors, printers, publishers, and other potential employers to meet with artists; they provided opportunities for professional advancement. But as one writer noted, without a trace of cynicism, "When a woman steps boldly beyond pretty copying and does work that is strong and imaginative, she is admitted to comparison with and the companionship of brother artists; she may not be elected to active membership in the Water Color Society, but she may hope for honorary membership in that august organization, and more than content herself with being an officer of high degree in the Water Color Club."[45]

The Society of Illustrators, founded in 1901, had ninety-six members by 1911, all male, and four associate members. The associate members were four of the most successful women illustrators of the time: Elizabeth Shippen Green, Violet Oakley, May Wilson Preston, and Jessie Wilcox Smith. When the society incorporated in 1920, however, these women became full members. One of the few clubs for professional female artists was founded in 1897 in Philadelphia. Led by Alice Barber Stephens, an illustrator and teacher at the School of Design, and by Emily Sartain, an artist and director of the school, the Plastic Club provided the same kind of community and publicity that male illustrators had found so useful.[46]

In the 1880s and 1890s the need for illustrations for magazine covers and stories, outdoor advertisements, and popular fiction swelled as the number of periodicals, newspapers, and advertising posters grew. Three notable chroniclers of the Golden Age of Illustration, Francis Hopkinson Smith, Frank Weitenkampf, and Henry Pitz, mentioned women illustrators in their discussions but always grouped them apart from men and singled out just two or three for praise.

Smith was himself an illustrator and contemporary of his subjects, and his *American Illustrators* (1892) was a dramatized account of the activities in the New York illustrators' clubs he frequented. He reviewed and praised American male illustrators and showed their work in beautiful reproductions, but because women were not members of the clubs, Smith mentioned them only in a review of the annual Water Color Society exhibition. Although he made fun of most female exhibitors, in "their devotion to the mild-eyed daisy and the familiar goldenrod standing erect in a ginger jar of Chinese blue," he allowed exceptions: Rosina Emmett, Mary Hallock Foote, and Alice Barber Stephens. These women are praised but their work is neither discussed or shown.[47]

In *American Graphic Art* (1912), Frank Weitenkampf also considered women illustrators in a separate division. Indeed, he remarked that the disruption of his chronological organization was "brought about by the convenient classification by sex." And he, too, commended the work of Foote and Stephens. Weitenkampf maintained that the illustrations of Howard Pyle's women students "exemplify various possibilities resulting from the application of the female temperament to illustration."[48]

Many female illustrators did specialize in domestic subjects, and some, though not all, worked in a decidedly decorative style. Howard Pyle was not only a famous illustrator but equally important as a teacher, at the Drexel Institute in Philadelphia and at his own school for professional illustrators at Chadds Ford, Pennsylvania. A third of Pyle's students at Chadds Ford were women. Pyle himself used a dramatic, realistic approach to illustrating, as did many of his male students. In *The Brandywine Tradition* (1968), Henry Pitz concluded that the women were naturally drawn to another style and subject matter: "The women artists, with a few exceptions, give the impression that they formed a consistent school some-what different from the men. . . . Their almost un-failing sense of the decorative, a shared technique and their natural inclination toward feminine, homely, re-poseful subjects are there in almost every picture."[49]

To what degree was Pyle responsible for the style and interests of his students? All were highly accomplished before they studied with Pyle, and many had some professional experience. One can also imagine that art directors encouraged a specific subject matter; illustrators then as now were classed as specialists in a particular genre. Nonetheless, this did not necessarily force women to concentrate on domestic subjects. In an autobiographical sketch, Jessie Wilcox Smith recalled that her first illustrating assignment was for a book about American Indians. Having successfully completed the first assignment, she was offered a second book on the same subject, and then a third. "I felt I must speak or forever after be condemned to paint Indians. So I wrote to the publishers that I did not know much about Indians and that if they had just an everyday book about children, I thought I could do it better. I was immediately rewarded with one of Louisa M. Alcott's stories, and a letter saying they were

Drawn for Eastman Kodak Co., courtesy Collier's Weekly. Copyright 1904, Collier's Weekly.

A Christmas Morning

Where there's a child, there should the Kodak be.
As a means of keeping green the Christmas memories,
or as a gift, it's a holiday delight.

KODAK

Kodaks from $5.00 to $97.00. Brownie Cameras (They work like Kodaks) $1, $2, $5.
Kodak Developing Machines, $2.00 to $10.00.

EASTMAN KODAK CO.

Catalogue free at the
dealers or by mail

Rochester, N. Y.

44. "Jessie Wilcox Smith. Kodak Advertisement." *Colliers* (November 26, 1904).
General Research Division, New York Public Library, Astor, Lenox
and Tilden Foundations.

glad to know I did other things, as they had supposed Indians were my specialty!"[50]

Women illustrators in the decade before and after the turn of the century were successful by any standard. Their work was published widely, they supported themselves and their families, and some were known by name to the public in an age when popular illustrators were celebrities. But in a newspaper article of 1912, "Qualities That Make for Success in Women Illustrators," the author was clear about what aspects of women's illustrations gained them adherents: "The field of illustration has been steadily widening for women since those days in the early 70's when Addie Ledyard's pictures of ideally pretty children with sweeping eyelashes won our young hearts and Mary Hallock Foote, whose quality of exquisite tenderness, rather than the strength of her drawing, brought her ardent admirers, was illustrating her own and other people's stories."[51]

Women graphic designers were allowed to work at jobs that took advantage of their culturally defined sex-specific skills. They were thought to be able typesetters because women generally have smaller hands than men. Their supposed affinity with decoration and domesticity made them illustrators of women and children. They were encouraged to participate in those careers in which they did not threaten male economic advantage. When they ventured beyond those limits, they were belittled or vilified or "disappeared" from history.

It is clear that women participated in significant though not overwhelming numbers in all aspects of work that would—by the first decade of the twentieth century—be recognized as the province of graphic design: in the printing industry, in advertising, and in illustration. Artistic theories during this period elevated the status of applied arts, including the decorative and domestic arts, and allowed women to participate more fully in them. Art and design schools were either open to women or established specifically to train women. Nonetheless, women were still seen as having specific abilities associated with their gender. The exceptions proved the rule; historians who praised a chosen few felt justified in ignoring the majority.

The graphic design process is a collective effort, and because women rarely headed art departments in advertising agencies, publishing houses, or magazines, their contributions are difficult to document. The record of women's participation in early graphic design is meager unless the researcher goes beyond standard design histories to statistical studies, to suffragist histories and histories of minorities, to documents and institutional histories of advertising agencies, publishing firms, art and design schools, and artists' clubs, to union histories, and to the trade journals. A comprehensive history of women in graphic design would right the old imbalance. It would also provide a more realistic view of the context in which graphic design began.

7. At the End of the "Mechanical Revolution"

In 1922 the *Boston Evening Transcript* published a special supplement in conjunction with a Graphic Arts Exposition held in the city. Several articles described the changes in printing technology and the work of printers' organizations. In addition, W. A. Dwiggins, by then a resident of the Boston area, contributed a column on the state of American graphic design.[1] In many ways Dwiggins's article sums up the themes covered in this book: the tremendous advances in printing and reproduction technology and its effect on the printing industry, the growth of a powerful advertising industry and mass media, and the recognition of a new profession facing new opportunities.[2]

Dwiggins believed that the technological revolution had ended and that designers had not fully appreciated its consequences. Printing as it had been understood and practiced for centuries was irrevocably changed. Dwiggins recognized, above all, that printing technology and the needs of advertising

45. "Three Advertisements." *Western
Advertising* (June 1919). Science,
Industry and Business Library,
New York Public Library, Astor, Lenox
and Tilden Foundations.

changed the nature of professional practice for commercial printers and graphic designers. With others in his generation, he revered the fine printing tradition continued by those in the private press movement and a few university presses. At the same time, he insisted that the true heirs of technological progress and advertising art worked in a new territory—the domain of graphic design. Further, the new means of production had necessarily changed the character of design:

> The revolution in technical practice is complete. Very little is left of the old methods. The standards of good printing as they stood from the beginning of the craft are suddenly superseded. There is thrust into the printer's hand a complex of new processes—half-tone engraving, machine composition, quadricolor, offset, fast running photogravure. The original conception of sound printing design as it stood until the age of the machines has very little bearing on these new processes. The impression of ink upon paper is an entirely new and different thing.

Dwiggins distinguished among three categories of printing: fine art printing, purely utilitarian printing, and printing for a purpose: graphic design. He called the impact of graphic design "so wide and so varied that you will have trouble choosing examples to represent it." Above all else, he characterized the new graphic object as ephemeral because it is inextricably associated with another new phenomenon—advertising. And like advertising its function is to persuade. Like advertising, "it is thoroughly democratic—goes everywhere and is read by everyone. It probably plays a larger part in forming the quasi-social state that we call civilization than all the books and newspapers and periodicals together. Its function is to prepare the ground for selling something, or to sell something directly itself. By hook or by crook, by loud noise or by subtle argument. It might fulfill its mission of getting something sold."

Although he acknowledged the pressures of commerce, Dwiggins charged his fellow practitioners with educating public taste: "Advertising artists are now their only teachers." He advised designers to pay attention to new graphic ideas from France, where he felt designers had "caught the spirit" of the ephemeral nature of advertising design. Like Earnest Calkins, Frank Parsons, and others interested in promoting a new design aesthetic, Dwiggins accepted responsibility for mass visual education. He also recognized that this was a dual responsibility—for artistic quality and for the integrity of the message communicated. His essay is an early contribution to what has become a continuing process of self-definition.

As we have seen, this discourse began during the transformation of publishing, reproduction technology, the printing industry, and advertising. Instances of splits between production and design functions produced a new kind of designer in the graphic arts; when compositors no longer designed the printed page, the layout man replaced them; when type manufacture was mechanized, the type designers emerged. Individual designers created new vocations by combining several designing skills. Some of this was reflected in trade journals that by the end of the second decade of the twentieth century combined the interests of printers and type designers in publication design with advertising directors and illustrators in advertising art. Other aspects of this transformation can be seen in the formation of new professional associations that provided separate traditions with a means of communication and at the same time expanded their interests to include other forms of design practice. By 1920 representatives of separate professional practices: printers, typographers, illustrators, art directors, photographers, calligraphers, engravers, and lithographers found a community in the same professional associations.

The relation between technology and American attitudes toward the visual arts forms the background of this story. The Aesthetic and Arts and Crafts movements were important to professional designers because they linked the craft trades with a larger view of life and because they made designers conscious of the meaning of style beyond superficial ornamentation. That they failed to transform the harsh conditions of industrial production is beyond question. They failed partly because neither John Ruskin nor Wiliam Morris nor their disciples could find a means of integrating the efficiencies of industrial production with design, a split that began in the last decades of the nineteenth century and has never been reconciled. Nevertheless, Morris's ideals encouraged those who designed graphic material and who worked in the world of commerce for a mass audience to find ways to enhance the quality of printed material and popular visual culture.

At the same time, designers were forced to defend and define their work as part of a larger debate on the role of popular art, fine art, and visual communication. Those involved in graphics began to look at the many strands of graphic design as parts of a larger entity, a visual art that had an extra-artistic function, that presented ideas in a visual form using both text and image to a mass audience. Theodore Low De Vinne, Henry Lewis Johnson, Frank Alvah Parsons, William Addison Dwiggins, and many others wrote books on the proper way to design advertisements, magazines, books, and other graphic material. The particulars of their work tell us a great deal about the ideas underlying the graphic styles of the late nineteenth and early twentieth centuries. Just as important, however, the very existence of their texts implies a readership who sought such advice in confronting this new kind of art called "graphic design."

Dwiggins underestimated the rate of technological development and how strongly it would continue to transform graphic design. In 1922 he could not foresee photoelectronic type composition or giant offset presses; he could not anticipate the allure of European Modernism for the American designer. But his

46. "Louis Braunhold, Designer and Illustrator."
Publishers' Weekly (September 26, 1872).
General Collection, Library of Congress.

generation, as well as the two previous ones, had participated in and recorded some of the great upheavals of the Industrial Revolution and its influence on design and mass culture.

Computer technology has, at the end of the twentieth century, again thrust the graphic design profession into a new relation with production processes. Software programs have conflated occupations once more. Nondesigners as well as professionals are designing publications—and appropriating and modifying typefaces, photographs, and illustrations for their own purposes. Again, designers confront the problem Dwiggins posed many decades ago: "Can we design this new printing with our minds trained in the standards that guided Aldus, or Bodoni, or De Vinne? Must all these things that we looked upon as good go overboard? How much of the old standard of quality can carry across the gap, and how can it be related to the new state of things?" Professional graphic designers, like their predecessors, find themselves redefining their roles and the function of graphic design in this new era.

Appendix A: Periodicals of Importance in

American Graphic Design, 1852–1920

*No matter it to these Visigoths that money and time is lavished to make these beautiful
to the eye, no matter that talent and scholarship sparkle in their pages; they are
consigned to the waste basket or cut into newspaper wrappers.*
JOHN SPRINGER, Iowa City Printer (1876)

*The successive issues of any printing trade publication in the United States, if
preserved and bound, will form a volume of interest and value. Even those devoted
primarily to advertising the wares of dealers in printing material, contain many
articles which are of practical or historical interest. . . . So little value has been
attached to them by unappreciative recipients, that a complete file is a rarity.*
"PRESERVE YOUR SPECIMEN," *Pacific Specimen* (1881)

The periodicals listed below are grouped in three categories: advertising, art and book
arts, and printing and typography. Within categories they are arranged in alphabetical
order by original title with cross-references under later titles. European periodicals of
particular importance to American graphic designers are included. In general, the list

does not include journals for their art work alone, and it does not include such mass circulation journals as *Century* or *Harper's Weekly*.

Publication data were obtained from the card catalogs of the Library of Congress and the Butler Library, Columbia University, from Carolyn F. Ulrich and Karl Küp's *Books and Printing: A Selected List of Periodicals, 1800–1942* (1943), and from Frank Luther Mott's five-volume *History of American Magazines* (1938–68). With the exception of the most popular journals, such as the *Inland Printer* and *Printing Art*, library runs are incomplete, and publication information, particularly for the earliest publications, is contradictory or incomplete. I have tried to reconcile discrepancies based on available material or noted them with a question mark. Although data cannot be uniformly presented, it seems more important to record all information available. I was unable to locate several journals listed in earlier compilations but chose to include them, without annotations, because they were regarded as useful in the past.

ADVERTISING JOURNALS

The Ad-School: A Practical Advertiser. Monthly. Chicago: Page-Davis, v. 1–10; January 1901–25. Name changed to *Common-sense.*

Also subtitled *A Monthly Journal Devoted to An Era of Better Publication.* Practical advice for the businessman ("Theory, like sentiment, seldom sells socks!"). Interesting for its defense of advertising practices.

Ad Sense. Chicago: Ad Sense Publishing Company, 1898–1906. Absorbed *Mail Order Bulletin*, 1901.

Subtitled *A Journal of Advertising and Business* and written for advertising professionals. See series by Alfred Bersback on the use of illustration in advertising.

Advertising and Selling. See *Profitable Advertising*

Advertising Experience. Chicago: Irving G. McColl, v. 1–12; 1893–1902. Merged into *Judicious Advertising.*

Advice to advertisers with a department of criticism to make advertisements more effective. Also included explanations of printing processes, descriptions of advertising campaigns, suggestions for dealing with illustrators, and the advantages of photography in advertising.

Advertising Ideas, Affiliated with Dry Goods Economist: A Practical Manual of the Busy Advertising Man in Dry Goods Stores and Newspaper Offices. New York: 1920–? Guy Hubbart, editor.

Models and samples of advertisements and pages of advertisements to show different kinds of layout, use of illustration, and type—with comments.

American Advertiser: How to Advertise Retail Stock. Chicago: Merchants Publishing Company, 1887–?

Articles on subjects ranging from vehement defenses of advertising practices to information on typography and color, discussions of different advertising techniques (e.g., "reason why advertising"), and profiles of agencies (e.g., agencies that specialized in

Appendix A

theatrical or subway advertising). Many model advertisements (see "Window Dresser" series) and cuts for sale.

American Journalist and Advertisers' Index. (First appeared as *American Journalist.*) Philadelphia: Coe, Wetherill and Company, v. 1–6, February 1872–July 1876; n.s., no.1–2, October 1876–January 1877. Absorbed *Advertisers' Index* in October 1876.

Good source of information on the business aspects of typefounding and on the industry's struggles with advertising agencies.

Art Directors Club. *Annual.* New York: Art Directors Club, 1922–present.

Record of the national exhibitions sponsored by the club, with introductory essays on the state of advertising art.

The Billposter and Distributor: Official Journal of the Associated Billposters and Distributors of the United States and Canada. Chicago: Outdoor Advertising Association of America, 1897–1931. Name changed to *Advertising Outdoors: A Magazine Devoted to the Interests of the Outdoor Advertiser*, v. 1–15, 1897–1910; *The Poster: The National Journal of Outdoor Advertising and Poster Art*, 1910–30; *Advertising Outdoors*, v. 1–2; 1930–31. Monthly.

Primarily concerned with the business and ethics of the trade; also held annual poster contests and published winning entries.

Charles Austin Bates Criticisms. New York: C. A. Bates, 1897–1902. Name changed to *Current Advertising*, March 1900–1902. Absorbed by *Profitable Advertising*, 1903.

Critiques using actual advertisements submitted by businessmen to improve advertising copy, illustration, and layout. Bates's highly opinionated, idiosyncratic voice dominated.

Common-Sense. See *Ad-School*

Direct Advertising and Sample Book of Mill-Brand Papers. Boston: Paper Makers' Advertising Association, 1912–13. Name changed to *Direct Advertising and House Organ Review*, 1914–?

Primarily concerned with marketing issues; during the 1920s, W. A. Dwiggins contributed articles on graphic designers and advertising.

Editor and Publisher: The Fourth Estate. New York: Editor and Publisher Company, 1901–? Name changed to *Editor and Publisher and Journalist*, June 10, 1911–April 22, 1916. Absorbed *Journalist*, Jan. 26, 1907; *Advertising* (formerly *Newspaperdom*), July 11, 1925; *Fourth Estate*, Dec. 5, 1927.

Of interest 1917–19 for the advertising industry's relation to the Committee for Public Information, with many examples of war posters.

Fame: A Journal for Advertisers. New York: Artemas Ward, March 1892–April 1938. Monthly.

Followed by one year the establishment of a journal of the same title in England and shared, in condensed form, many articles. Directed at the professional advertiser, with information on trademark protection, space costs, and advertising practices. Several articles examined the relationship between advertiser and advertising artist.

Appendix A

George P. Rowell and Company's American Newspaper Report and Advertiser's Gazette.
New York: The Company, 1868–84; in 1877 sold to W. H. Woodcock, owner of a printers' supply business. Name changed to *American Reporter and Printers' Gazette*, then *Woodcock's Printers' and Lithographers' Weekly Gazette and Newspaper Reporter*, 1879–84.

Interesting pieces of information from the era; for example, the highest price for a cartoon was $350, paid by *Harpers Bazaar* to Thomas Nast in 1871. Also included many type specimens and articles by Theodore Low De Vinne.

The Graphic Arts: A Magazine for Printers and Users of Printing. Boston: Graphic Arts Publishing Company, v. 1–3; 1911–15. Imprint varied, issued 1911–12 by the National Arts Publishing Company. Monthly. Subtitle varied: v. 1–3, *A Monthly Magazine Representing Progressive Developments in Engraving, Printing, Publishing and Advertising*, v. 4, *The Monthly Magazine of the Craftsmanship of Advertising*.

Edited by Henry Lewis Johnson. Substantial articles by distinguished members of the profession on all aspects of graphic design. Included profiles of individual designers and beautiful reproductions.

Judicious Advertising. Chicago: Lord and Thomas, 1902–April 1925. Merged with *Advertising Experience* in 1903 and title changed to *Judicious Advertising and Advertising Experience*. Resumed as *Judicious Advertising* in 1912.

An important advertising journal of its day, with articles and news on advertising design and designers. See, for example, W. Livingston Larned's series "The New Era of Advertising Art," which appeared in 1918.

Mahin's Magazine. Chicago: John Lee Mahin, 1902–4; v. 1–3, no.1–2. Merged into *Judicious Advertising*. R. S. Thain, editor.

Proponent of "scientific advertising"; the editor's goal was "to bring the truths of psychology and advertising into closer harmony." Walter Dill Scott was a regular contributor. Also addressed issues of advertising effectiveness and the need for professional standards and ethics.

Mail Order Journal. New York: 1897–1925; name changed to *Advertising Age*, 1916–22; then to *National Advertising*.

Not seen by compiler.

Mertz Magazine. See *Pacific Coast Advertising*

Modern Advertising. Chicago: Frederic Goudy, 1892–93.

Goudy's short-lived magazine. Not seen by compiler.

Pacific Coast Advertising: A Monthly Exponent of Western Publicity. Los Angeles: W. D. Curtis, 1901–5, 5 vols. Continued as *Mertz Magazine*.

An advertising magazine for professionals with emphasis on advertising California products and businesses; good examples of advertisements combining photography with line drawing.

Pettengill's Reporter, 1851–59.

First advertising magazine. Not seen by compiler.

Appendix A

Poster: The National Journal of Outdoor Advertising and Poster Art. See *The Billposter and Distributor*

Printers' Ink: A Journal for Advertisers. New York: Printers' Ink Publishing Company, 1888–1967. Succeeded by *Marketing/Communications,* 1967–72. Frequency varied: semi-monthly, 1888–89; weekly, 1890–1964; semi-monthly, 1965–67.

Begun by George P. Rowell, the pioneer advertising agent, it was one of the earliest and certainly among the most successful and widely imitated advertising journals of the nineteenth century. At first concerned solely with newspaper advertising, it later broadened in scope to include all media. It featured stories that reinforced its ardent boosterism and closely monitored government policies that affected advertising. A great deal of advertising history is recorded in its pages. For a complete publication history, see Mott, *History of Advertising,* 4:246–47.

Profitable Advertising. Boston: C. F. David 1891–April 1924; name changed to *Advertising and Selling with the Advertising News,* New York: Kate E. Griswold, September 1918–March 1919; *Advertising and Selling: A National Journal of Marketing,* 1919–24. Absorbed *Selling Magazine,* June 1909; *Advertising News,* September 1918; *Business World,* December 1910. Absorbed by *Advertising Fortnightly,* May 1924.

Its motto: "We show you how to do it." Written originally for the businessman, later for

47. "Contest Entry." *Signs of the Times* (August 1906). General Collection, the Library of Congress.

the advertising professional, with practical advice on design and copy as well as marketing. Kate E. Griswold, manager and publisher, edited the journal until 1919, and was often cited as a model for women in publishing. George French, who succeeded her as editor, was the author of an advertising text. Of special interest are the reviews of advertisements. A successful and influential journal.

Print: Direct-by-Mail Advertising and Selling Ideas for Printers. Boston: Brad Stephens and Company, 1911–17? House organ.

Not seen by compiler.

Reklame: Zeitschrift des Deutschen Reklame-Verbandes. Berlin: 1908–?

Not seen by compiler.

Signs of the Times: Journal of Advertising Devoted to the Interests of the Advertiser, the Agency and the Purveyor of Publicity. Cincinnati: Signs of the Times Publishing Company, 1906–present. Subtitle varies: *The National Journal of Signs and Advertising Display.*

The premier magazine of outdoor advertising. In early years, it included sign contests, profiles, how-to articles, "signologues" ("dissertations on outdoor publicity" by "recognized exponents of profitable advertising"), and news of the Billposters Association. A treasury of styles.

Western Advertising. San Francisco: Ramsey Oppenheim Company, February 1919–?

A journal for the advertising industry with occasional notes on advertising art and good examples of color printing used in advertising.

ART AND BOOK ART JOURNALS

Aldine Press: A Typographic Art Journal. New York: James Sutton and Co., v. 1–9; September 1868–December 1879; name changed to *Aldine, a Typographic Art Journal,* 1871–73; *Aldine: The Art Journal of America,* 1874–79.

Notable for its original wood engravings and typography, *Aldine* was, and still is, regarded as one of the most beautifully illustrated American journals. Began in 1868 as a modest house organ distributed free to customers by the printer Sutton, Browne and Company of New York, it soon became a showcase for fine illustration, prints, and typography and grew into a substantial sixteen-page publication. See Mott, *History of Advertising,* 3:410–12, for a complete publication history.

American Art Review: A Journal Devoted to the Practice, Theory, History and Archaeology of Art. Boston: D. Estes and C. E. Lauriat, v. 1–2; 1879–81. Edited by S. R. Koehler.

Although this journal ceased after two volumes, it remains a monument to the highest standards of writing and scholarship. Elegantly produced, *American Art Review* is notable for beautiful typography and illustrations and the quality of its paper and printing. W. J. Linton's *History of Wood Engraving in America* was published in serial form over several issues in the first volume. The work of American printmakers, shown with original etchings, figured prominently.

Appendix A

Art Age. New York: Turnure and Gilliss Brothers, v. 1–10; April 1883–October 1889. Monthly. Edited by Arthur B. Turnure.

Originally focused on "artistic printing" for printers, publishers, and booksellers, *Art Age* soon became a lively journal that reviewed all developments in the fine and applied arts and literature, particularly in the New York area.

Art and Progress. Washington, D.C.: American Federation of Arts, v. 1–46; November 1909–53. Name changed to *American Magazine of Art,* January 1916–36; *Magazine of Art,* 1936–53. Absorbed *Creative Art,* January 1934.

See column "In the Magazines" for reviews of illustrations in major periodicals. Occasional articles about the job market for illustrators.

Art Interchange. New York: Art Interchange Company, v. 1–53; 1878–November 1904.

This monthly journal of opinion and information originally concentrated on interior decoration. It was part of the Arts and Crafts movement and one of the few art journals to attain a high circulation, "as much as ten thousand," according to Mott (4:146). Arthur B. Turnure was editor from 1880 to 1883; Josephine Redding succeeded him. The journal closely followed the poster craze of the 1890s.

The Artist: An Illustrated Monthly Record of Arts, Crafts and Industries. New York: Truslove, Hanson and Comba, 1898–1902.

The American edition of an English publication devoted to the Arts and Crafts movement. Each issue began with "The American Survey," edited by Charles H. Caffin. Its mission was "to seek out and record all the instances, of which so many exist in this country, of art applied to crafts without the hindrance of commercialism" (23, no. 226 (October 1898), ix).

Bradley: His Book: A Monthly Magazine Devoted to Art, Literature and Printing. Springfield, Mass.: May 1896–February 1897.

A one man tour-de-force; Bradley wrote many of the articles, designed the advertisements, and contributed illustrations for the "literary features," written by others. He promised in the first issue that "the art will bear slightly toward decoration, a field but little developed here. Each number will be as widely different from the previous one, in colors, paper and types, as it is practical to make it." Of special interest is a regular column, "Primer of Ornament and Design," for which Bradley showed how he turned a realistic drawing of one object, such as a dandelion, into decorative and repeating patterns.

Brush and Pencil: An Illustrated Magazine of the Arts of Today. Chicago: Phillips and Company, v. 1–19; September 1897–May 1907; suspended August–November 1904.

Articles and news items on a variety of arts and artists related to the Midwest, including profiles of illustrators and professional associations. "A magazine devoted to the interests of the students of the Art Institute," it also represented the views of the Chicago Arts and Crafts Society.

The Commercial Illustrator. Minneapolis: The Federal Schools, Inc., 1916–. Name changed to *The Illustrator,* 1917; *The Federal Illustrator,* September 1917–Summer 1941.

Organ of the Federal School of Commercial Designing and, in 1917, the Federal School

171

VOL. XXIII.

SEPT.-DEC., 1898.

·THE·

·ARTIST·

·AN·ILLVSTRATED· MONTHLY·RECORD· ·OF·ARTS·CRAFTS· AND·INDVSTRIES·

·PVBLISHED·BY·
·TRVSLOVE·HANSON·&·COMBA·
·67·FIFTH·AVENVE·
·NEW·YORK·

48. "Cover." *Artist* (September–December 1898). General Collection, Library of Congress.

Appendix A

of Applied Cartooning, two important correspondence schools for aspiring graphic designers. "A Chat with the President," biographical articles by and about teachers and graduates, and news of competitions and results (with reproductions) were regular features. Exhortations to work hard with promises of success and riches predominated.

The Craftsman. Eastwood, N.Y.: G. Stickley, v. 1–31; October 1, 1901–December 1916. Merged with *Art World,* New York: Art Society of America, January 1917.

Edited and published by Gustav Stickley, a proponent of the Arts and Crafts movement and interpreter of William Morris's aesthetics in the United States. Professor Irene Sargent of Syracuse University was responsible for the early issues. For a complete publication history and examples of its pages, see Barry Sanders, *The Craftsman: An Anthology* (Santa Barbara, Calif.: Peregrine Smith, 1978).

The Crayon: A Journal Devoted to the Graphic Arts. New York: William James Stillman and J. Durand, editors and publishers, v. 1–8; January 1855–July 1861. Weekly during 1855, monthly thereafter.

A leading art magazine of the period, concentrating on aesthetics and championing the ideas of John Ruskin, who was a contributor. See "Ruskinism in America: *The Crayon,*" in Roger Stein's *John Ruskin and Aesthetic Thought in America, 1840–1900* (Cambridge: Harvard University Press, 1967), 101–23.

Federal Illustrator. See *Commercial Art Illustrator*

Handicraft. Boston: Society of Arts and Crafts, v. 1–2; April 1902–April 1903; 1910–12.
Not seen by compiler.

Lithograph. New York: Charles Hart, 1874.
Not seen by compiler.

Magazine of Art. (American edition.) New York: Cassell and Company, v. 1–28; May 1878–July 1904 (v. 27–28 also numbered n.s. 1–2). Numbering in American and English editions is the same.

Brought the latest art news and examples of new styles from Europe, including Art Nouveau. A "Monthly Record of American Art" was added in 1882.

Magazine of Art. (Washington, D. C.: 1909–53.) See *Art and Progress*

Modern Art. Indianapolis: Joseph M. Bowles; Boston: L. Prang and Company, v. 1–5, no. 1; 1893–97. Quarterly.

Edited by Bowles. Notable for its William Morris–inspired ornaments and full-page illustrations. A youthful Bruce Rogers worked on its layout and contributed illustrations when *Modern Art* was published in Indianapolis.

Monthly Illustrator. See *Quarterly Illustrator*

The Poster. New York: W. M. Clemens, v. 1, 1–5, January–May 1896. Monthly.

William Montgomery Clemens published and edited this short-lived journal during the height of poster collecting. Filled with news, opinions, reviews, and quotations in no discernible order. In black and white with red, black, and white reproductions.

Appendix A

Poster Lore: A Journal of Enthusiasm Devoted to the Appreciation of Modern Posters. Kansas City: Red Pale Press, Frederic Thoreau Singleton, v. 1, 1–4; 1896. Irregular.

Singleton did most of the writing and all of the production and printing of this small but elegant magazine. He concentrated on poster collecting but included reviews of books, magazines, and exhibitions celebrating poster art. Tiny reproductions of posters were issued as supplements.

Prang's Chromo: A Journal of Popular Art. Boston: Louis Prang, v. 1–2; 1868–69. Five issues.

Louis Prang's house organ, used to advertise the company's reproductions. It featured articles on the process of chromolithography with examples in vivid color and price lists.

Quarterly Illustrator. New York: Harry C. Jones, 1893–95. Name changed to *Monthly Illustrator*, February 1895–1897. Absorbed *Home and Country*, October 1895.

A mine of information about individual illustrators, reviews of published work and exhibitions, and histories of major illustrated journals and art schools. Heavily illustrated.

The Studio: An Illustrated Magazine of Fine and Applied Art. London: National Magazine Company, April 1893–1988; American edition, March 1897–October 1921; name changed to *International Studio*, November 1921–1931. Absorbed *Scrip*, June 1908; absorbed by *Connoisseur*, September 1931. Monthly.

Founded by Charles Holme and C. Lewis Hind. Hind and later Gleeson White were editors during the period under study. The *Studio* introduced Art Nouveau, particularly the work of Aubrey Beardsley, Japanese art, French posters, and artistic photography, to the United States.

Western Camera Notes: A Monthly Magazine of Pictorial Photography. Minneapolis: n.p., v. 1–8; December 1899–December 1907. Absorbed *Young Photographer*, 1901; *Paine's Photographic Magazine*, 1902. Merged into *Camera Craft*. Organ of the Minneapolis Camera Club, 1899–1900; other societies, including the National Association of Amateur Photographers, March–December 1907.

Edited by C. F. Potter. A journal of advice to amateur photographers and those interested in professional careers. See especially Harvey S. Lewis' twenty-part course, "Commercial Photography and Its Adaptation to Modern Advertising," beginning in the October 1904 issue.

PRINTING AND TYPOGRAPHY JOURNALS

American Art Printer: Devoted to the Typographic Art and Kindred Industries. New York: C. E. Bartholomew, v. 1–7, nos. 1–4; January 1887–1893. Bimonthly and monthly.

A magazine for those who aspired to become artist-printers, with many articles of advice and criticism.

American Bookmaker. New York: Howard Lockwood, July 1885–January 1897; title varied: *Printer and Bookmaker*, March 1897–December 1899; *American Printer and Bookmaker*, January–February 1900; *American Printer*, March 1900–1958. John Clyde Oswald became publisher in 1899. Absorbed *Western Printer*, 1902; *International*

174

Printer, 1906; *Master Printer* and *Printing Trade News*, 1915. Absorbed by *Inland and American Printer and Lithographer*, September 1958. Monthly. The periodical had been a continuation in part of the *Paper Trade Journal*, begun in May 1872. Subtitled *A Journal of Technical Art and Information for Publishers, Bookbinders, Printers, Lithographers, Blank-book Manufacturers and All Others Connected with or Interested in Bookmaking*.

Lockwood, head of the printing firm Lockwood and Company, was an active member of the United Typothetae of America, and this journal served at times as the organization's official organ. It chronicled Typothetae activities but also featured articles of technical information, studies of historical and contemporary printers and presses, and information about book club activities. J. Clyde Oswald continued to address these interests. See especially "School of Typography," a regular column.

American Bulletin: Published in the Interests of the American Type Founder Company and Publishers and Printers Everywhere. New York: American Type Founder Company, May 1910–June 1918; suspended November 1911–February 1912. House organ.

Notable for type specimens and the series "Biographies of Famous Printers," by Henry Lewis Bullen.

American Chap Book. Jersey City, N.J.: American Type Founders Company, vols. 1–2; 12 nos.; 1904–5. House organ.

The work of Will Bradley. Each number was devoted to one subject, for example: "Use of Borders and Ornaments" (November 1904); "Cover Designs" (March 1905); "Advertising Display" (June 1905); "Title Pages" (August 1905). Each began with Bradley's written considerations and was followed by his design solutions.

American Model Printer: A Journal Devoted to the Typographic Art and Kindred Trades. New York: Kelly and Bartholomew, 1879–85. Official publication of the International Typographical Union of North America. Irregular. Edited by W. J. Kelly.

An influential magazine for job-printers working in smaller communities throughout the United States. It dispensed both technical and aesthetic advice and is blamed by some for the proliferation of exotic letterforms and composition, particularly "Egyptianism," popular in the 1880s.

American Newspaper Reporter and Printers Gazette. See *George P. Rowell's American Newspaper Reporter and Printers Gazette*

American Pressman. Chicago: F. Pampusch, 1897–98; St. Louis: T. F. Galoskowsky, 1898–?

Organ of the International Printing Pressman and Assistants Union. Primarily union news and proceedings of meetings.

American Printer. See *American Bookmaker*

Ars Typographica. New York: Marchbanks Press, 1918–20; New York: Press of the Wooly Whale, 1934. (v. 1, nos. 1–3 [1918–20], no. 4 [1934], edited by Frederic W. Goudy; v. 2–3 [1925–26], edited by Douglas C. McMurtrie. Rpt. in 2 vols., Westport, Conn.: Greenwood Press, 1970; v. 1 [1918–20, 1934] and v. 2 [1925–26].)

Appendix A

Typographical history, modern typographical design, and professional issues addressed in substantial essays.

Artist Printer. June 1889–April 1893. St. Louis. Absorbed by *National Printer Journalist,* May 1893. Subtitle varies: *A Monthly Journal; A Journal for the Progressive.* Monthly.

Written for unionized printers and owners of printshops: "For the dissemination of ideas, a medium through which employer and employee may commune, and any distinction be only a matter of brains." Varied fonts with each issue to "give our subscribers a more practical idea of the utility of new faces than can be obtained from specimen sheets."

Bruce Printers' Cabinet. New York: Bruce Type Foundry, 1904–? Subtitle varies: *A Modern Journal of Printing and Type Making; Devoted Entirely to the Interests of the Printing Fraternity.*

House organ of a family-owned typefoundry notable for its use of color inks and attention to "artistic composition."

The Chicago Printer: A Medium of Intercommunication between Printers, Journalists, Publishers, Paper Makers, Type Founders, Printing Press Manufacturers, Printing Ink Makers, and the Trade Generally. Chicago: Henry R. Bose, v. 1, 1–4, 1883.

The editor-publisher proposed to produce "a first-class technical journal," but he defined his mission broadly to include histories of presses and the profession, employment problems, and issues raised by new technology. He vigorously defended the advertising industry.

The Chicago Specimen: A Quarterly for Printers and Publishers. Chicago: Marder, Luse and Co. (name varies), January 1867–November 1891. House organ for the Chicago Type Foundry. Quarterly.

Primarily a catalog of book and newspaper faces and cuts, some full page, prefaced with news items and comments by the publisher.

Composing Stick: A Quarterly Magazine Devoted to the Interests of Printers and Manufacturers. Cleveland: H. H. Thorp and Co., v. 1, 1–2; October 1875–January 1876. House organ.

Thorp sold printing presses and other print equipment and supplies. Notable for illustrations, some in multiple colors.

Chromatic Art Magazine: For the Elevation of the Typographic and Lithographic Arts. New York: John Henry (editor and publisher), v. 1–2, no. 5; August 1879–Summer 1884; suspended 1881–83. Bimonthly, then quarterly.

Lengthy, detailed articles on presses, typefounding and ink-making processes, and the careers of printers and typefounders. Embellished with beautiful wood engravings.

Electrotype Journal: A Quarterly Magazine of Graphic Arts. Chicago: A. Zeese and Company, later by Franklin Engraving and Electrotyping Company, April 1874–October 1901. Quarterly house organ.

A journal concerned with the reproduction of illustrations, particularly by means of electrotype. Featured news of general interest to the trade, detailed descriptions of electrotyping processes, and "the best specimens of cuts, ornaments and other designs."

Engraver and Printer: A Monthly Magazine of Progress in Illustration; later *A Monthly Magazine of Progress in Illustration and Typography.* Boston: Boston Photogravure Company, v. 1–4; February 1891–1896. Edited by Henry Lewis Johnson, 1891–94; Albert Gould Glover, 1895–96.

Conceived as a house organ but transformed by its first editor, Henry Lewis Johnson, into a pioneering effort by combining information on the technology of engraving and printing with design. For a complete publication history and an assessment of its importance, see John Bidwell, *"The Engraver and Printer,* a Boston Trade Journal of the Eighteen Nineties," *Papers of the Bibliographical Society of America,* vol. 71 (New York: The Society, 1977), 29–48.

Franklin Printer. San Francisco: 1908–September 1909. Name changed to *Pacific Printer and the Franklin Printer,* December 1909; *Pacific Printer,* January–May 1910; *Pacific Printer, Publisher, and Lithographer,* June 1910–August 1952. Subtitle varies.

Although the magazine concentrated on the technical aspects of printing, articles on design appeared regularly. Included many examples of three-color halftone printing.

The Graphic Arts: A Magazine for Printers and Users of Printing. See under "Advertising."

Graphic Arts and Crafts Year Book: The First American Annual Review of Engraving, Printing and Allied Industries. Hamilton, Ohio: Republican Publishing Company, 1907–14.

Edited by Joseph Meadon. Short, summary essays on the year in magazine photography and illustration, book arts, and advertising, as well as technical articles on halftone processes, lithography, papermaking, and printing. Also included reviews of trade journals.

The Inland Printer: Leading Business and Technical Journal of the World in the Printing and Allied Industries. Chicago: MacLean-Hunter Publishing Company, 1883–1958. Name changed to the *Inland and American Printer and Lithographer,* 1958–1961.

The premier trade journal in American printing and recognized as such from its first issue. The magazine provided trade news and technical information, and it served as a forum of opinion for job compositors and pressmen. It was also an unofficial organ for the unions. Now a rich source of materials on printing history. For a study of the early years of the magazine, its history and scope, and well-chosen examples of its pages, see Maurice Annenberg, *A Typographical Journey through the Inland Printer, 1883–1900* (Baltimore: Maran Press, 1977).

International Printer. See *Paper and Press*

Mail Order Journal. See *National Editorial Journalist and Printer and Publisher*

Mirror of Typography: Reflecting the Beautiful in the Art. New York: T. H. Senior, March 1869–74. Quarterly, then monthly.

The editor's stated intention was to give "the American printer a Magazine devoted to his interests, and to the further development and improvement of his art." The magazine emphasized technology, especially the evolution of the cylinder press. Editorials presented the typefounders' response to attacks on protective tariffs by George Rowell and others in the advertising industry.

Model Printer's Guide. Philadelphia: J. W. Daughaday and Co., Winter 1877–1880. Subtitle varies: *A Journal Devoted to the Advancement of Printing; A Journal of Typography and Literature.*

Not seen by compiler.

Modern Engraver. Chicago: Blomgren Brothers and Co., v. 1, 1–3; March, July, October 1890. House organ.

"While the aim of this publication is solely to introduce to the notice of our friends . . . the variety and excellence of the Engraving done by BLOMGREN BROS. & CO., we, at the same time, thought it best to surround the illustrations with reading matter that treats of the live subjects of interest to thinking men." (1, no. 2 [July 1890]).

Interesting articles on engraving technology with good examples.

Monatshefte für Graphisches Kunstgewerbe. Berlin, n.p.: 1902–9.

Comprehensive treatment of all aspects of printing, illustration, and advertising with articles on typefaces and layout and including beautiful specimens.

Monotype: Journal of Composing Room Efficiency. Philadelphia: Lanston Monotype Machine Company, 1913–30. House organ.

Information for the users of the company's products; also included articles on type design, type specimens, and advertising.

Pacific Printer. See *Franklin Printer*

Pacific Specimen. San Francisco: Pacific Type Foundry until October 1876; Marder, Luse and Company, Summer 1877–1881. v. 1–6; 1875–81. Volume 1, number 1, was preceded by an introductory number called "First Number, January 1875" (issued November 1874). Quarterly.

A house organ for the Pacific Type Foundry and later the San Francisco branch of Marder, Luse and Company's typefoundry. It was modeled after their *Chicago Specimen*. Introducing the first number, the editor wrote, "We offer the *Pacific Specimen*, not as an art journal neither as merely an advertising sheet, but as a medium of business and social intercourse between the publishers and printers of the Pacific Coast and ourselves."

Paper and Press. Philadelphia: 1885–January 1906. Title changed to *International Printer: A Modern Journal of Printing and the Illustrative Arts.* Philadelphia: International Printer Company, 1896–February 1906. Absorbed by *American Printer*.

Articles primarily of technical interest with good examples of reproduction processes; some touched on design. See especially John V. Sears's contributions on the history and use of ornament, typographic styles, and bookbinding.

National Editorial Journalist and Printer and Publisher. Springfield, Mass.: 1883–. Name changed *National Journalist for Editors . . .* , 1889; to *Mail Order Journal*, 1940. Absorbed *Artist Printer*, 1893?; *Proofsheet*, 1896; *United States Publisher*, 1931; *Mail Order Journal*, 1940.

VOL .1 APRIL 1913 NO. 1

MONO TYPE

F.B.

A Journal of Composing Room Efficiency

LANSTON
MONOTYPE
MACHINE
COMPANY

PHILA-
DELPHIA

"THE word Monotype means much more than the name of a machine; it includes a complete system of composing room practice based on the work of the Monotype both as a composing machine and as a type caster."

49. "Cover." *Monotype* (April 1913). General Collection, Library of Congress.

Appendix A

Early issues included obituaries of notable printers. Of relevance to graphic design only during the early 1900s, when newspaper design and advice on advertising design for job printers, publishers, and engravers were significant issues.

Paper World: A Monthly Journal of Information, Discussion, and Recital as to Paper. Holyoke, Mass.: Clark W. Bryan, 1880–? Moved to Springfield, Mass., and later to New York.

"Devoted to the paper interest in its broadest sense, not simply to its manufacture, but in all the departments of trade and commerce of which paper forms a component part, which broadens and deepens as the world progresses, to an almost boundless extent." Histories of the major papermaking companies, press manufacturers, publishers, and typefoundries and biographies of successful papermakers and others associated with the paper trade.

Penrose Annual: Review of the Graphic Arts. See *Process Yearbook: Penrose's Pictorial Annual*

Printer: A Monthly Newspaper Devoted to the Interests of the "Art Preservative of All Arts." New York: Henry and Huntington, v. 1–6; 1858–86.

The editors were aware that their journal was one of the first in the field and claimed a wide scope: new technology as well as the history of typefounding, papermaking, printing presses, illustration, and all forms of publications. Good examples of type and cuts.

Printers' Bulletin. See *Printers' Monthly Bulletin*

Printer's Circular: A Record of Typography, Literature, Arts and Sciences. March 1866–79; subtitle changed to *A Record of Typography, Paper-making, Lithography, Bookbinding, and Publishing;* in 1890 it became *The Printers' Circular and Stationers' and Publishers' Gazette: A Monthly Record of Events of Interest to Printers, Publishers, Stationers, Lithographers, Bookbinders, Paper-makers, and Kindred Industries.* Philadelphia: R. S. Menamin, v. 1–25, no. 6; 1866–90.

One of the most important early printers' journals. According to Bigmore and Wyman, Mrs. Jessie E. Ringwalt was responsible for the historical and literary articles, and its editor-publisher was a "type-broker, printers'-engineer and agent" (*Bibliography of Printing*, 1:184). It featured type specimens, columns on the "State of the Trade" in American cities and in Europe, and miscellaneous notes on numerous subjects. It was an organ of the National Typographical Union.

Printers' Monthly Bulletin. Boston: Boston Type Foundry, John K. Rogers and Co., January 1858–1868. Name changed to *Printers' Bulletin*, 1891. House organ.

Edited by Samuel Nelson Dickinson (b. 1801), who designed "Scotch-face." According to Roy Nash, Dickinson edited an earlier magazine called *Typographic Advertiser*, begun in November 1845, which preceded the Johnson Foundry publication of the same name (*Printing as an Art*, 17–18, n. 17).

Printing Art: An Illustrated Monthly Magazine of the Art of Printing and of the Allied Arts. Cambridge: Harvard University Press, v. 1–69; 1903–27; Dartnell Corporation,

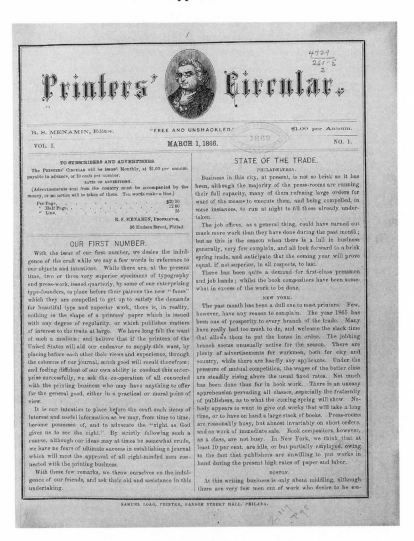

50. "Cover." *Printers' Circular* (March 1, 1866). General Collection,
Library of Congress.

1927–41. Name changed to *Printing Art Quarterly* in 1935. Merged with *Print*, Summer
1942.

An important journal for graphic design that combined substantial articles by leading
practitioners and educators in graphic design, printing, and advertising with actual
printed materials. Will Bradley, Theodore Low De Vinne, and Carl Purington Rollins
were among its distinguished contributors. Henry Lewis Johnson served as editor from
March 1903 to October 1910.

The Printing Press: A Journal of Typography and Accessory Arts. Chicago: Franklin

Society of Chicago, v. 1–2; July 1875–October 1876. Quarterly July 1875–April 1876; bimonthly June–October 1876. Edited by Henry Rush Boss.

Subtitled *An Organ of Intercommunication between Printers, Type Founders, Editors, Journalists, Reporters, Correspondents, Ink and Paper Makers, Bookbinders, Readers, Advertising Agents, Engravers, Book Sellers, Book Buyers and Book Lovers.* A journal of sketches, news items, amusing notes, "forthcoming books," and information about the Franklin Society.

Process Yearbook: Penrose's Pictorial Annual. London, 1895–. Name changed to *Penrose Annual: Review of the Graphic Arts,* 1916–present.

A major British publication; its early emphasis on technical aspects of printing changed to a broader consideration of layout and design. It included beautiful specimens of color printing.

Proof Sheet. Philadelphia: Collins and McLeester, July 1867–?. Edited by Eugene H. Munday. Biweekly, then monthly, bimonthly. House organ.

Featured articles on the history of printing, new technology, and the apprenticeship system. Also published many interesting cuts, some quite large, for sale by the publisher.

Publishers and Stationers' Trade Circular: A Journal Devoted to the Interests of the Publishing, Printing, Book, Stationery, News, Music, Art and Fancy Trades, and Associated Branches. New York: F. Leypoldt, v. 1–present; January 18, 1872–present. Absorbed *American Literary Gazette and Publishers' Circular,* 1872.

The official organ of the Publishers' Board of Trade and, shortly after its first number, of the Book Trade Association of Philadelphia. During its early years, Leypoldt, who was both editor and publisher, focused on printing technology, business practices, copyright law, tariffs, and postal rates and regulations and included reviews of published and forthcoming books and "literary and trade gossip."

Publishers' Weekly. See *Publishers and Stationers' Trade Circular*

Quadrat: Devoted to the Interests of the Craft. Pittsburgh: A. C. Bakewell, then Allan C. Kerr and Co., v. 1–5; February 1873–December 1877. Edited by J. F. Marthens. Monthly.

House organ for a type and press supplier serving western Pennsylvania. Notable for its "Typographical Bibliography" column.

Round's Monthly Printers' Cabinet. Chicago: Sterling P. Rounds, January 1857–March 1858?; changed name to *Rounds' Printers' Cabinet,* December 1856–1888. House organ; monthly, then quarterly.

Of interest for wood-engraved spot illustrations, with articles on printing, typefounding, and papermaking.

Superior Printer: A Technical Journal for the Advancement of Compositors and Pressmen. Cincinnati: Earhart and Richardson, May 1887–April 1888.

Articles on design and layout as well as type specimens.

Type. New York: American Type Founders Company, January 1889–December 1894? House organ.

Not seen by compiler.

Appendix A

The Type-Founder. Chicago: Barnhart Brothers and Spindler, Great Western Type Foundry, 1876–1908? House organ.

Represented industry viewpoints, especially on the tariff question.

Typographic Advertiser: Published for the Advancement of Typography and Type-founding. Philadelphia: L. Johnson and Company 1855–92. The MacKellar, Smiths and Jordan Company was the publisher beginning in 1866, followed by Lay and Brothers, year unknown. Publication ceased in 1892. There were 42 vols. in all.

Admired in this country and abroad, it was the prototype of many other periodicals on type. It began as a marketing device, and the early issues are primarily type and spot specimen pages, but this format soon gave way to substantial articles and news items, book reviews, and profiles of contemporary printers and printing practices. Edited by Thomas MacKellar and later by his son, William Brasher MacKellar.

Typographic Messenger: A Bi-Monthly Magazine of the Typographic Art. New York: James Conner's Sons, v. 1–10, November 1865–October 1875. Bimonthly 1865–69; quarterly 1870–75. House organ.

This journal included both metal and wood type specimens, many advertisements for presses, and color advertisements for color inks. Especially notable for profiles/obituaries of leading printers, type founders, and publishers and for editorials in defense of tariffs on types imported from Europe.

Typographica. Marlborough on the Hudson, N.Y.: Frederic W. Goudy, 1911–1927. Irregular.

A variation on a house organ, this journal was used by Goudy to promote his typefaces and ideas about design. Its pages are themselves a demonstration of Goudy's design skills.

The Typographic Journal: Official Paper of the International Typographical Union of North America. Indianapolis, Ind.: W. S. McClevey, July 15, 1889–?

"Organ of communication to subordinate unions." Primarily concerned with reporting changes in policy, convention proceedings, official news of member unions, and the state of the trade.

The Typos' Guide. Washington, D.C.: H. L. Pelouze and Company, July 1874–? Bimonthly.

The publisher frankly introduced this journal as "a medium to advertise and display our merchandise" but embellished it with news and practical information for printers, such as different kinds of paper, explanations of printing terms, and notices about useful books.

Appendix B: "New Kind of Printing Calls

for New Design"

"Old Standards of Excellence Suddenly Superseded Because
of the Complex of New Processes in the Industry—Still the
Opportunity, However, for Blending Commonsense
with Artistic Taste"

BY W. A. DWIGGINS

Enthusiasts of a sentimental turn of mind, inspired by a verbal formula—The Printing Art—and misled by a false interpretation of the same, have worked great confusion with the boundary that divides art from printing. The subtle intoxication of the third word of the phrase induces them to materialize vague near-aesthetic halos upon the heads of various people who undertake to print.

How printed matter looks makes no conscious difference to anybody except to the

From the *Boston Evening Transcript*, August 29, 1922, Graphic Arts Section, 3:6

184

designer and the connoisseur of printing. When placards are put up at the corner garage announcing the current price of gasoline they do not need to be fine art. They do their work just as they are. All the main purposes of printing can be served without calling upon the help of art. The manufacturer with something to sell has ideas about the good looks of his printing, but his ideas are peculiar unto himself, and do not usually claim any relationship with art. He may be under the illusion that his printing is art. We are not. But as a charitable act let us add him to the printing designer noted above to complete the roster of those who care how printed matter looks. Oftentimes printing seems to tell its story just as well without art.

ARTISTS STAMP THE HISTORY OF PRINTING

Make a record of these two facts—printing is not an art, and art is not essential to printing—and against them as a background let us project the following surprising conclusions. The history of printing is largely a history of individual artists. The names that stand foremost in the biography of the craft are the names of men conspicuous for a fine taste for design. Out of all the mass of printing that must have been done since the invention the only noteworthy relics are those few books and documents that were made by men of artistic mind. Printed paper has been collected and cherished for three hundred years, not because it was printing but because it was printed art.

Artists have tampered with printing and diverted it to their own ends ever since Gutenberg devised moveable types. All through the course of the industry they have brought their faculties to bear upon the problem of turning printing into fine art. They have tampered with it in such a thoroughgoing fashion that—so far as the old work is concerned—the practical reasons for doing printing have been lost sight of, and printed paper is noteworthy chiefly because artists did meddle with it.

It will be perceived at once by the most complex that here are two groups of facts that do not fit together at all. There is more to this matter than appears at first blush. It would seem that there are several distinct classes of things to be examined under the title "printing." There are, verily.

Let us get down to cases and pick the industry apart. We want to find out what art has to do with printing—not historic printing but printing here and now. There are plain lines of cleavage in the modern industry. Working on these we are able to pry the business apart into three rough classes—plain printing; printing as a fine art; and a third large intermediate class of printing more or less modified by artistic taste. Town reports and hand-bills, telephone directories and school catalogs stand in the first class. The second might be represented by books printed for the Grolier Club by Bruce Rogers. The third class of printing is so wide and so varied that you will have trouble choosing examples to represent it.

Appendix B

Printing of the first class—the plain variety—is the backbone of the industry. This class outbulks the others by an overwhelming tonnage. It performs an imposing and valuable work and performs it in a thoroughly workmanlike manner. The technical excellence of the product of the "plain" printing plant is all that anyone could ask. This class of printing proves the truth of the deduction of the third paragraph. It gets no help from art and does not need it. It is outside the domain of art.

Printing as a fine art is not—as one might rashly assume from a review of the industry—a matter of history only. The thing is still happening. The man of taste—whom our sentimentalist would extinguish by calling him a "printer-artist"—is still to be discovered in the craft. Scattered all through the industry are men of fine artistic taste pursuing printing as an art. And it is to be noted that they do it, in many instances, on an entirely practical basis, and find little handicap, indeed, in their adherence to distinguished traditions. They produce printing that is fine art because they want to—because—one is constrained to say—they are artists.

But the consideration of printing as fine art is not quite the purpose of this note. Printing on that plane is, by its very nature, removed into the province of a critic of the fine arts, and cannot be examined on an equal footing with the product of the industry at large. What contact the industry at large has with art is the question on which we are engaged. We have narrowed our examination down to the third group of printing. We may look for that contact there.

This last group has certain noteworthy characteristics. For one thing it is not made to be sold, it is made to be given away—with a very canny purpose behind the gift. Then, it is a new thing—as new as advertising. It is thoroughly democratic—everybody takes a hand in making it, it goes everywhere and is read by everyone. It probably plays a larger part in forming the quasi-social state that we call civilization than all the books and newspapers and periodicals together. Its function is to prepare the ground for selling something, or to sell something directly itself. By hook or by crook, by loud noise or by subtle argument. It might fulfill its mission of getting something sold.

It is really a kind of super-printing. Its requirements have forced the industry to expand itself, to include new and strange functions—critical study of clients' markets—preparation of "literature," descriptive, educational, argumentative—sales always in view at the end. One of the functions that the press has been forced to include is performed by a section known as the art department or art service.

The art department produces something. It is what is called "art work." The expression "art work" is advertising agents' slang. "Art work" might be defined as drawings, decoration, etc., made to complicate the advertiser's message. It seems that in some advertising a plain straight-forward statement of the facts will not serve. Little indiscretions must be committed, little naive slips and false starts need to be contrived, to catch the victim's eye. Or he must have his back rubbed and his foibles exploited before he can be coaxed into just the right position for the dead-fall to get him. One infers that it is the function of the art service to provide these inducements, indirections and subterfuges.

Appendix B

The ingenues of the art services work most skilfully at making pictures and ornamental designs. Their products rank sufficiently high as drawings and designs. But the application of their work slips up in some peculiar way. The big carnival on Main street needs their help to be a complete affair but their art is off up a side alley doing clever tricks.

In view of the excellent work done by some of the art departments of printing plants the foregoing comment may seem to be pitched too strong. But these people hold a key position in the whole question of art and printing and the public taste, and what they do or missdo is of great moment to the artist. You can almost say that the future of printed graphic art rests in their hands. Illustration used to be spoken of as "the people's art" but advertising "art work" has supplanted it in popular esteem. Estimate how many more people know about Coles Phillips than know about Raleigh or George Wright. If all the talk about the importance of art to the industries of a nation is anything but buncombe it is of the highest importance that the advertising draughtsmen be made conscious of their influence and of their opportunity. Art will not occur in the industries until our fellow citizens learn to know the real thing when they see it. Advertising artists are now their only teachers. Advertising design is the only form of graphic design that gets home to everybody.

The implication is that the advertising artists fail to set the proper tone. The conduct of an art as an adjunct to business is always difficult. These artists, however sound as artists they may be in themselves, are under a pressure from outside that is almost bound to make them unfit as exponents of sound standards. It is unlucky that the job of setting styles for printing should be in their hands because they are bound by the conditions of their service to set styles on a level lower than the best.

ADVERTISING ARTISTS CAN DO BETTER

But they can better their performance. They have the chance to work ably within the limitations of their handicap. They can bring some pressure to bear at least upon making salesprinting a clearer and more precise medium for the merchant's message. They need to relearn the rules of their game. Let them give ear to the words of the prophet and mend their ways. They have a moral code set down for the department of the just typographer made perfect:

Cultivate simplicity. Have simple styles of letters and simple arrangements.

In the matter of layout forget art at the start and use horse-sense. The printing-designer's whole duty is to make a clear presentation of the message—to give it every advantage of arrangement—to get the important statements forward and the minor parts placed so that they will not be overlooked. This calls for an exercise of common sense and a faculty for analysis rather than for art.

Have pictures consistent with the printing process. Printers' ink and paper are a convention for light and shade and color. Stay inside the convention.

Be niggardly with decorations, borders and such accessories. Do not pile up ornament like flowers at a funeral. Scheme the white spaces—paper is indeed a "part of the picture." Manipulate the spaces of blank paper around and among the printed surfaces to make a pleasing pattern of areas.

Get acquainted with the shapes of the type letters themselves. They are the units out of which the structure is made—unassembled bricks and beams. Pick good ones and stick to them.

It is easy to formulate rules. It is not so easy to apply them. As a matter of fact, the new kind of printing calls for a new kind of design. The revolution in technical practice is complete. Very little is left of the old methods. The standards of good printing as they stood from the beginning of the craft are suddenly superseded. There is thrust into the printer's hand a complex of new processes—half-tone engraving, machine composition, quadricolor, offset, fast running photogravure. The original conception of sound printing design as it stood until the age of the machines has very little bearing on these new processes. The impression of ink upon paper is an entirely new and different thing.

In one generation of printers the continuity of tradition has "faulted." Can we design this new printing with our minds trained in the standards that guided Aldus, or Bodoni, or DeVinne? Must all these things that we looked upon as good go overboard? How much of the old standard of quality can carry across the gap, and how can it be related to the new state of things? Typesetting by hand is about to become as obsolete as spinning thread by hand. Machine composition is a settled fact. How is it to be made good in the old sense? Or is the old sense to be discarded?

Of course all these questions will be answered. The right way will be worked out and a new standard evolved. The point to be stressed is that the new standard must not be a mechanical standard merely, it must also be an aesthetic standard. Artists must take a part in thinking it out—not the art services only, but artists—artists in terms of Holbein and Tory.

HINTS FOR ARTISTS IN MODERN PRINTING

There are hints in the new printing that the artist can profit by. Its material suggests a slighter and sketchier style than we at present affect—things that look like here today and gone tomorrow. Such things can still be good design and good art. The butterfly is justly admired for its good looks but is admittedly scheduled for only a brief stay. Our way of using decorative drawings that appear to have consumed months in their preparation is somehow inconsistent with the fact that the things they decorate are meant to last only for an hour. The enduring volumes of the ancients are a wrong source of inspiration for decorative styles that are to serve a purpose so ephemeral.

The French have caught the spirit of this kind of design. The leakage of their styles over into our picture making will serve us a good turn if we are able to perceive what they are about. The drawing of accessories for the new kind of printing and the layout of the printing itself need to be done at a higher rate of vibration than we are accustomed to. Some few have caught the pitch. The art director of Vogue and Vanity Fair schemes pages that are consistent with the demands of the new craft.

Appendix B

The problem is stimulating through the very condition of its novelty. New lines have to be run and new charts made. For the time being all fences are down and all rules off. So at least it would seem. But in spite of the completeness of the mechanical revolution, the law of art still runs. Sound design is still sound design even though it be in novel material. The underlying purpose of printing has not been changed, neither has the fundamental problem for the artist. An orderly and graceful disposition of parts continues to be desirable and printed pages are still intended to be read. On these terms the designer will attempt to do for the new printing what he undertook to do for the old. His success will still depend upon a suitable blending of common sense with artistic taste.

Notes

INTRODUCTION

1. W. A. Dwiggins, "New Kind of Printing Calls for New Design," *Boston Evening Transcript* (August 29, 1922), Graphic Arts Section, 3:6; reprinted as Appendix 2.

2. William Dunlap, *A History of the Rise and Progress of the Arts of Design in the United States* (New York: G. P. Scott, 1834, 2 vols.; Boston: C. E. Goodspeed, 1919, 3 vols.), 1:1–3.

3. Ellen Shapiro, "The Name Game," *AIGA Journal of Graphic Design* 11,1 (1993), 1–3, 14.

4. "Arts Club Warned of 'Thought Trust,'" *New York Times* (November 13, 1913): 9.

5. Claire Hoertz Badaracco, *Trading Words: Poetry, Typography, and Illustrated Books in the Modern Literary Economy* (Baltimore: Johns Hopkins University Press, 1995); Michele H. Bogart, *Artists, Advertising, and the Borders of Art* (Chicago: University of Chicago Press, 1995); Jules Lubbock, *The Tyranny of Taste: The Politics of Architecture and Design in Britain, 1550–1960* (New Haven: Yale University Press, 1995).

6. Richard Hollis, *Graphic Design* (London: Thames and Hudson, 1994), 8.

7. I have tried to follow Victor Margolin's counsel in maintaining the distinctions between the different strands of graphic design practice amid a changing context. See Margolin's "Narrative Problems of Graphic Design History," *Visible Language* 28,3 (July 1994): 234–243.

CHAPTER 1: CONTEXTS AND CONNECTIONS

1. Ralph Fletcher Seymour, *Some Went This Way: A Forty-Year Pilgrimage Among Artists, Bookmen, and Printers* (Chicago: Ralph Fletcher Seymour, 1945), 33.

2. Rita R. Gottesman, "Early Commercial Art," *Art in America* 43,4 (December 1955): 34.

3. Bureau of the Census, *The United States by Industries: Twelfth Census of the United States*, vol. 7, *Manufacturers*, pt. 1, *United States by Industries* (Washington, D.C.: Government Printing Office, 1900), clii.

4. Bureau of the Census, *Thirteenth Census of the United States Taken in the Year 1910*, vol. 4, *Population Occupation Statistics* (Washington, D.C.: Government Printing Office, 1914), 378.

5. Clive Ashwin, *History of Graphic Design and Communication: A Source Book* (London: Pembridge Press, 1983), 4. According to Nash, "Previously the designer with respect to printing had been one who added illustrations or ornamental features to it. Now, in the new light of the 'revival,' the designer could find a place to stand in the printing field analogous to that occupied by the architect in building." Ray Nash, *Printing as an Art* (Cambridge: Harvard University Press, 1955), 53.

6. Joseph Blumenthal, *Typographic Years* (New York: Frederic C. Beil, 1982), 30.

7. Gottesman, "Early Commercial Art," 34; Rob Roy Kelly, *American Wood Type, 1828–1900* (New York: Van Nostrand Reinhold, 1969; New York: Da Capo Press, 1977), 186; Frank Presbrey, *The History and Development of Advertising* (New York: Doubleday, 1929; New York: Greenwood Press, 1968), 251–52. For a stylistic analysis of early advertising, see William G. Gabler, "The Evolution of American Advertising in the Nineteenth Century," *Journal of Popular Culture* 11,4 (Spring 1978): 763–71.

8. Kelly, *American Wood Type*, 166–67. Dates for the Golden Age Illustration vary: Michele Bogart prefers a longer time frame, 1880–1930; see her *Artists, Advertising, and the Borders of Art* (Chicago: University of Chicago Press, 1995), 51. Frank Luther Mott, *A History of American Magazines*, 5 vols. (Cambridge: Harvard University Press, 1938–1968), 3:191; Henry Martyn, "The Illustrations of the Quarter," *Quarterly Illustrator* 1,1 (January–March 1893): 13.

9. Peter Marzio, *The Democratic Art* (Boston: David Godine, 1979), 3; Robert Jay, *The Trade Card in Nineteenth-Century America* (Columbus: University of Missouri Press, 1987), 1; Helena E. Wright, *With Pen and Graver: Women Graphic Artists Before 1900*, exhib. cat. (Washington, D.C.: National Museum of American History, Smithsonian Institution, 1995), 10. For a comprehensive study of Prang's life and work, see Larry Freeman,

Louis Prang: Color Lithographer, Giant of a Man. (Watkins Glen, N.Y.: Century House, 1971).

10. The freedom occasioned by the lithographic process is noted in Clarence P. Horn-ung and Fridolf Johnson, *Two Hundred Years of American Graphic Art* (New York: George Braziller, 1976), 50, and in Philip B. Meggs, *A History of Graphic Design*, 2d ed. (New York: Van Nostrand, Reinhold, 1992), 158.

11. Mott, *History of American Magazines*, 4:153.

12. Engravers split over their role: members of the "New School" saw their work as translators, reproducing the effects of one medium in another. W. J. Linton, the most vocal in opposition, argued that engravers were creators of art in a different medium. For examples of the controversy, see "Wood-engraving and the 'Scribner' Prizes," *Scribners Monthly Illustrated* 21,6 (April 1881): 937–45, and William J. Linton, *American Wood Engraving* (Boston: Estes and Lauriat, 1882; rpt. with intro. by Nancy Carlson Schrock, Watkins Glen, N.Y.: American Life Foundation, 1976), 69–71.

13. Estelle Jussim, *Visual Communication and the Graphic Arts* (New York: R. R. Bowker, 1974), 82–83.

14. Susan E. Meyer, *America's Great Illustrators.* (New York: Harry N. Abrams, 1978), 12; "Artist Pays Tribute to the Enterprising Gentlemen in the Engraving Busi-ness," *Pacific Printer* 2,9 (December 1909): 13.

15. Mott, *History of American Magazines*, 3:191; Louis Levy, quoting from an article he wrote for the *Photographic Times Almanac of 1890*, "The Growth of Photo-Engrav-ing," *Printing Art* 28,2 (October 1916): 27; Robert Taft, *Photography and the American Scene* (New York: Macmillan, 1938), 445. For an exploration of the cultural significance of halftone, see Neil Harris, "Iconography and Intellectual History: The Halftone Effect," in *Cultural Excursions* (Chicago: University of Chicago Press, 1990), 304–17.

16. *Critic*, 3,135 (March 24, 1883), quoted by Mott, *History of American Magazines*, 3:191; Albin H. Hutchings, "From the Woodcut to the Half-Tone with Personal Reminis-cences," *Printing Art* 28,4 (October 1916): 24, 28.

17. Mott, *History of American Magazines*, 4:153; C. A. Collins, "Art Usage Curves Shoot Up," *Inland Printer* 70,6 (March 1923): 857–58.

18. This paragraph is based on the first chapter, "Beginnings, 1865–1921," in Robert A. Sobieszek's *Art of Persuasion* (New York: Harry N. Abrams, 1988), 16–22, and the exhibition catalog, Amon Carter Museum of Western Art, *Photography in Nineteenth-Century America*, ed. Martha A. Sandweiss (New York: H. N. Abrams, 1991), 216–20.

19. Kelly, *American Wood Type*, 108,146; Dard Hunter, *Papermaking: The History and Technique of an Ancient Craft* (New York: Alfred A. Knopf, 1947), 380–81.

20. For an explanation of the skills required in traditional typesetting, see Roger Levenson, *Women in Printing: Northern California, 1857–1890* (Santa Barbara, Calif.: Capra Press, 1994), 13–23; for stereotype and electrotype, see H. A. Maddox, *Printing: Its History, Practice and Progress* (London: Sir Isaac Pitman and Sons, 1923), 75–79; Leven-son, *Women in Printing*, 16.

21. John S. Thompson, *History of Composing Machines* (Chicago: Inland Printer, 1904; New York: Arno Press, 1972), 106. For a modern history of composing machines, see

Richard E. Huss, *Printer's Composition Matrix* (New Castle, Del.: Oak Knoll Books, 1985).

22. For a comprehensive history of the pantograph, see Huss, *Printer's Composition Matrix*, 8–12; a brief version can be found in Beatrice L. Warde, "Cutting Types for Machines: A Layman's Account," *Dolphin* 2 (1935), 66–68; Bureau of the Census, *Twelfth Census*, 7, pt. 1:clii.

23. For a detailed description of monotype in its various stages of development and its operation, see Thompson, *History of Composing Machines*, 120–26.

24. Kelly, *American Wood Type*, 146, 207–9; Frederick W. Hamilton, *Type and Presses in America* (Chicago: United Typothetae of America, Committee on Education, 1918), 28.

25. John Tebbel and Mary Ellen Zuckerman, *The Magazine in America, 1741–1990* (New York: Oxford University Press, 1991), 18, 26; Mott, *History of American Magazines*, 3:5, 4:11.

26. Mott, *History of American Magazines*, 3:25–45.

27. Presbrey, *History and Development of Advertising*, 472–73. Collins believed that photographs accounted for less than 10 percent in 1895 to almost 30 percent in 1920 ("Art Usage," 858). For a different view, see a recent analysis of the *Ladies' Home Journal*. According to Bogardus, by 1895 photographs appeared frequently in 1894 and quickly increased in number; by 1890 a third of the articles and columns were illustrated with photographs, as were almost 80 percent of the advertisements. Ralph F. Bogardus, "Tea Wars: Advertising Photography and Ideology in the *Ladies' Home Journal* in the 1890s," *Prospects* 16 (1991): 299–300.

28. Presbrey, *History and Development of Advertising*, 590.

29. *Chicago Printer*, 1,3 (June 1883): 1; Earnest Elmo Calkins and Ralph Holdern, *The Art of Modern Advertising* (London: Sidney Appleton, 1905), 2.

30. The classic advertising histories, Henry Sampson's *History of Advertising from the Earliest Times* (London: Chatto, 1874; Detroit: Gale Research, 1974), and Frank Presbrey's *History and Development of Advertising*, ignore advertising artists, although Presbrey includes information on the development of art departments in agencies. Daniel Pope, *The Making of Modern Advertising* (New York: Basic Books, 1983), describes the increased use of illustration in advertising but not the illustrators themselves. For an unsympathetic but searching treatment, see Jackson Lears, "The Problem of Commercial Art in a Protestant Culture," in his *Fables of Abundance* (New York: Basic Books, 1994), 261–98, and for an alternate interpretation, see Michele H. Bogart, "The Problem of Status for American Illustrators," in her *Artists, Advertising, and the Borders of Art*, 15–78.

31. Editors of *Advertising Age*, comp., *How It Was in Advertising* (Chicago: Crain Book, 1976), 10; Richard A. Foley, "The Philadelphia Advertising Agencies," *Profitable Advertising* 17,5 (October 1908): 491.

32. Victor Margolin, Ira Brichta, and Vivian Brichta, *The Promise and the Product: Two Hundred Years of American Advertising Posters* (New York: Macmillan, 1979), 35.

33. Bureau of the Census, *The Statistical History of the United States from Colonial*

Times to the Present (Stamford, Conn.: Fairfield Publishers, 1965), 526. The bureau's numbers were based on information supplied by Printer's Ink Publications.

34. The importance of the Centennial in American industrial design was eloquently addressed by Isaac Edwards Clarke in his introduction to "The Democracy of Art," *Art and Industry*, 6 vols. (Washington, D.C.: Government Printing Office, 1885), 1:xxxi–cclviii.

35. For a discussion of postal rates, especially the RFD and mail order businesses, see Daniel J. Boorstin, *The Democratic Experience* (New York: Random House, 1973), 111–29. For the economics of advertising in magazine, see *Printers' Ink, a Journal for Advertisers: Fifty Years, 1888–1938* (New York: Printers' Ink, 1938), 41, 44.

36. [Henry Lewis Johnson], "Catalog Making," *Engraver and Printer* 2,4 (April 1892): 68, 71.

37. George P. Rowell, *Forty Years an Advertising Agent, 1865–1905* (New York: George Presbrey, 1906; New York: Garland, 1985), 158–59. We should also note that it was not until 1906 that the Pure Food and Drug Act became law. The act forbade not only adulteration but also fraudulent labeling of food and drugs sold in interstate commerce. This changed the nature of advertising that had heretofore relied heavily on the patronage of patent medicine companies.

38. John Ruskin, *The Stones of Venice*, 3 vols. (London: Smith, Elder, 1851–1853; New York: Garland, 1979), 2:165.

39. For a detailed critique of Arts and Crafts ideology in America, see T. J. J. Lears, *No Place of Grace* (New York: Pantheon, 1981), 60–97, and Thorstein Veblen, *The Theory of the Leisure Class: An Economic Study of Institutions* (New York: Macmillan, 1899; New York: New American Library, 1953), 116–17. Veblen excoriated the Kelmscott-inspired books published by the private presses and their fetish of hand production, which he argued resulted in illegible, unwieldy tomes whose function was to advertise the wealth of their owner.

40. Nathaniel C. Fowler, Jr., *About Advertising and Printing: A Concise, Practical, and Original Manual on the Art of Local Advertising* (Boston: A. M. Thayer, 1889), 6.

41. During 1902 and 1903, Scott contributed a series of twenty-four articles called "The Psychology of Advertising" to *Mahin's Magazine* and published them as *The Theory and Practice of Advertising* (Boston: Small, Maynard, 1903). In 1908, he followed with *The Psychology of Advertising: A Simple Exposition of the Principles of Psychology in Their Relation to Successful Advertising* (Boston: Small, Maynard, 1908); Henry Foster Adams, *Advertising and Its Mental Laws* (New York: Macmillan, 1916), 19. The textbooks include: Frank Alvah Parsons, *Principles of Advertising Arrangement* (New York: Prang, 1912), and *Art Appeal in Display Advertising* (New York: Harper and Brothers, 1921); Daniel Starch, *Advertising: Its Principles, Practice, and Techniques* (Chicago: Scott, Foresman, 1914); and George French, *How to Advertise: A Guide to Designing, Laying Out, and Composing Advertisements* (New York: Doubleday, Page for the Associated Advertising Clubs of the World, 1917). See Ellen Mazur Thomson, "'The Science of Publicity': An American Advertising Theory, 1900–1920," *Journal of Design History* 9,4 (1996): 253–72.

42. W. A. Dwiggins, "New Kind of Printing Calls for New Design," *Boston Evening Transcript* (August 29, 1922), Graphic Arts Section, 3:6; reprinted in Appendix 2.

CHAPTER 2: THE TRADE JOURNALS

1. In 1940, the first issue of *Print* contained a checklist of periodicals the editors considered basic for the graphic design professional. The list shows that trade journals written primarily for publishers, printers, and artists continued to be an important source of information for graphic designers well into this century. See "Checklist of Current Graphic Arts Periodicals," *Print* 1,1 (June 1940): 117–19.

2. The influence of William Morris and the Arts and Crafts movement on American printing is described by Susan Otis Thompson, *American Book Design and William Morris* (New York: R. R. Bowker, 1977).

3. Printing and typography journals are considered together because they were often addressed to the same audience. Some printers produced their own type and publishers of house organs for type foundries hoped to sell their products to printers. See Maurice Annenberg, *Type Foundries of America and Their Catalogs* (Baltimore: Maran Printing, 1975; New Castle, Del.: Oak Knoll Press, 1994).

4. *Typographic Advertiser* 1,1 (April, 1855): 1.

5. *Printer* 1,1 (May 1859): 1.

6. *Printers' Circular* 1,10 (December 1, 1866): 133. Although minorities and women worked as printers and compositors from colonial times, they are rarely mentioned in the trade literature except as a trade union issue. See chapter 6, below. However, according to E. C. Bigmore and C. W. H. Wyman, Jessie E. Ringwalt "has for many years written almost invariably the first articles, chiefly of a biographic, historical, or literary character" in the *Printers' Circular* and many were reprinted in the *American Encyclopedia of Printing* by J. Luther Ringwalt, her husband. *A Bibliography of Printing* (London: 1880–86; London: Holland Press, 1978), 184.

7. *Will Bradley: His Chap Book* (New York: Typophiles, 1955); Will Bradley, "Notes Toward an Autobiography," in *Will Bradley: His Graphic Art*, ed. Clarence P. Hornung (New York: Dover, 1974), xix.

8. "Fancy Jobbers," *American Art Printer* 2,5 (September–October 1888): 1.

9. A. Jay, "Artistic Printing," *Artist Printer* 7 (December 1889): 27.

10. John Bidwell, *"The Engraver and Printer*, a Boston Trade Journal of the Eighteen Nineties," in *Papers of the Bibliographical Society of America* (New York: The Society, 1977), 71:29–48. This article, based on Johnson's papers in the collection of Ray Nash and Nash's own *Printing as an Art* (Cambridge: Harvard University Press, 1955) are the two sources I have found with information about Johnson.

11. "Publisher's Announcement," *Engraver and Printer* 1,1 (February 1891).

12. *Printing Art* 10,2 (April 1903): xix.

13. Ibid., 22.

14. Will A. Bradley, "Design in Magazine Make-up," *Printing Art* 16,6 (February 1911): 456–57.

15. For a detailed analysis of early advertising magazines and their contribution to professionalization, see Quentin J. Schultze, "The Trade Press of Advertising: Its Content and Contribution to the Profession," *Information Sources in Advertising History*, ed. R. W. Pollay (Westport, Conn.: Greenwood Press, 1979), 49–62.

16. Rob Roy Kelly, *American Wood Type, 1828–1900* (New York: Van Nostrand Reinhold, 1969; New York: DaCapo Press, 1969), 209. For the typefounders' defense of the tariffs, see "The Tariff on Type," *Type-Founder* 2,7 (Spring 1878): 106–7; E. A. Wheatley, "Printers and Advertisers," *Inland Printer* 9,11 (August 1892): 945.

17. George P. Rowell, *Forty Years an Advertising Agent, 1865–1905* (New York: George Presbrey, 1906; New York: Garland, 1985), 364, 159.

18. Ibid., 354–55. Rowell reported that he had originally intended to attach his name to the publication and created a logo for it: "At one time I thought of giving it my own name. I even went so far as to get up a heading composed of the word ROWELL with a small picture over it representing the act of hiding a candle under a bushel and which, may be, had the word DON'T cut into it in some way. It was surprising how well the name and design looked, and I am by no means confident that it would not have been a success; but it was a little too personal."

19. *Profitable Advertising* 1 (1891): 251.

20. Ibid., 250.

21. *Charles Austin Bates Criticisms* 1,5 (May 1897): 69.

22. *Advertising Experience* 5,1 (May 1897): 2.

23. In a lecture he delivered in 1925, Albert Davis Lasker, the head of Lord and Thomas, a leading advertising agency, credited John E. Kennedy with the definition of advertising as "salesmanship in print"; the story appears in *The Lasker Story as He Told It* (Chicago: Advertising Publications, 1963), 21. T. Russell, "The Living Model as an Advertising Basis," *Penrose Pictorial Annual* 18 (1912–13): 188.

24. *Mahin's Magazine* 1,1 (April 1902): 1. Parson's articles appeared in *Advertising and Selling* 21 (1911). The series was later published as *The Principles of Advertising Arrangement* (New York: Prang, 1912).

25. For an analysis of the intellectual response to text illustration, realism, and photography, see Neil Harris, *Cultural Excursions: Marketing Appetites and Cultural Taste in Modern America* (Chicago: University of Chicago Press, 1990), especially "Iconography and Intellectual History: The Halftone Effect," 304–17, and "Pictorial Perils," 337–48.

26. John Sartain, *Reminiscences of a Very Old Man, 1808–1897* (New York: D. Appleton, 1899), 251.

27. Henry Martyn, "The Illustrations of the Quarter," *Quarterly Illustrator* 1,1 (January–March 1893): 4, 13–14.

28. *Art Age* 1,1 (November 1883): 29.

29. *Art Age* 3,28 (November 1885): 1.

CHAPTER 3: CAREER TRANSFORMATIONS

1. Edward S. Smith, "The Field of Commercial Art," *Commercial Illustrator* 1,4 (March 1916): 10–11; Reginald B. Miller, "The Silent Salesman That Sells—Commercial Art," *Western Advertising* 1,3 (April 1919): 9.

2. Robert Grayson, "Design and Display in Job-Work," *American Art Printer* 6,9 (April 1893): 389 (reprinted from the British periodical *British Printer*); F. W. Thomas, "Illustrated Advertising for Printers," *Inland Printer* 10,3 (December 1892): 213–14.

3. F. T. Olsaver, "Art Printing," *Inland Printer* 14,6 (March 1895): 535–37.

4. Bruce Rogers, *Paragraphs on Printing: Elicited from Bruce Rogers in Talks with James Hendrickson on the Functions of the Book Designer* (New York: William E. Rudge's Sons, 1943; New York: Dover, 1979), 2.

5. For a detailed description of printshop culture, see William S. Pretzer, "The Printers of Washington, D.C., 1800–1880" (Ph.D. diss., Northern Illinois University, 1986); Harry Kelber and Carl Schlesing, *Union Printers and Controlled Automation.* (New York: Free Press, 1967) 9; W. B. Prescott, "Technical Trade Education," in George A. Tracy, *History of the Typographical Union* (Indianapolis: International Typographical Union, 1913), 1104.

6. Dorr Kimball, *Composing Room Management* (Berkeley, Calif.: n.p., 1918), 73, italics added.

7. Carl Purington Rollins, *American Type Designers and Their Works*, exhib. cat. (Chicago: Lakeside Press, 1947), 3.

8. William E. Loy, "Designers and Engravers of Type," *Inland Printer*: series of articles published in various issues, 1898–1900.

9. Beatrice Warde, "Cutting Types for Machines: A Layman's Account," *Dolphin*, 2 (1935): 68.

10. Robin Kinross, *Modern Typography* (London: Hyphen Press, 1992), 43–51; 43, 46; Frederic W. Goudy, "Introduction," in Peter Beilenson, *The Story of Frederic W. Goudy* (Philadelphia: Lanston Monotype Machine Company for the Distafff Side, 1939), unpaginated.

11. For this description of Goudy's career, I have relied on Beilenson, *The Story of Frederic W. Goudy*, and D. J. R. Bruckner, *Frederic Goudy*, Masters of American Design series (New York: Harry N. Abrams, 1990), 41–74.

12. Alice Rouillier, "The Work of Elizabeth Colwell," *Graphic Arts* 4,4 (March 1913): 237–48.

13. Harvey S. Lewis, "Commercial Photography and Its Adaptation to Modern Advertising: A Course of Twenty Illustrated Lessons on the Subject," *Western Camera Notes* 5–6 (October 1904–June 1905); "Photography in Advertising," *Photo-Era* (February 1903): 73–74; ibid. (March 1903): 114–16. See biographical sketches of advertising artists in Robert A. Sobieszek, *The Art of Persuasion. The Art of Advertising Photography* (New York: Harry N. Abrams, 1988); P. G. Hubert, Jr., "Occupations for Women," *Woman's Work*, 2 vols. (New York: Charles Scribner's Sons, 1894), 1:12. See also Michele Bogart,

Notes to Pages 69–73

"The Rise of Photography," in her *Artists, Advertising, and the Borders of Art* (Chicago: University of Chicago Press, 1995), 171–204.

14. René Hassner, "Photography and the Press," in *A History of Photography*, ed. Jean-Claude Lemagny and André Rouille (New York: Cambridge University Press, 1986), 76; "Engraving on Wood," *Scribner's Monthly* 18,3 (July 1879): 456–57; William J. Linton, *American Wood Engraving* (Boston: Estes and Lariat, 1882; rpt. with intro. by Nancy Carlson Schrock, Watkins Glen, N.Y.: American Life Foundation, 1976), 71; Joseph Pennell, *Modern Illustration* (London: George Bell and Sons, 1895), 40, 115.

15. Will Bradley, "The Art of Illustration," *Nation* 97,2523 (July 10, 1913): 42–23; Ann Barton Brown, *Alice Barber Stephens: A Pioneer Woman Illustrator*, exhib. cat. (Chadds Ford, Pa.: Brandywine River Museum, 1984), and Foote's autobiography, Mary Hallock Foote, *A Victorian Gentlewoman in the Far West* (San Marino, Calif.: Huntington Library, 1972).

16. Judy L. Larson, "Introduction," in *American Illustration, 1890–1925: Romance, Adventure, and Suspense* (Calgary, Alta.: Glenbow Museum, 1986), 19–45; Michele H. Bogart, "Problem of Status for American Illustrators," in her *Artists, Advertising, and the Borders of Art*, 15–78.

17. For accounts of Sloan's career, see John Sloan, *American Art Nouveau: The Poster Period of John Sloan* (Lock Haven, Pa.: Hammerwell Paper, 1967); *John Sloan's New York Scene from the Diaries, Notes, and Correspondence, 1906–1913*, ed. Bruce St. John (New York: Harper and Row, 1965); Sloan, *American Art Nouveau*, unpaginated.

18. Letter dated October 8, 1917, Dehn Papers, Archives of American Art, Smithsonian Institution, as quoted in Rebecca Zurier, *Art for the Masses: A Radical Magazine and Its Graphics, 1911–1917* (Philadelphia: Temple University Press, 1988), 189, n. 15.

19. Gene Mitchell, *The Subject Was Children: The Art of Jessie Wilcox Smith* (New York: E. P. Dutton, 1979), 1–2.

20. Pennell, *Modern Illustrators*, 114–15; from a letter written by Penfield, dated December 7, 1895, as quoted in David W. Kiehl, "American Art Posters of the 1890s," *American Art Posters of the 1890s* (New York: Metropolitan Museum of Art, 1987), 13.

21. For a history of Harper and Brothers and especially the relationship between art editor and illustrator, see Eugene Exman, "Charles Parsons and His School of Artists," in his *The House of Harper* (New York: Harper and Row, 1967), 102–20; *Charles Parson and His Domain*, exhib. cat. (Montclair, N.J.: Art Museum, 1958), 17. For biographical material on Drake, see the posthumous tributes in Alexander W. Drake, *Three Midnight Stories* (New York: Century, 1916); William W. Ellsworth, *A Golden Age of Authors* Boston: Houghton Mifflin, 1919); Arthur John, *The Best Years of the "Century": Richard Watson Gilder, "Scribner's Monthly," and the "Century" Magazine, 1870–1909* (Urbana: University of Illinois Press, 1981), especially "Alliance of Art and Morality," 76–93; Robert Underwood Johnson, *Remembered Yesterdays* (Boston: Little, Brown, 1923), 99–102; James J. Best, *American Popular Illustration: A Reference Guide* (Westport, Conn.: Greenwood Press, 1984), 76, 118.

22. Frank Presbrey, *The History and Development of Advertising* (New York:

199

Doubleday, Duran, 1929; New York: Greenwood Press, 1968), 525. The quotation appears in Peirce Johnson, "It Started With the Art Directors Club of New York . . . The Future Is in Our Past," *Art Directing for Visual Communication and Selling* (New York: Hastings House, 1957), 208–9.

23. Miles Stanton, "Facilities of the West: Where Engravings Are Made—Sketch of the Franklin Engraving and Electrotyping Company's Plant," *Advertising Experience* 5,4 (August 1897): 5–8. The Stanton article describes in some detail a leading Chicago company that was established in 1861 as an electrotype foundry and later added zinc etching, half-tone engraving, and an art department.

24. Ralph Fletcher Seymour, *Some Went This Way: A Forty-Year Pilgrimage Among Artists, Bookmen, and Printers* (Chicago: Ralph Fletcher Seymour, 1942), 35, 58. Seymour tells us that all these men went to art school at night to increase their skill, including Leyendecker, who attended the Art Institute.

25. *Profitable Advertising* 18,5 (October 1908): 477.

26. John, *Best Years of the "Century,"* 76–93; Johnson, *Remembered Yesterdays*, 99–102.

27. "Exclusively for *Collier's*," *Collier's* 36,1 (October 14, 1905): 1, 21.

28. *Printers' Ink, a Journal for Advertisers: Fifty Years, 1888–1938*, section 2 (New York: Printers' Ink, 1938), 165; Ralph M. Hower, *History of an Advertising Agency: N. W. Ayer and Son at Work, 1869–1939* (Cambridge: Harvard University Press, 1939; New York: Arno Press, 1978), 54, 329–30, 95.

29. "Running an Art Department," *Federal Illustrator* 4,3 (Fall 1916): 19.

30. Frank Presbrey, *The History and Development of Advertising* (New York: Doubleday, Duran, 1929; Westport, Conn.: Greenwood Press, 1968), 525–27; *Printers' Ink: a Journal for Advertisers*, 161–72. According to Calkins, the typical agency was divided into seven departments: commercial research, plan (campaign designing), mediums and rates, copy, art (including layout and typography), placing and checking, soliciting or business-getting. Calkins distinguished the power of the production manager in setting schedules to comply with "physical requirements" called for in the campaign plan from "the professional and artistic requirements" that were the domain of the art director. "The art department must give way to the production manager's authority on the former, but with respect to the latter, the art director is 'supreme' and answerable only to the campaign manager or agency head." Earnest Elmo Calkins, *The Advertising Man* (New York: Scribner's Sons, 1922), 70–72, 83–87.

31. Harry T. Peters, *Currier and Ives: Printmakers to the American People* (Garden City, N.Y.: Doubleday, 1942), 18–31.

32. Rob Roy Kelly, *American Wood Type, 1828–1900* (New York: Van Nostrand Reinhold, 1969; New York: Da Capo, 1977), 186; H. C. Bunner, "American Posters, Past and Present," in Arsène Alexandre et al., *The Modern Poster* (New York: Charles Scribner's Sons, 1895), 72.

33. Bunner, "American Posters," 88.

34. Ibid, 91–92.

35. The description of poster designers is based on a study by Jacquelyn Days Server,

"The American Artistic Poster of the 1890s" (Ph.D. diss., City University of New York, 1980); "Picture Posters," *Inland Printer* 19,2 (May 1897): 208. This article was condensed from an address given by George R. Sparks at a Chicago poster exhibition.

36. Percy V. Bradshaw, *Art in Advertising* (London: Press Art School, 1925), 446, 482.

37. John Thayer, *Astir: A Publisher's Life Story* (Boston: Small, Maynard, 1910), 31; Presbrey, *History and Development of Advertising*, 474.

38. This description of Bradley's career is based primarily on his autobiography *Will Bradley: His Chap Book* (New York: Typophiles, 1955). It was reprinted as "Notes Toward an Autobiography," in *Will Bradley: His Graphic Art*, ed. Clarence P. Hornung (New York: Dover, 1974), xi–xxxi. See also Anthony Bambace, *Will H. Bradley: His Work: A Bibliographical Guide.* (New Castle, Del.: Oak Knoll Press, 1995).

39. Bradley, "Notes Toward an Autobiography," xxvi–xxvii.

CHAPTER 4: PROFESSIONALIZATION

1. Magali Sarfatti Larson, *The Rise of Professionalism: A Sociological Analysis* (Berkeley: University of California Press, 1977), x.

2. Samuel Haber, *The Quest for Authority and Honor in the American Professions, 1750–1900* (Chicago: University of Chicago Press, 1991), 361.

3. In attempting to define their roles, professional associations at times must have argued over the kinds of professions they considered for admission into their ranks. The only public discussion I have found in club records occurred when Joseph Pennell, the illustrator and writer, questioned the inclusion of photographers as members in the newly formed American Institute of Graphic Arts. In response to a membership prospectus, Pennell is reported to have asked, in "his characteristically caustic manner," "By what stretch of imagination could photography be included as one of the graphic arts?" John Clyde Oswald, "How the Institute Began," *News-letter of the American Institute of Graphic Arts* 36 (February 1935): 2.

4. The names of individual printers and illustrators have rarely been identified. For a study of Afro-American publishing, see Penelope L. Bullock, *The Afro-American Periodical Press, 1838–1909* (Baton Rouge: Louisiana State University Press, 1981). For the Douglass case, see Philip S. Foner and Ronald L. Lewis, eds. *Black Workers: A Documentary History* (Philadelphia: Temple University Press, 1989), 144–49.

5. "The Negro in the Printing Office," *Inland Printer* 7,3 (December 1889): 268; Joseph Pennell, *The Adventures of an Illustrator* (Boston: Little, Brown, 1925), 53–54.

6. "The Heathen Chinee as a Competitor" *Inland Printer* 2,12 (September 1885): 536. Native Americans in the Southwest also ran printing establishments, with schools to train students located on reservations. These groups were marginalized, and their work is still largely unrecognized.

7. "Constitution and Bye-laws of the Franklin Society of the City of Chicago, Chicago: 1870," F. C. Bigmore and C. W. H. Wyman, *Bibliography of Printing* (London: Bernard Quaritch, 1880; London: Holland Press, 1978), 235; Adolf Growoll, *American Book Clubs:*

Their Beginnings and History and a Bibliography of Their Publications (New York: Dodd, Mead, 1897), 152–55.

8. *Publishers' Weekly* 634 (March 22, 1884): 352; John T. Winterich, *The Grolier Club, 1884–1967: An Informal History* (New York: The Club, 1967); "The Grolier Club," *American Bookmaker* 1,1 (July 1885): 3.

9. For a detailed history of this organization and its key documents, see Leona Margaret Powell, *History of the United Typothetae of America* (Chicago: University of Chicago Press, 1926), 13.

10. Powell argued that the Typothetae united as a response to unfair competition rather than antiunionism, but contemporaries emphasized the issue of union demands. See Powell, *History of the United Typothetae*, 193–94; 207–13. Everett Waddey contended the group formed in opposition to an nine-hour day and what printers considered to be micromanagement by the union. See "One Decade of the United Typothetae of America," *Printer and Bookmaker* 25,2 (October 1897): 73–81.

Howard Lockwood, publisher of the *Printer and Bookmaker*, was an active member of the United Typothetae, and his publication often served as an organ for it. H. O. Shepard's *Inland Printer* attempted to be impartial, although it was, for a time, the official organ of the pressmen's unions in the United States and Canada.

11. Waddey, "One Decade of the United Typothetae," 73–81.

12. For information on the society, see Ray Nash, *Printing as an Art* (Cambridge: Harvard University Press, 1955), 35–69; Charles A. Rheault, *S. P. at Seventy-Five: The Society of Printers, 1955–1980* (Boston: The Society, 1981); and *The Society of Printers for the Study and Advancement of the Art of Printing* (Boston: The Society, 1895).

13. *The Graphic Group: A Brief Sketch of the Graphic Group Organized in 1911 for the Betterment of the Graphic Arts* (New York: William Edwin Rudge, 1929): 5–7.

14. Ibid., 6–7.

15. Oswald, "How the Institute Began," 2.

16. The National Arts Club acted as midwife to the AIGA, the Art Directors Club, and supported the Society of Illustrators' exhibitions. The Club, located in New York City, was founded in 1898 as a national organization to "stimulate, foster and promote public interest in the arts." The arts were defined broadly, and the organization provided exhibition space for fine arts, applied arts, and industrial arts. In 1905 it launched an annual exhibition of "artistic and commercial posters"; in 1906, the "Books of the Year" show began. For a comprehensive documentary history, see Catherine Stover, *Inventory of the Records of the National Arts Club, 1898–1960* (Washington, D.C.: Archives of American Art, Smithsonian Institute, 1990); Oswald, "How the Institute Began," 1–2.

17. "Arts Club Warned of 'Thought Trust,'" *New York Times* (November 13, 1913): 9, italics added. The announcement appeared as a brief notice before a lengthy report of a diatribe on nouveau riche aspirations.

18. The quotation is from the institute's constitution, as reprinted in Oswald's "How the Institute Began," 1.

19. "Too Many Printing Shows?—You're Wrong!" *News-letter of the American Institute of Graphic Arts* 16 (February 25, 1925): 2.

20. Francis Hopkinson Smith's *American Illustrators* (New York: Scribners, 1892) is a hortatory, semifictionalized account of five imaginary evenings at the clubs where illustrators gathered to discuss professional problems and praise each other's work. For modern descriptions and analysis, see James J. Best, *American Popular Illustration* (Westport, Conn.: Greenwood Press, 1984), 117–29.

21. William Henry Shelton, *The Salmagundi Club* (New York: Houghton Mifflin, 1918), 13. Shelton also wrote an article on the club's history, "The Salmagundi Club," *New York Herald Tribune* (December 18, 1927): 14–15, 31.

22. Best, *American Popular Illustration*, 120–21; Michele H. Bogart, *Artists, Advertising, and the Borders of Art* (Chicago: University of Chicago Press, 1995), 35–39, 70–71. Sloan's diary entry for April 26, 1907, began, "Sent $5 (which I can little afford) to the secretary of the Society of Illustrators to which I have recently been elected (oh joy!!?)." *John Sloan's New York Scene from the Diaries, Notes, and Correspondence, 1906–1913*, ed. Bruce St. John (New York: Harper and Row, 1965), 124, 180.

23. For the history of Arts and Crafts philosophy and a description of individual clubs, see Eileen Boris, *Art and Labor: Ruskin, Morris, and the Craftsman Ideal in America* (Philadelphia: Temple University Press, 1986).

24. Mary Spain, *The Society of Arts and Crafts, 1897–1924* (Boston and New York: The Society, 1924), 5–6, 8.

25. Ibid., 11–12; Nancy Findlay, *Artists of the Book in Boston* (Cambridge: Harvard College Library, Houghton Library, Department of Printing and Graphic Arts, 1985), xii–xiv.

26. Boris, *Art and Labor*, 44–45.

27. For general information on advertising clubs, see *Printers' Ink, a Journal for Advertisers: Fifty Years, 1888–1938* (New York: Printers' Ink, 1938), 78–79, 142–43.

28. Ibid., 78; *The Sphinx Club* (New York: The Club, 1910), 9–13.

29. *Printers' Ink, a Journal for Advertisers*,142–46.

30. Peirce Johnson, "It Started with the Art Directors Club of New York . . . The Future Is in Our Past," in *Art Directing for Visual Communication and Selling* (New York: Hastings House, 1957), 206–17.

31. Ibid., 207.

32. Ibid., 208.

33. The Art Directors Club, *Annual* (New York: Publishers Printing, 1921), vii, ix. For an alternate interpretation, see Bogart, *Artists, Advertising, and the Borders of Art*, 128–32.

CHAPTER 5: THE GREAT DIVIDE

1. Carroll D. Wright, "The Practical Value of Art," *Munsey's Magazine* 17,4 (July 1897): 562.

2. Ibid., 566.

3. This paragraph and the next builds on the thesis propounded by Lawrence Levine in *Highbrow/Lowbrow: The Emergence of Cultural Hierarchy in America* (Cambridge: Harvard University Press, 1988). Levine argued that at the beginning of the nineteenth century the appeal of popular arts surmounted class and geographical boundaries, bringing disparate groups together. Over the course of the century, he traced the evolution of a high/low chasm in the performing arts, in art education, and in the creation of public museums, parks, and libraries. At the same time Levine described attempts by representatives of elite culture to instruct and elevate the general population.

4. Peter Marzio, *The Art Crusade* (Washington, D.C.: Smithsonian Institution Press, 1976). John Rubens Smith (1775–1849), Rembrandt Peale (1778–1860), and John Gadsby Chapman (1808–89) are the men Marzio called the "art crusaders." For a different view of this same process, see Diane Korzenik, *Drawn to Art: A Nineteenth-Century American Dream* (Hanover, N.H.: University Press of New England, 1985). Using the drawings, student work, magazines, and instruction books belonging to the Cross family, Korzenik traced this New England family as it moved from farming in New Hampshire to careers in Boston's printing establishment and schools. The Crosses, like many others, regarded art education as preparation for work in a new industrial era.

5. William Minifie, *Popular Lectures on Drawing and Design Delivered at the Public Meetings of the School of Design of the Maryland Institute* (Baltimore: The Institute, 1854), 2–3,12–13,18–19. Minifie's curriculum was arranged in a six-level sequence, beginning with pencil sketching and proceeding through drawing machinery, drawing buildings, and topographic drawing to landscape and figure painting.

6. For a study of the application of Ruskin's theories in the United States, see Mary Ann Stankiewicz, "'The Eye Is a Nobler Organ': Ruskin and American Art Education," *Journal of Aesthetic Education* 18,2 (Summer 1984): 51–64; John Ruskin, "Preface" (1857), *The Elements of Drawing*, vol. 15 of *The Works of John Ruskin* (London: George Allen, 1904; New York: Dover, 1971), 12.

7. John Ruskin, "Preface," *The Laws of Fésole*, Vol. 15 of *The Works of John Ruskin* (London: George Allen, 1904), 344; Ruskin, *Elements of Drawing*, 13.

8. For a history of Smith's struggle to establish a system of art education in the American public schools, see Harry Green, "Walter Smith: The Forgotten Man," *Art Education* 19,1 (January 1966): 3–9.

9. Walter Smith, *Art Education: Scholastic and Industrial* (Boston: James R. Osgood, 1873), 189, 6.

10. Ibid., 14.

11. Arthur D. Efland, *A History of Art Education* (New York: Teachers College Press, 1990), 113.

12. Ibid., 71–72. Smith's *Art Education*, appendix 4, provides general information as well as details of curricula for: the National Academy of Design (New York), Cooper Union for the Advancement of Science and Art (New York), the Boston Normal Art School, Lowell Institute (Boston), the Yale School of the Fine Arts (New Haven), and the Philadelphia School of Design for Women. See also Foster Wygant, *Art in American Schools in the Nineteenth Century* (Cincinnati: Interwood Press, 1983), 97.

13. Maurice H. Needham et al., *The Book of Oz Cooper: An Appreciation* (Chicago: Society of Typographic Arts, 1949), 7, 30, 39–42; Ralph Fletcher Seymour, *Some Went This Way: A Forty-Year Pilgrimage Among Artists, Bookmen, and Printers* (Chicago: Ralph Fletcher Seymour, 1942), 39, 47; Nancy Findlay, *Artists of the Book in Boston* (Cambridge: Harvard College Library, Houghton Library, Department of Printing and Graphic Arts, 1985), xi–xii; "The Scudder School for Girls, New York City," an advertisement that appeared in *Vogue* (August 15, 1915): 5.

14. For Dow's aesthetic theory, see Efland, *History of Art Education*, 177–81; Foster Wygant, *School Art in American Culture* (Cincinnati, Ohio: Interwood Press, 1993), 26–27; and Frederick C. Moffatt, *Arthur Wesley Dow (1857–1922)* (Washington, D.C.: National Collection of Fine Arts, Smithsonian Institution Press, 1977). For the Clarence H. White School, see Susan Doniger, "The Clarence H. White Schools of Photography," in *A Collective Vision*, exhib. cat. (Athens: Ohio University Art Gallery, 1986), 17–26, and Bonnie Yochelson, "Clarence H. White Reconsidered: An Alternative to the Modernist Aesthetic of Straight Photography," *Studies of Visual Communication* 9,4 (Fall 1983): 23–44.

15. Quoted in Doniger, "Clarence H. White Schools of Photography," 19. The school invited leading figures in the world of art to lecture, including Frederic Goudy (20).

16. Edward S. Smith, "The Field of Commercial Art," *Commercial Illustrator* 1,4 (March 1916): 10; Meyer Booth College of Commercial Art, *Success in Commercial Art* (Chicago: The College, 1919), 9, 21, 8. Meyer Booth was also a commercial art and publishing company, employing over one hundred artists in its art department.

17. "Chromo Civilization," *Nation* 482 (September 24, 1874): 201–2; Peter Marzio, *The Democratic Art: Chromolithography* (Boston: David Godine, 1979), 202. See Michele H. Bogart, *Artists, Advertising, and the Borders of Art* (Chicago: University of Chicago Press, 1995), 15–78, for a comprehensive treatment of the problems of status.

18. Walter Benjamin, "The Work of Art in the Age of Mechanical Reproduction," *Illuminations* (New York: Schocken Books, 1968), 217–51. See also Miles Orvell, *The Real Thing: Imitation and Authenticity in American Culture, 1880–1940* (Chapel Hill: University of North Carolina Press, 1989), xv–xxvi.

19. Oscar Lovell Triggs, "Arts and Crafts," *Brush and Pencil* 1,3 (December 1897): 48.

20. Louis Levy, "The Growth of Photo-engraving," *Printing Art* 28,2 (October 1916): 26.

21. Neil Harris, "Pictorial Perils: The Rise of American Illustration," in his *Cultural Excursions: Marketing Appetites and Cultural Tastes in Modern America* (Chicago: University of Chicago Press, 1990), 337–48.

22. Ralph M. Hower, *The History of an Advertising Agency: N. W. Ayer and Son at Work* (Cambridge: Harvard University Press, 1939), 331.

23. H. C. Bunner, "American Posters, Past and Present," in Arsène Alexandre et al., *The Modern Poster* (New York: Charles Scribner's Sons, 1895), 72.

24. Jacquelyn Days Server, "The American Artistic Poster of the 1890s" (Ph.D. diss., City University of New York, 1980), 15–23.

25. "The American Poster," *New York Times* (January 24, 1896): 4.

26. "The Artistic Pictorial Poster: High Art in Advertising," *Profitable Advertising*

4,10 (March 15, 1895): 291; Smith quoted in H. E. Johns, "Art in Printing," *American Art Printer* 6,2 (September 1892): 58.

27. "The Artistic Pictorial Poster," *Profitable Advertising*, 4,10 (March 15, 1895): 297.

28. "Introduction," *Poster Show*, exhib. cat. (Richmond, Va.: n.p., 1896), unpaginated; Louis J. Rhead, "The Moral Aspect of the Artistic Poster," *Bookman* 1 (June 1895): 312–14.

29. S. de Soissons, "Some American Posters," *Artist* 23,225 (September 1898): 16.

30. Nathaniel C. Fowler, Jr., *Fowler's Publicity* (New York: Publicity, 1897), 749.

31. Walter Dill Scott, *Theory and Practice of Advertising* (Boston: Small, Maynard, 1903), 2–3.

32. "Illustrative Advertising," *Inland Printer* 14,1 (October 1894): 63. Parson's articles appeared in 1911 in *Advertising and Selling* and were published as *The Principles of Advertising Arrangement* (New York: Prang, 1912); George French, *How to Advertise: A Guide to Designing, Laying Out, and Composing Advertisements* (New York: Doubleday, Page, for the Associated Advertising Clubs of the World, 1917), 87; "Structure and Typography," *Advertising and Selling* 21,5 (October 1911): 43; A. Rowden King, "Art Versus Commercial Art," *Advertising and Selling* 21,5 (October 1911): 51.

33. Earnest Elmo Calkins, *Business the Civilizer* (Boston: Little, Brown, 1928), 138–40.

34. "From the Inside," *Fame* 10,10 (October 1901): 479; Will B. Wilder, "'Art' and Advertising," *Fame* 18,10 (October 1909): 218. Jackson Lears contends that Calkins knew that advertising artists had little freedom, although he never stated so publicly. See his *Fables of Abundance: A Cultural History of Advertising in America* (New York: Basic Books, 1994), 313.

35. "Car Cards and Several Kinds of Posters," *Profitable Advertising* 18,11 (April 1909): 1102; King, "Art Versus Commercial Art," 49.

36. "Mr. Ogden to the Sphinx," *Fame* 7,5 (May 1898): 179, 180; "Art Commercialized and Commercial Art," *Fame* 20,9 (September 1911): 206–7.

37. Max Wineburgh, "Subway Advertising," *American Advertiser* 21,1 (January 1905): 65.

38. Levine, *Highbrow/Lowbrow*, 182–83,185,186; Albert Davis Lasker, *The Lasker Story as He Told It* (Chicago: Advertising Publications, 1963), 21–22.

39. Kurt Varnedoe and Adam Gopnik, *High and Low: Modern Art and Popular Culture* (New York: Museum of Modern Art, 1990), 15.

40. See Stephen Vaughn, "Advertising America—and Advertising," in his *Holding Fast the Inner Lines* (Chapel Hill: University of North Carolina Press, 1980), 141–92; Susan E. Meyer, *America's Great Illustrators* (New York: Harry N. Abrams, 1978), 229; George Creel, *How We Advertised America* (New York: Harper and Brothers, 1920; New York: Arno Press, 1972), 165.

CHAPTER 6: WOMEN IN GRAPHIC DESIGN HISTORY

1. Linda Nochlin, "Why Have There Been No Great Women Artists?" *Art News* 69,9 (January 1971): 22–39, 67–71. This article also appeared as "Why Are There No Great

Women Artists?" *Women in Sexist Society: Studies in Power and Powerless*, ed. Vivian Gornick and Barbara Moran (New York: Basic Books, 1971), and *Art and Sexual Politics*, ed. Thomas B. Hess and Elizabeth C. Baker (New York: Colliers, 1971). Feminist art historians have expanded Nochlin's agenda considerably. For a overview of feminist art criticism and art history in the 1970s and 1980s, see Thalia Gouma-Peterson and Patricia Mathews, "The Feminist Critique of Art History," *Art Bulletin* 69,3 (September 1987): 326–57.

2. Martha Scotford Lange, "Is There a Canon of Graphic Design History?" *AIGA Journal of Graphic Design* 9,2 (1991): 3–5, 9.

3. See Lange's article, cited above, for the omission of women designers from major graphic design texts. The two most useful biographical references for women in graphic design are concerned with women artists: Chris Petteys, *Dictionary of Women Artists: An International Dictionary of Women Artists Born before 1900* (Boston: G. K. Hall, 1985), and Charlotte Steifer Rubinstein, *American Women Artists from Early Indian Times to the Present* (Boston: G. K. Hall, 1982).

One of the problems encountered in any attempt to track women is that of multiple surnames. Cross-references are not always used. In addition, many women and men signed their work with initials instead of first names and some first names are gender neutral—a problem in identifying signatures in published work in cases when it is signed. Most advertisements and magazine illustrations were not signed.

4. Cheryl Buckley, "Made in Patriarchy: Toward a Feminist Analysis of Women and Design," *Design Discourse: History Theory Criticism*, ed. Victor Margolin (Chicago: University of Chicago Press, 1989), 262.

5. Virginia Penny, *The Employments of Women: A Cyclopaedia of Woman's Work* (Boston: Walker, Wise, 1863), vii, 53.

6. "Woman's Position in Art," *Crayon* 8,2 (February 1861): 28.

7. Basic information on Fanny Palmer can be found in Henry T. Peters's *Currier and Ives: Printmakers to the American People* (Garden City, N.Y.: Doubleday, 1942), 26–29. Peters summarizes her life and identifies the prints known to be hers. Otherwise she is absent from graphic history until Mary Bartlett Cowdrey's "Fanny Palmer, An American Lithographer," in *Prints: Thirteen Illustrated Essays on the Art of the Print*, ed. Carl Zigrosser (New York: Holt, Rinehart and Winston, 1962), 219–34, and her entry in *Notable American Women*, ed. Edward T. James, 3 vols. (Cambridge: Belknap Press of Harvard University Press, 1971), 3:10–11. Charlotte Steifer Rubinstein included Palmer in *American Women Artists* (Boston: G. K. Hall, 1982), 68–70, and wrote in depth about her in "The Early Career of Frances Flora Bond Palmer (1812–1876)," *American Art Journal* 17,4 (Autumn 1985), 71–88. Penny, in an obvious reference to Palmer ("Mrs. P. Brooklyn, an English lady"), writes that "she is probably the only lady professionally engaged in this business in the United States." *Employments of Women*, 69.

8. For bibliographical information, see Martha Jane Soltow and Mary K. Wery, *American Women and the Labor Movement, 1825–1974* (Metuchen, N.J.: Scarecrow, 1976). Especially useful histories on women in the printers' union include Elizabeth F. Baker, *Technology and Women's Work* (New York: Columbia University Press, 1964); Mary

Notes to Pages 137–38

Biggs, "Neither Printer's Wife Nor Widow," *Library Quarterly* 50,4 (1980): 431–52; Eleanor Flexner, *Century of Struggle* (Cambridge: Belknap Press of Harvard University Press, 1959), especially "Women in Trade Unions, 1860–1975," 131–41; Belva Mary Herron, "Labor Organization Among Women," *University Studies* 1,10 (May 1905), and *University of Illinois Bulletin* 2,12 (July 1, 1905): 15–25; Philip Sheldon Foner, *Women and the American Labor Movement*, vol. 1 (New York: Free Press, 1979); George A. Stevens, *New York Typographical Union No. 6* (Albany: J. B. Lyon, 1913), 421–40; and Barbara Mayer Wertheimer, *We Were There* (New York: Pantheon Books, 1977). Roger Levenson's *Women in Printing: Northern California, 1857–1890* (Santa Barbara, Calif.: Capra Press, 1994) not only restored the Women's Cooperative Printing Union (1868–80) in San Francisco to American type history but greatly increased our knowledge of a significant number of women typographers and printers in the West.

9. For guides to women's periodicals, see Maureen E. Hady, *Women's Periodicals and Newspapers from the Eighteenth Century to 1981* (Boston: G. K. Hall, 1982); Nancy K. Humphreys, *American Women's Magazines* (New York: Garland, 1989); Mary Ellen Zuckerman, *Sources on the History of Women's Magazines, 1792–1960* (New York: Greenwood Press, 1991). See also Lynne Masel-Walters, "To Hustle with the Rowdies," *Journal of American Culture* 3,1 (Spring 1980), on the history of the suffragette press. A study of women cartoonists who worked for prosuffrage publications is the subject of Alice Sheppard's *Cartooning for Suffrage* (Albuquerque: University of New Mexico Press, 1994).

10. A fine example is the work of Carroll D. Wright, then chief of the Bureau of Statistics of Labor, whose study appeared in 1889 as *The Working Girls of Boston* (Boston: Wright and Potter, 1889; New York: Arno Press, 1969). It was undertaken "to ascertain the moral, sanitary, physical and economic conditions of the working girls of Boston," including those in the printing trades (1). Wright concluded that, "the working girls are as respectable, as moral, and as virtuous as any class of women in our community; that they are making as heroic a struggle for existence as any class is a fact which all the statistics prove" (120). And in case anyone missed the point, he spelled it out: "girls cannot work hard all day and be prostitutes too" (121).

See also Edith Abbott and Sophonisba P. Breckinridge, "Employment of Women in Industries," *Journal of Political Economy* 14 (January 1906): 14–40; Joseph A. Hill, *Women in Gainful Occupations 1870 to 1920*, Department of Commerce, Bureau of the Census, Census Monographs, 9 (Washington, D.C.: Government Printing Office, 1929; Westport, Conn.: Greenwood Press, 1978); Helen L. Sumner, *Report on Condition of Woman and Child Wage-Earners in the United States: History of Women in Industry in the United States*, vol. 9 (Washington, D.C.: Government Printing Office, 1910), 212–21; *Women at Work: A Century of Change*, no. 161 (Washington, D.C.: Government Printing Office, 1933).

11. Roger B. Stein, "Artifact as Ideology: The Aesthetic Movement in Its American Cultural Context," in *In Pursuit of Beauty*, exhib. cat. (New York: Metropolitan Museum of Art, 1986), 22–51; Anthea Callen, *Women Artists of the Arts and Crafts Movement*,

1870–1914 (New York: Pantheon, 1979), and "Sexual Division of Labor in the Arts and Crafts Movement," *Woman's Art Journal* 5 (Fall–Winter 1984–85): 1–6.

12. Leona M. Hudak, *Early American Women Printers and Publishers, 1639–1820* (Metuchen, N.J.: Scarecrow Press, 1978), 2. Elizabeth Harris Glover established the Cambridge Press, the first press in North America, in 1639. Her husband, Jose Glover, wishing to set up a printing business, boarded a ship from England with his family, a press, and printing supplies. He died en route. See Hudak, 9–19. See also Ava Baron, "An 'Other' Side of Gender Antagonism at Work: Men, Boys, and the Remasculinization of Printers' Work, 1830–1920," in *Work Engendered* (Ithaca, N.Y.: Cornell University Press, 1991), 47–69.

Mary Biggs notes that the percentage of female apprentices in printing was high compared to women in other skilled trades and that there is some reason to believe the percentage of men who actually underwent a six-year apprenticeship was relatively small. Certainly the trade journals complained of this and supported technical education for boys to make up the deficiency. Biggs, "Neither Printer's Wife Nor Widow," 438.

13. *Typographic Advertiser* 14,3 (April 1869): 1.

14. Edith Abbott, "Harriet Martineau and the Employment of Women in 1836," *Journal of Political Economy* 14 (1906): 615; Penny, *Employments of Woman*, 490. This average is for New York and New England; Wertheimer, *We Were There*, 92; Wright, *Working Girls of Boston*, 82–83.

15. Foner, *Women and the American Labor Movement*, 145; H. Dewey Anderson and Percy E. Davidson, *Occupational Trends in the United States* (Palo Alto, Calif.: Stanford University Press, 1940), 300–301. The authors note that although printing material increased by more than 760 percent from 1899 to 1929, only 120 percent more workers were employed (309). Lois Rather, *Women As Printers* (Oakland, Calif.: Rather Press, 1970), 25.

16. Herron, "Labor Organization Among Women," 16.

17. Ibid., 15–16.

18. *Inland Printer* 1,6 (March 1884): 10.

19. In the 1880s and 1890s, the *Inland Printer* regularly attacked women in the printshop. See *Inland Printer* 1,1 (October 1883): 1; 2,12 (September 1885): 534; 7,1 (October 1889): 108–9; 7,9 (June 1890): 819–20; 9,10 (July 1892): 875–76; 10,5 (February 1893): 195; and 10,6 (March 1893): 501. Charles J. Dumar, president of the New York Typographical Union, argued that union women were given preferential treatment: see 8,10 (July 1891): 1001–2. F. M. Cole, "Lady Compositors," *Inland Printer* 7,2 (November 1889): 109. *Inland Printer* 1,6 (March 1884): 10.

The rhetoric used by both sides is instructive. A printshop owner recommended hiring women as typesetters and wood-engravers because they were more obedient, did not use foul language, and cost considerably less. He concluded, "At least let women have a fair opportunity to do something else besides get married. What man is there who would not resent being told that his chief ambition in life should be to be a father? Yet women are told daily that they should devote twenty years of a lifetime in the preparing for motherhood, at least ten years in bearing children, and the rest of their lives in recovering from the effects. If they prefer to think that the world is populated sufficiently, or that to bear a child does not call for the sacrifice of a lifetime, they are snubbed, and especially so when they show any inclination to compete with men in trades." "Male Versus Female Labor," *Art Age* 3,25 (August 1885): 14.

20. "Proceedings, National Labor Union, August 1869," *Workingman's Advocate* 6,5 (September 4, 1869), reprinted in *America's Working Women*, ed. R. Baxandall, L. Gordan, and S. Reverdy (New York: Random House, 1976), 112–13.

21. From a report given by Lewis at the International Typographers convention in 1871 and cited by Stevens, *New York Typographical Union*, 437.

22. Cole, "Lady Compositors," 109.

23. "Woman as Compositors," *Inland Printer* 7,8 (May 1890): 820.

24. Baker, *Technology and Women's Work*, 45. The experience of women printers in the territories and states in the West was somewhat different. In a pictorial study of frontier journalism, numerous photographs from state archives show women working as editors, printers, and compositors. See Robert F. Karolevitz, *Newspapering in the Old West* (Seattle: Superior, 1965), especially "Printers in Petticoats," 173–80. Karolevitz also includes photographs of women in printing classes in state universities as well as in a special school for American Indians. Sherilyn Cox Bennion, *Equal to the Occasion: Women Editors of the Nineteenth-Century West* (Reno: University of Nevada Press, 1990), estimates that in western regions there were 344 women printers (5 percent of the total) in 1890 and 959 women (10 percent) in 1900 (10). Levenson's *Women in Printing*, though ostensibly limited to northern California, is an invaluable source of information on all women in American printing with extensive documentation on women who worked in California.

25. Edna Martin Parratt, "Women Printers," *Bulletin of the New York Public Library* 56,1 (January 1952): 42–43. Often cited, this was only a brief reply to an item on women printers. The names of other women printers can be found in Rather, *Women as Printers*. See also Susan Otis Thompson, *American Book Design and William Morris* (New York: R. R. Bowker, 1977), 206. The exception is a profile in an exhibition catalog published by Women in Design, Chicago, *Ten Years: Women in Design Chicago Anniversary Exhibition*, 1988. It is clear, however, that the authors were unable to determine the extent of Bertha Goudy's contribution to the design of books issued by the press.

26. For information on Armstrong, see Charles B. Gullans, *A Checklist of Trade Bindings Designed by Margaret Armstrong*, UCLA Library Occasional Papers, no. 16 (Los Angeles: University of California Library, 1968), and her obituary, *New York Times* (July 19, 1944). Whitman is one among several women in Nancy Findlay's *Artists of the Book in Boston* (Cambridge: Harvard College Library, Houghton Library, Department of Printing and Graphic Arts, 1985). Starr is quoted in *Notable American Women*, 352.

27. *The Craftsman* 2,1 (April 1902): 33–34; Alice C. Morse, "Women Illustrators," in *Art and Handicrafts in the Woman's Building of the World's Columbian Exposition*, ed. Maud Howe Elliot (Paris: Goupil, 1893), 75.

There are several examples of work by women in Susan Otis Thompson's "Arts and

Crafts Book," in *The Arts and Crafts Movement in America, 1876–1916*, ed. Robert Judson Clark (Princeton, N.J.: Princeton University Press, 1972), 93–116, and her *American Book Design*. See also Wendy Kaplan, *"The Art That Is Life:" The Arts and Crafts Movement in America, 1875–1920* (Boston: Little, Brown for the Museum of Fine Arts, 1987), for reproductions of work by women with extensive captions by Thompson.

28. *The Society of Arts and Crafts, 1897–1924* (Boston: The Society, 1924), 7,8; Charles A. Rheault, Jr., *S. P. at Seventy-Five: The Society of Printers, 1955–1980* (Boston: The Society, 1981), unpaginated; Martha Scotford, "The Tenth Pioneer," *Eye* 18 (Autumn 1995): 56–57; "Newly Admitted Members," *News-letter of the American Institute of Graphic Arts* 19 (July 10, 1926): 2.

29. "Editorial Squibs," *Profitable Advertising* 1,1 (June 1891): 9.

30. In addition to Kate Griswold, who eventually became publisher of *Advertising Experience*, several other women gained prominence in journalism at the turn of the century. See "No Sex in Success?" *The Ad-School: A Practical Advertiser* 1,7 (July 1901): 11. See also *Inland Printer* 8,7 (April 1891): 680, for profiles of Mrs. Frank Leslie, who edited her father and her husband's publications, and Mary Louise Booth, who worked at *Harper's Bazaar*. Quotation from "Women in the Business World," *Profitable Advertising* 3,1 (June 15, 1893): 37.

31. "Photography in Advertising," *Advertising Experience* 6,4 (February 1898): 24; *Printers' Ink, a Journal for Advertisers: Fifty Years, 1888–1938* (New York: Printers' Ink, 1938), 118.

32. Clarence Bloomfield Moore, "Women Experts in Photography," *Cosmopolitan* 14,5 (March 1893): 580–90; C. Jane Gover, *The Positive Image: Women Photographers in Turn of the Century America* (Albany: State University of New York Press, 1988), xvii. See also Naomi Rosenblum, "Not Just for Fun: Women Become Professionals, 1880–1915," in her *A History of Women Photographers* (New York: Abbeville Press, 1994), 55–70.

33. Jacquelyn Days Server, "The American Artistic Poster of the 1890s" (Ph.D. diss., City University of New York, 1980), 92; *Poster Show*, exhib. cat. (Richmond, Va.: n.p., 1896).

34. S. C. de Soissons, "Ethel Reed and Her Art," *Poster* (November 1898): 199–202.

35. "Ethel Reed, Artist," *Bradley: His Book* 1, 3 (July 1896): 74. (Reed went to England and has disappeared from subsequent histories.)

36. Alice Rouillier, "The Work of Elizabeth Colwell," *Graphic Arts* 4,4 (March 1913): 237–48; Petteys, *Dictionary of Women Artists*.

37. "A Declaration of Art in Advertising," *Arts and Decoration* 14,6 (April 1921): 464–65, 498; M. R. Edmondson, "Where Woman Fits in the Advertising World," *American Advertiser* 21,3 (March 1905): 56–57.

38. Helen Woodward, *Through Many Windows* (New York: Harper and Brothers, 1926; New York: Garland, 1986), 147.

39. Taylor Adams, "Early Women in Advertising—All Uphill," in *How It Was in Advertising, 1776–1976*, comp. editors of *Advertising Age* (Chicago: Cain, 1976), 30.

40. Walter Smith, *Industrial Art*, Vol. 2 of *The Masterpieces of the Centennial International Exhibition Illustrated* (Philadelphia: Gebbie and Barrie, 1877), 95–96. In this

catalog of works appearing in the Philadelphia Centennial, Smith praised Englishwomen for their expertise in needlework, a skill learned at new schools of applied design.

41. *First Annual Report of the Committee on the School of Design for Women* (Philadelphia: The School, 1852): 2–4; *Proceedings of the Franklin Institute of the State of Pennsylvania, for the Promotion of the Mechanic Arts, Relative to the Establishment of a School of Design for Women* (Philadelphia: The Institute, 1850), 1, 5. The school's history can be found in T. C. Knauff, *An Experiment in Training for the Useful and Beautiful* (Philadelphia: The School, 1922), and Nina de Angeli Walls, "Art and Industry in Philadelphia: Origins of the Philadelphia School of Design for Women, 1848 to 1875," *Pennsylvania Magazine of History and Biography* 117, 3 (July 1993): 177–99. The curriculum was divided into three departments: drawing (a basic course for all students), industrial design (including textile, wallpaper, oil cloth, carpet, and furniture design), and wood engraving and lithography (illustration for the arts, sciences, and natural history). From its first year in existence, students obtained patents and sold their work to manufacturers and publishers.

42. Walter Smith, *Art Education*, 110–19 and appendixes with detailed description of curricula, 370–80; Peter Cooper, *To the Legislature of the State of New-York, in Senate and Assembly Convened* (New York: n.p., 1856). The importance of many of these institutions in graphic design education remains to be explored. The best sources I have found on early design education are Isaac Edwards Clarke, *Art and Industry*, 6 vols. (Washington, D.C.: United States Office of Education, 1885–98), and Arthur D. Efland, *A History of Art Education: Intellectual and Social Currents in Teaching the Visual Arts* (New York: Teachers College Press, 1990); Penny, *Employments of Women*, 55–58; Thomas Woody, *A History of Women's Education in the United States*, 2 vols. (New York: Science Press, 1919), 2:75–80.

43. Penny, *Employments of Women*, 57–58, 104.

44. See Alice Sheppard, *Cartooning for Suffrage* (Albuquerque: University of New Mexico Press, 1994), and Trina Robbins, *A Century of Women Cartoonists* (Northampton, Mass.: Kitchen Sink Press, 1993). For a rare personal note on the strength it took for a woman to enter the profession, see "Fay King, Cartoonist," *Federal Illustrator* 2,2 (Midwinter 1917–18): 12–13.

45. Frances M. Benson, "Five Women Artists of New York," *Quarterly Illustrator* 1,1 (January–March 1893): 34.

46. James J. Best, *American Popular Illustration: A Reference Guide* (Westport, Conn.: Greenwood Press, 1984), 120; "About the Society of Illustrators" (New York: The Society, n.d.), single sheet; Ann Barton Brown, *Alice Barber Stephens: A Pioneer Woman Illustrator* (Chadds Ford, Pa.: Brandywine River Museum, 1984), 24–25.

47. Francis Hopkinson Smith, *American Illustrators* (New York: Scribners, 1892), 54.

48. Frank Weitenkampf, *American Graphic Art* (New York: Holt, 1912; Johnson Reprint, 1970): 189–90.

49. Rubinstein, *American Women Artists*, 159. For a comprehensive list of students and references, see *"A Small School of Art": The Students of Howard Pyle*, ed. Rowland

Elzea and Elizabeth H. Hawkes (Wilmington: Delaware Art Museum, 1980); Henry Pitz, *The Brandywine Tradition* (Boston: Houghton Mifflin, 1969), 178.

50. "An Autobiographical Sketch" was published in *Good Housekeeping* in October 1917 and reprinted in Gene Mitchell, *The Subject Was Children* (New York: E. P. Dutton, 1979), 4–5.

51. Frances R. Marshall, "Qualities That Make for Success in Women Illustrators," *Public Ledger* [Philadelphia] (December 15, 1912): 1.

CHAPTER 7: AT "THE END OF THE MECHANICAL
REVOLUTION"

1. W. A. Dwiggins, "New Kind of Printing Calls for New Design," *Boston Evening Transcript* (August 29, 1922), Graphic Arts Section, 3:6; reprinted in Appendix 2. All subsequent quotations are from this article.

2. Dwiggins was himself an illustrator, advertising artist, typographer, and book designer. Born in Martinsville, Ohio, he went to Chicago in 1899. There he studied printing with Frederic Goudy at the Frank Holme School of Illustration and returned to run his own press in Cambridge, Ohio, from 1903 to 1904. He then followed Frederic and Bertha Goudy to Higham, Massachusetts, where he remained for the rest of his life. Until 1923, when he met Alfred A. Knopf, Dwiggins worked in advertising design. Knopf hired Dwiggins to oversee the design of his books, and Dwiggins became one of the most influential book designers of his time. He also designed type for the Mergenthaler Linotype Company, notably *Metro*, *Electra*, and *Caledonia*. He was an active member of the Society of Printers, where he met Updike, Rollins, and other members of the Boston printing elite. In his writing he combined a lightly borne erudition, a passionate commitment to design issues, and a self-deprecating, wry sense of humor. Under the pseudonym Thedam Püterschein and under his own name, Dwiggins contributed to journals and wrote a textbook on advertising art, *Layout in Advertising* (1928). He designed, wrote, and published the *Fabulist*, a magazine that appeared at erratic intervals when its creator was satisfied with his materials. He was known also a calligrapher and puppeteer. When he first used the phrase "graphic designer" he was describing himself. A bibliography of work by and about Dwiggins can be found in Paul A. Bennett, ed., *Postscripts on Dwiggins*, 2 vols., Typophile Chap Books, 35, 36 (New York: Typophiles, 1960).

Index

References to illustrations are italicized

Adams, Henry Forster, 35
Advertising, *26, 28;* agencies, 26–27, 50,
  76–78; associations, 51, 101–4; in
  magazines, 24–25; populism, 128–29;
  psychology applied to, 34–35, 124–
  25; trade journals, 49–55; during
  World War I, 103, 129–30, *131. See
  also* Outdoor advertising
Advertising Experience, 53
Aesthetic movement, 31–33, 107–8, 138,
  162. *See also* Ruskin, John
African Americans in the graphic arts,
  42, 88–89

American Art Printer, 43, *44*
American Bookmaker, 92
American Chap-Book, 84
American Indians in graphics, 88
American Institute for Graphic Arts, 4–
  5, 84, 95, 96–98, 104
*American Institute for Graphic Arts
  News-letter,* 67, 97
American Type Founders Association,
  23, 67, 84
Anderson, Alexander, 12
Anthony, Susan B., 137, 142
Applied arts and high culture, 105–7

215

Index

Apprentices, 138, 140, 142
Armory Show, 102, 129–30
Armstrong, Margaret, 59, 144
Art Age, 57–58
"Art crusaders," 108
Art directors, 27, 72–73, 102–4
Art Directors Annual, 55
Art Directors Club of New York, 73, 102–4, 149
Artist, 172
Artist Printer, 45, *56*
Art journals, 55–59
Art Nouveau, 34, 58–59, 83
"Art of printing," 34, 45–49
Arts and Crafts movement, 31, 33–34, 53, 100–101; antimachine bias, 116–17; educational theory of, 110–12; style of, 48; women in, 138, 162
Arts and Craft societies, 33, 100–101. *See also* Society of Arts and Crafts of Boston
Associations: of advertisers, 101–4; Arts and Crafts, 100–101; of illustrators, 98–100; of printers, 90–100; racism in, 88–89; woman in, 88, 145, 154–55
Ayer and Sons. *See* N. W. Ayer and Sons

Bailey, Lydia R., 138–39
Bates, Charles Austin, 53, 54, *54*, 76, 167
Beardsley, Aubrey, 34, 83
Benton, Linn Boyd, 20
Black and White Society. *See* Salmagundi Club
Bloomer, Amelia Jenks, 137, 139
Book Club of California, 91
Book clubs, 90–91
Book designers, 63
Bradbury and Houghteling, 27
Bradley, Will, 45, 60, 69, 94, 100, *121;* aesthetics, 48, 84; career, 58–59, 83–84; covers for *Inland Printer*, 42, 83, 119; on women designers, 149

Bradley: His Book, 83
Bunner, H. C., 78–79, 119–22
Buscha, Samuel L., 68

Caffin, Charles, 105, 117, 171
Calkins, Earnest Elmo, *12*, 76–78, 96, 102, 104, 125
Cartooning and cartoonists, 115, 153
Catalogs, 18, 30
Caxton Club, 91
Century Magazine (Scribner's Monthly), 55, 68, 72, 75
Charles Austin Bates Criticism, 53, *54*
Chéret, Jules, 34, 122, 123
Chicago Columbian Exposition of *1893*, 29, 116
Chinese-American printers, 89
Chiswick Press, 11
Chromolithography, 13–14, 78, 116
Clarence H. White School of Photography, 113–15
Club of Odd Volumes, 91
Cobden-Sanderson, T. J., 33, 95, 144, 145
Collier's, 75, *127*
Colwell, Elizabeth, 68, 149, *150*
"Commercial art": definitions of, 61–62
Commercial studios, 81
Committee on Public Information (CPI), 130
Compositors. *See* Typesetters and typesetting
Cooper, Oswald B., 67, 68, 112
Correspondence schools, 112, 115
Crane, Walter, 71, 83, 107
Crayon, 55, 57
Creel, George, 130
Currier and Ives, 13, 78, 135–36
Curtis Publishing Company, 74, *75*
Cuts, 12, 38, *41*

Darley, Felix O. C., 16, 70
Design education, 108–15, *111, 113*
Design schools, 31, 110–12; correspon-

Index

dence, 112, 115. *See also* Clarence H. White School of Photography

Deskilling, 61

De Vinne, Theodore Low, 75, 91–93, 163, 168

Douglass, Lewis H., 88–89

Doves Press, 33, 95, 144

Dow, Arthur Wesley, 103, 113–14

Drake, Alexander W., 72, 73; on engraving, 69; at *Scribners (Century)*, 55, 75, 91, 97

Dryden, Helen, 147

Dwiggins, William Addison, 35, 45, 112, 159–63, 167; career, 213n; "New Kind of Printing Calls for New Design," 184–89

Education. *See* Design education; Design schools

Electrotype, 4, *5*, 19–20, *20*

Engraver and Printer, 45–46

Engravers and engraving, *2*, *3*, 9, 12, 55–57, 193n; demise of profession, 15–18, 68–69; women, 135

Engraving houses, 74

Federal School of Applied Cartooning, 115, 171–72

Federal School of Commercial Designing, 115, 171–72

Foote, Mary Hallock, 69–70, 155, 157

Fowler, Nathaniel, 124

Frank Holme School of Illustration, 112

Franklin Engraving and Electroplating Company, 74

Franklin Society of Chicago, 90–91

Frost, A. B., 75, *127*

Galaxy, 24

Gibson, Charles Dana, *70*, 75, 99, 103, *127*, 130, 149

Gilder, Richard W., 68–69, 72

Golden Age of Illustration, 12, 134. *See also* Illustrators and illustration

Goodhue, Bertram Grosvenor, 100

Goudy, Bertha Sprinks, 66, 67, 144

Goudy, Frederic W., 49, 66–67, *67*, 96, 104, 112

Graham's Magazine, 56–57

Graphic Arts, 59, 149

Graphic design: attacked in press, 116–19; defined, 4–5, 35, 61–62; separation from printing, 11; separation from production, 11–12, 60–71; influence of technology, 8–9, 11–23

Graphic Group, 84, 95–96

Griswold, Kate E., 51, 146, 169–70

Grolier Club, 91

Halftone process, 16–18, *17*

Harper and Brothers, New York, 72–73

Harper's Monthly, 55

Harper's Weekly, 55

Henri, Robert, 71, 103

Hoe, Robert, Jr., 91

Hoke Process Sign Works, *80*

Holme, Frank, 42, *152*

Holme, Ida Van Dyke, 112

Homer, Winslow, 70, 73

Hutchings, Albin H., 18

Illustrators and illustration, 15–18, 55–57, 68–72, 75; for advertising, 124–28; associations, 98–100; use in magazines, 12–13, 24–25, 56–57, 70; technology, effects of, 12–19, 71. *See also* Engravers and engraving; *Quarterly Illustrator*

Inland Printer, 42, 49, 83, 119

International Studio, 58

Ives, Frederick, 16, 96

Job printers, 9, *10*, 92

Johnson, Henry Lewis, 45–48, 59, 95, 100, 149, 163, 168

Johnson, Peirce, 102

Index

Kemble, E. W., 75, *127*

King, A. Rowden, 125

Ladies Home Journal, 82

Lanston, Tolbert, 20, 22

Lanston Monotype Company, 67

Lasker, Alfred, 129

Layout men, 63–64

Lee Lash Company, *79, 80*

Letterers, 68

Levy, Louis, 16, 117

Levy, Max, 16

Lewis, Augusta, 142

Leyendecker, Frank X., 75, 99, *127*

Leyendecker, J. C., 74, 99, 149

Linotype, 20, *21*, 63, 143

Linton, William James, 69, 170, 193n

Lithographers and lithography, 3, *4*, 13–14, 116

Lithography houses, 78–81

Lockwood, Howard, 92

Low, Will H., 98, *99*, 130

Magazines, 36–59; advertising in, 24; circulation, 23–24; illustration used in, 12–13; publishers, 74–75. *See also* Trade journals

Mahin's Magazine, 54

Maurer, Louis, 78

McManus, Blanche, 147

Mechanization, 8–9, 32, 33

Mergenthaler, Ottmar, 20, 31

Mergenthaler Type Company, 67

Meyer Booth College of Commercial Art, 115

Minifie, William, 108–9

Minorities in graphic design, 42, 88–89

Modernism, 5–6, 129–30

Monotype, 22, *22*, 63

Morris, William, 33–34, 83, 100, 162; influence on American Arts and Crafts, 101, 144; influence on design education, 110–11; influence on mag-azine design, 38, 48; influence on magazine editorials, 57–58; influence on printing associations, 90, 91, 93

Morse, Alice C., 145

Nast, Thomas, 70, 73

Nation, 55, 116

National Arts Club, 95, 96, 102, 202n

N. W. Ayer and Sons, Philadelphia, 26, 27, 76, *77*

Ogden, R. C., 128

Ostertag, Blanche, *152*

Outdoor advertising, 9, 27, 101–2, *118*

Outdoor Advertising Association of America, 101–2

Palmer, Fanny, 31, 78, 135–37, *136*

Palmer, Volney, 26

Pantograph, 20, 22, 65

Paper manufacture, 18–19

Parrish, Maxfield, 75, *127*, 130

Parson, Charles, 72–73, 163

Parsons, Frank, 34, 54, 78–81

Penfield, Edward, 72, 99, 119

Pennell, Joseph, 69, 72, 89, 103, 130, 201n

Penrose's Annual, 43, 53

Peter, Sarah, 152–53

Philadelphia Centennial Exposition of *1876*, 28, 107, 116

Philadelphia School of Design for Women, 70, 152–53

Philobiblon Club, 91

Photographers and photography, 14–18; commercial, 68; use in magazines, 24, 68; school of, *15*, 113–15

Pickering, William, 11

Postal system, 29–30

Poster designers and poster houses, 14, 79–81, *79, 80*, 119–23, *120, 121*

Prang, Louis, 13–14, 31, 110

Presbrey, Frank, 73, 77, 78, 82, 102

Printer, 40

Index

Printers and printing, 50; apprentices, 86, 93, 138, 140, 142; associations, 90–98; specialization, 43, 63–68; training, trade journals, 38–49. *See also* "Art of printing"

Printers' Circular, 40

Printers' Ink, 50–51

Printing Art, 46–49, *47*

Private press movement, 33, 90, 144

Professionalization, 85–90

Profitable Advertising, 51, *52*

Proof-Sheet, *41*

Publishing companies, 74–76

Punch-cutting machine. *See* Pantograph

Pyle, Howard, 98, 99, 155

Quarterly Illustrator, 12, 57

Ransom, Will, 112

Reed, Ethel, 112, 119, 147–48, *148*

Remington, Frederic, 73, 75, 99, *127*

Rhead, Louis, 31, 122, 123

Rogers, Bruce, 11, 63, 64, 95, 173

Rollins, Carl Purington, 45, 64

Rowell, George P., 30, 50, 102, 168, 169

Rowfant Club, 91

Ruskin, John, 32, 57, 107, 109, 152, 173

Sacker, Amy M., 100

Salmagundi Club, 98–99

Sartain, Emily, 154

Sartain, John, 56–57, 82

Schools. *See* Design schools

Scott, Walter Dill, 34, 54, 124, 168

Scribner's Monthly (Century Magazine), 55, 68, 72, 75

Senefelder, Alois, 13

Seymour, Ralph Fletcher, 8, 74, 105, 112

Sloan, John, 59, 70–72, 100, 119

Smith, Francis Hopkinson, 122, 154

Smith, Jessie Wilcox, 72, 75, *127*, 149, 154–57, *156*

Smith, Walter, 31, 109–12, 151–52

Smith's Academy, 112

Society of Arts and Crafts of Boston, 45, 84, 100–101

Soissons, S. de, 123

Society of Illustrators, 99–100, 130, 154

Society of Printers, 45, 93–95

Sphinx Club, 102, 128

Stanford Briggs, Inc., New York, 81

Starr, Ellen Gates, 144–45

Stephens, Alice Barber, 70, 154, 155

Stereotyping, 4, 19–20

Stone and Kimball's *Chap Book*, 57, 66, 83, 119

Thayer, John Adams, 82–83, 102

Thompson, J. Walter, 26

Tonnesen, Beatrice, 146–47

Trade journals, 36–59, 165–83; for advertisers and agents, 49–55; for illustrators, 55–59; for printers and typefounders, 38–49

Trademarks, 28

Triggs, Oscar Lovell, 116–17

Turnure, Arthur B., 57, 91

Type designers and type design, 23, 64–68, *65*

Typefoundries, 22–23; trade journals, 38–49

Typesetters and typesetting, 19–23; racism, 88–89; women as, 138–45

Typographica, 49, 67

Typographic Advertiser, 38–40, *39*

Typographische Monatsblätter, 43

United Typographical Union, 31, 92, *93*, 141

United Typothetae of America, 31, 91–93, *94*

Updike, Daniel Berkeley, 45, 95, 100

Veblen, Thorstein, 33

219

Index

Walsh, Richard, 73
Water Color Society, 154
Weber, Max, 96, 114
White, Clarence H., 113–15
Whitman, Sarah Wyman, 100, 144
Wineburgh, Max, 128–29
Women graphic designers, 133–58; cartoonists, 31, 153; in advertising, 145–51; in associations, 88, 145, 154–55; in book binding, 144; design education for, 152–54; illustrators, 151–57; in printing trades, 138–45; in private press movement, 144
Women's suffrage, 137, 138–39
Women's Typographical Union (WTU), 143
Woodward, Helen Rosen, 151
Wright, Carroll D., 105–6, 208n

Youth's Companion, 24